Flat 5, Ras Branscombe,
Salcombe Regis,
Nr. Sidmouth.
25th Dec. 1943.
S. Bevan.

My darling Son,

Very many thanks to your two letters dated 30.F. November and I'm hoping here are a few here & the way, Sorry about the cable but as I hadn't heard for 2 months, I had every right to be anxious (consider yourself squashed).

I've been in hospital for 20th inThing a & brochitis, as I was reasoning and around to my Christmas home. My hospital came. The place I don't work improved, I give almost anything to be back here, darling you have no idea how miserable I am)

to have Sep's home and to my sister home in Bournemouth. You are I complaining, and you, poor dear, have been away for fifteen months. Now I have just heard you 2 go on an Admin course (2 week) as being in New Guinea Eve!

Darling, I will let you have a photo as soon as I can get Mellie Express, as apparently there is not a decent photographer in Sidmouth. We are on a three barrel system (which is killing me) and I haven't had an opportunity to get away. Can I possibly let me have you some Snaps (just want to mate sure you haven't grown a beard!) please do if there is a chance I'll try and send you Snaps as they are more natural than the other things — here I breathe heavy.

Lieut. J. S. Bickerton,
R.N.V.R.
Coastal Force Base,
Malta.

Sender's name and address:-

I hope you are having a
lovely Christmas, lots of dances,
parties, etc.: — but not too
much to drink. Please write
soon and tell me about it.
I wonder what you'll be doing
New Years' eve, I expect you'll be doing
it up at sea.

Poor old Mr Dudley Ormond
thinking he would be home
for Christmas, what a shocking
disappointment. Nice work
Richie taking his place, please
give him my love. (I bet he's had
and type Sidche is not enjoying
like without Irene Ormond (!)
and I hope his fiancée stays will
be up the next time I see him.

By the way have you received
released in which I told you
that R.N. are not commuting
their supervisors in the rocket
apparently they have enough.
Still and no future in it.

My love to Gladys etc
Yanks, folks —

You'll never change.

PARENTS AT WAR

Parents at War

DAVID BICKERTON

MARVELLOUS BOOKS

MARVELLOUS BOOKS
www.marvellousbooks.com
info@marvellousbooks.com

First Edition 2018

Every effort has been made to trace copyright holders and to obtain permissions, where applicable. The author would be pleased to hear, through the publisher, from anyone in possession of additional, relevant material that might be included in a future edition of this book.

ISBN: 978-1-909900-11-0

Contents

Foreword

I was pleased to be invited to provide a foreword for this interesting book which provides an insight to the personal lives of those many thousands of families separated during the course of the Second World War. I have a personal interest in that my father's career in the Royal Navy followed a very similar pattern to that experienced by Lt Donald Bickerton, and indeed he took part in some of the same actions. I have also had the pleasure of knowing the late Geoffrey Searle (author of *At Sea Level*) and Sir Derrick Holden-Brown who both became Lieutenant-Commanders (RNVR) in Coastal Forces.

David Bickerton has succeeded very well in demonstrating the difficulties of communication at that time when one had to rely on ticking that which applied on pre-written postcards for quick messages or the occasional letter if one was lucky. These were censored and obviously could give no clue as to where they were sent from, or what one was doing. Read against a backdrop of a censored press which understandably contained mis-information ("fake news" is not a recent invention), it could only give rise to apprehension about the safety of one's family. This is hard to understand in the 21st century where we have instant communication and the "news" can be created by anyone with a smart phone.

In order to provide an historical context to his parents' correspondence, David Bickerton has interspersed it with details of what was happening at the time. In that he has drawn from previously published sources and has been given access to personal correspondence of those mentioned above.

Coastal Forces were unlike the permanent Royal Navy. They had few "professional" crews and officers as they were mainly civilians drafted in for the hostilities. They were also very young – boys could enlist at the age of 16, and some of them had become officers before they even had the right to vote. Some older officers had been reservists before the war, training on *HMS President* – a First World War sloop moored in the Thames. These men were called up immediately at the outbreak of war and allocated to ships – often merchant ships taken over by the Admiralty. There they would get to learn shipboard routine and those suitable would be selected to attend officer training at *HMS King Alfred* – which was Lancing College taken over for the duration.

It follows there was a different ethos among Coastal Forces crews. The ships were obviously smaller with crews as few as ten. There was no room for "pomp and circumstance" – you had to live together in a very small space and work as a team.

Friendships made at this time were enduring – even 75 years later. I can do no better than to quote the late Sir Derrick Holden-Brown:

> "Within Coastal Forces there was a brotherly relationship founded on adversity which came from the sea and from the enemy, and in such small craft as we served the ships' companies were very close. I served in two "Dog-boats" as Pilot, First Lieutenant and CO – *MGB 663* and *MGB 655* – both lost on mines in the Adriatic, and was lucky to survive. Yet I look back on that wonderful feeling of Brotherhood, and realise that the Royal Navy was my University, than which [sic] there could be no better."

David Carter
Secretary, Coastal Forces Veterans Association (London Branch)

Preface

Before they died, my parents had a good sort out and did not hoard excessively. I am guilty of the opposite but intend, over the next few years, to follow in their footsteps. For the sake of my three children, let us hope I survive, of sound mind, long enough to achieve this ambition.

When I emptied my parents' house on the Isle of Wight, the boxes of memorabilia that they had retained found their way into my loft. There they remained until after my retirement at the end of September 2010. When I did start to examine the contents, I discovered 30 or 40 love letters, written during the war, that I found intriguing. The passion with which they were written aroused my interest, and I had a growing desire to learn more about their lives during this period. Their handwriting, especially my mother's, could not be described as reader friendly, so I spent some time typing up these letters (initially with one finger but eventually I progressed to two digits). The task for me, bearing in mind my typing speed and the legibility of the script, became colossal as I found several more bundles of wartime letters and then there was the post-war correspondence. I finished up typing some 150 wartime and another 80 post-war letters. In this book, I concentrate on the former.

Unfortunately, most of the surviving letters have had their postage stamps removed. I have to admit to being the culprit as, when I was aged around eight or nine, I was a keen stamp collector. Quite why I might require dozens of identical, franked stamps I am not certain. It must have been in order to swap with friends who had something different in exchange.

As the letters are very personal, I wondered whether my parents would mind me reading them and sharing them with others. On reflection, I decided, that they had been deliberately left for that purpose. So many other documents had been cleared out.

Only 22 of the wartime letters were from my mother. She seems to have been less prolific than my father but, even so, many more of her letters appear to be lost to time. I was told at the Portsmouth Naval Museum that this is common as sailors, like my father, would have limited space aboard ship and, when they returned to UK, all their belongings would have to fit into one kitbag. I also sometimes wonder whether my mother might have destroyed some letters that she might have considered too personal for the inquisitive eyes of the next generation.

I decided to research some of the subject matter within the letters, from the six invasions in which my father was involved to the five radar stations to which my mother was posted. To me, by far the most exciting discovery was the 'pact of friendship' signed by nine members of the Maquis – a French resistance group – during the invasion of Southern France. I discovered the 'pact' quite by chance and eventually managed to find a local historian in France who was equally as intrigued. This is all detailed in Chapter Eleven of this book.

With the help of my parents' wartime records, I also attempted to find out more about their exploits. It is to my regret that I did not ask questions during their lifetimes. They spoke very little of the war. There are so many gaps in my knowledge that I will never fill.

Whilst I have compiled the letters with a narrative for my own benefit, I am hopeful that the contents will be of interest not only to family members but also to those who might be fascinated by the lives of two ordinary people who volunteered to do their bit during the Second World War.

I have read up about the war in the Mediterranean between 1942 and 1945. Whilst I have made every effort to ascertain the facts, I am a long way from being knowledgeable in the subject and apologise to the reader for any inaccuracies.

Glossary of Acronyms and Abbreviations

ACS2	Aircraft Woman Second Class
ACW	Aircraft Woman
AM	Air Ministry
AMES	Air Ministry Experimental Station
AMG	Allied Military Government
AWOL	Absent without Leave
BBC	British Broadcasting Corporation
BIGOT	British Invasion of German Occupied Territory
CBE	Commander of the British Empire
CCF	Commander Coastal Forces
CF	Coastal Forces
CO	Commanding Officer
CW	Commission and Warrant
DSC	Distinguished Service Cross
DVD	Digital Video Disc
E-boat	Schnellboot or S-Boot (*German*)
EEC	European Economic Community
ENSA	Entertainments National Service Association
GPO	General Post Office
HDML	Harbour Defence Motor Launch
HMML	Her Majesty's Motor Launch
HMS	Her Majesty's Ship (also used for naval shore establishments)
HQ	Headquarters
I/C	In Charge of
IMDb	Internet Movie Database
LACW	Leading Aircraft Woman
LCA	Landing Craft, Assault
LCI	Landing Craft, Infantry
LS	Landing Ship
LST	Landing Craft, Tank
Lt	Lieutenant
Lt Cmdr	Lieutenant Commander
MGB	Motor Gun Boat
MGM	Metro-Goldwyn-Meyer
M of H	Ministry of Health

M of I	Ministry of Insurance
MID	Mention in Despatches
ML	Motor Launch
MTB	Motor Torpedo Boat
NCO	Non-Commissioned Officer
NMRN	The National Museum of the Royal Navy
OLQ	Officer-Like-Qualities
PD	Pembroke Dock
PDC	Personnel Despatch Centre
P/O	Petty Officer or Pilot Officer
POW	Prisoner of War
PT	Patrol Torpedo (boat) *(US)*
RAF	Royal Air Force (also used for shore establishments)
RN	Royal Navy
RC	Roman Catholic
RNR	Royal Naval Reserve
RNVR	Royal Naval Volunteer Reserve
SCSN	Central Society of Rescue of the Shipwrecked *(French)*
SNSM	National Society for Rescue at Sea *(French)*
SO	Senior Officer
SOP	Standard Operating Procedures
Sub Lt	Sub-Lieutenant
TT	Teetotal
U-boat	Unterseeboot (undersea boat) *(German)*
US	United States
VAT	Value Added Tax
VE	Victory in Europe
WAAF	Women's Auxiliary Air Force
WRNS	Women's Royal Naval Service (commonly known as Wrens)
WW2	World War 2
YMCA	Young Men's Christian Association

Acknowledgements

With thanks to:

Philip Andrews for providing research material

David Carter, son of Lt F L Carter RNVR, for providing photographs and other information

Hubert Guillois for making contact with José Valli and for his translation skills

Marianne Guillois for her translation skills

Simon Hancock of the *Haverfordwest Town Museum* for assistance in research

Kristy Howell for her guidance and editing

Heather Johnson of the *National Museum of the Royal Navy, Portsmouth* for assistance in research

Roger Shore, Archivist of the Moordown Local History Society, for providing images of Metropole Hotel in Bournemouth from around 1910 and 1943, the latter belonging to **John Goslin**

Rod Suddaby of the *Imperial War Museum, London* for assistance in research

José Valli for research material on Port-Saint-Louis-Du-Rhône

Chapter One

DON BICKERTON

Frank Donald Bickerton, known as 'Don' was born in Liverpool on 22nd June 1917. His father was manager of a printing firm and he had a younger brother, Leslie. He went to Bray Street Junior School, where his Aunt Bertha (who lived to 108) was a teacher. He was keen on football and used to spend many Saturday afternoons at Anfield. His interest in Liverpool Football Club stayed with him all his life. As a boy, he was also keen on the sea. In the school holidays he would buy a season ticket for the cross-Mersey ferry and, on his own, visit Birkenhead and New Brighton. His senior school was Liverpool Collegiate.

He left school at 16 and found a job as a packer, wrapping such items as overalls. He enjoyed life to the full, with his circle of friends, and was especially keen on tennis. He was, however, eager to better himself and get away from home, so he attended evening classes. He took and passed the Civil Service examinations and, at the age of 18, moved to digs in London and started work in a clerical position at the Ministry of Health. His first break came when someone went on leave and he was asked if he knew anything about public relations. He said that he had been involved in PR when he was working in Liverpool. This was a slight misrepresentation as he had only been packing publicity leaflets! However, he grasped the opportunity and created a favourable impression. That was the start of a career in PR that was to culminate in him becoming Director General of the Central Office of Information.

In 1940 he volunteered for the Royal Naval Volunteer Reserve (RNVR). His service record is shown below:

CERTIFICATE of the Service of

SURNAME. (In Block Letters)	CHRISTIAN NAME OR NAMES.
BICKERTON	Frank Donald

in the Royal Navy.

NOTE.—The corner of this Certificate is to be cut off where indicated if the man is discharged with a "Bad" character or with disgrace, or if specially directed by the Admiralty. If the corner is cut off, the fact is to be noted in the Ledger.

		Man's Signature on discharge to Pension
Port Division	Chatham.	
Official No.	JX 203168	

Date of Birth 22 June 1917

Nearest known Relative or Friend. (To be noted in pencil.)
Relationship: FATHER
Name: FRANK McDOWELL BICKERTON

Where born — Town or Village Fairfield Liverpool — County Lancashire
Address: FAIRFIELD, THOMAS LANE, BROAD GREEN, LIVERPOOL 14

Trade brought up to Civil Servant

Religious Denomination Church of England

All Engagements, including Non-C.S., to be noted in these Columns.

Swimming Qualifications.

Date of actually volunteering	Commencement of time	Period volunteered for	Date.	Qualification.	Signature.
1. 26 June 1940		Until the end of the period of the present emergency NS/AF/A 1939	1.		
2.			2.		

Description of Person	Stature Feet	In.	Chest, In.	Colour of Hair	Eyes	Complexion	Marks, Wounds, and Scars
On Entry as a Boy							
On advancement to man's rating, or on entry under 28 years......... On re-engagement or re-entry for C.S. or for Non-C.S. after attain-	5	9	32⅞	Fair	Blue	Fair	Scar on right knee

2.

Name _Frank Donald BICKERTON_

Name of Ship. (Tenders to be inserted in brackets)	Substantive Rating	Non-Substantive Rating	From	To	Cause of Discharge and other notations authorised by Article 606, Clause 9, K.R. and A.I.
Raleigh	Ord Sea		26 June '40	2 Sep 40	
Pembroke	— " —		3 Sep 40	28 Oct. 40	
Calliope (Mauritius)	—do—		29 Oct 40	13 Dec. 40	
Mauritius	— " —		14 Dec '40	9 May. 41.	
Victory	— " —		10 May '41	4 July '41	
King Alfred	— " —		5 July '41	10 Sept 41	Granted temporary commission as Sub. lieutenant R.N.V.R.

4.

Name _Frank Donald BICKERTON_   Conduct.

Second Class for Conduct (inclusive dates)		Character and Efficiency on 31st December yearly, on final discharge, and other occasions prescribed by regulation. If qualified by service and recommended for Re-engagement or for Medal and Gratuity, "R.R." or "R.M.G." to be awarded on 31st December and final discharge, if not, a line to be drawn across column. Character is assessed as follows:—V.G., Good, Fair, Indifferent, Bad.
From	To	Note as to method of assessing Efficiency.
		Superior—above average efficiency. Satisfactory—average efficiency. Moderate—less than average efficiency. Inferior—inefficient. } in substantive rating, held at the time, without regard to fitness for advancement.
		Variations in efficiency are often explained by the fact that the man had recently been promoted—see pages 2 and 3—and had not gained sufficient experience in his new position to justify a higher award than that actually assessed.

Good Conduct Badges			Character	Efficiency in Rating, noting substantive rating in brackets	Whether R.R. R.M.G. or not	Date	Captain's Signature
Date	1st, 2nd, 3rd	Granted, Deprived, Restored					
			V.G.	Sat (Ord Sea).		31 Dec 40.	W. O. Stephens
			VG	Sup. (—"—)		10 Sept 41	

Don's Certificate of Service

Don's first posting, commencing on 26th June 1940, was to _HMS Raleigh_, a shore establishment at Torpoint, Cornwall (see **Map A,** over the page). He was ranked as an Ordinary Seaman and was aged just 23. _HMS Raleigh_ had been established just 6 months earlier on 9th January 1940 as a basic training facility. It had been commissioned following the Military Training Act, which required that all males aged 20 and 21 years old be called up for six months' full-time military training, before being transferred to the RNVR.

After two months, on 2nd September 1940, he left _HMS Raleigh_ and, the following day, began further training at _HMS Pembroke_, a shore establishment at Chatham, Kent (see **Map A**).

MAP A

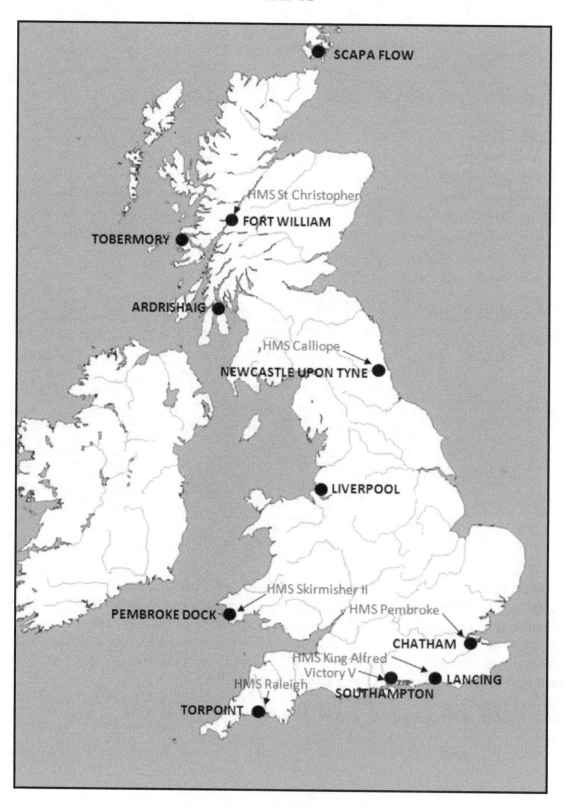

SCAPA FLOW

HMS St Christopher

FORT WILLIAM

TOBERMORY

ARDRISHAIG

HMS Calliope

NEWCASTLE UPON TYNE

LIVERPOOL

HMS Skirmisher II

HMS Pembroke

PEMBROKE DOCK

CHATHAM

HMS King Alfred

Victory V

LANCING

HMS Raleigh

SOUTHAMPTON

TORPOINT

The shore barracks at Chatham that Don would have entered was commissioned in 1878, moving ashore in 1903 and was decommissioned in 1983. The buildings, designed by Sir Henry Pilkington, now house the University of Medway. Whilst at *HMS Pembroke*, Don's training included seamanship, knots, boat handling, gun drill and shooting on the rifle range. Trainees slept either in bunks in the barracks block or in an extension that was tunnelled into the bank behind.

Don left there, also after two months, on 28th October 1940. The next day he started at *HMS Calliope*, a training ship that had been based at Newcastle upon Tyne (see **Map A**, on page 4) since 1907. This was clearly specific training in advance of being a crew member of the battle cruiser, *HMS Mauritius*, the construction of which was nearing completion on Tyneside. His service record shows that he left *HMS Calliope* on 13th December 1940.

HMS Calliope (1884) in port at Portsmouth
US Naval Historical Center [public domain], via *Wikimedia Commons*

On 14th December 1940, the construction of *HMS Mauritius* was officially completed. Acceptance Trials were scheduled to start and Don's service record shows him joining this brand-new battle cruiser. She was built by Swan Hunter and Wigham Richardson on the Tyne and engined by the Wallsend Slipway and Engineering Company. Her standard displacement was 8,000 tons, and she had an extreme length of 555½ feet, extreme breadth of 62 feet and mean draught of 16½ feet. She was originally armed with twelve 6-inch guns in four triple turrets. Geared turbines of 65,000 horse-power driving four shafts gave her a designed speed of 31½ knots. She had one Walrus aircraft and a crew of 730 men.

On 7th January 1941, Don sailed on her to Scapa Flow (see **Map A**) for service with the 10th Cruiser Squadron, Home Fleet. After all his training, Don was at last at sea. In mid-February 1941 she joined military convoy WS 6B as ocean escort during passage to Freetown, Sierra Leone from the Clyde. On 5th March 1941, and upon arrival in Freetown, she was detached from this convoy which was destined for the Middle East round the Cape of Good Hope and the Horn of Africa. A week later she left Freetown, escorting convoy SL 68 en route to the UK. She continued, over the following weeks, shuttling convoys SL 69 and SL 70 to and from Freetown, and on 9th May 1941 she again arrived in Freetown with Middle East troop convoy WS 8A.

HMS Mauritius in Malta circa 1946

HMS Dorsetshire from the Wright & Logan Collection (© by permission *NMRN*)

Don's service record shows that he left *HMS Mauritius* on 9th May 1941 after six months' duty. This was because he had been identified as having officer-like-qualities (OLQ). This may have been decided before he was posted to *HMS Mauritius* when he was undertaking basic training and had been earmarked to transfer to the Coastal Forces division of the Royal Navy. He was therefore required to return to UK for officer training and his service record shows that he was attached to *HMS Victory*, the Portsmouth onshore establishment from 10th May 1941. In practice, he first had to return to UK and this was facilitated by his transfer to another battle cruiser, *HMS Dorsetshire*, which had arrived in Freetown the day before the arrival of *HMS Mauritius*. He would have been embedded with her crew and given specific tasks; there was no room for passengers in the Navy. On 11th May 1941 she left Freetown and, the following day, she joined convoy SL 74 as an escort.

In the meantime, the Navy was pursuing the massive 50,000-ton German battleship *Bismark* which had sunk the British 49,000-ton battle cruiser *HMS Hood* on 24th May 1941. 1,415 sailors were lost and there were only three survivors. Two days later *HMS Dorsetshire* was detached from the convoy and sent to join the search for the *Bismark*. On 27th May 1941 she, along with *HMS Maori*, helped sink *Bismark* and rescued 110 German survivors from the sea. She was forced to leave the remaining German sailors behind after reports that there were U-boats and enemy aircraft in the vicinity. Most of *Bismark*'s 2,200 crew died. Don said that some of the British sailors were 'not suited' by the decision to evacuate the area before the remaining survivors had been rescued. However, he seemed to concur that the captain had no choice. On 29th May 1941 one German sailor, who had died of his injuries, was buried at sea. The following day the remaining prisoners were landed and handed to a military escort at South Shields.

Presumably Don then travelled to Southampton, probably after a short period of leave. The *World Naval Ships* website shows that *Victory V*, at that time, was based in the South Western Hotel in Southampton, as *HMS Victory* at Portsmouth was being affected by heavy German bombing. His service record indicates that he left *HMS Victory* on 4th July 1941.

On 5th July 1941 Don commenced his officer training at *HMS King Alfred*, which was based in Lancing College, Sussex (see **Map A**, on page 4). There would also have been a spell on the Officers' Training Ship at nearby Hove. *Coastal Forces at War* by David Jefferson records that this establishment was commissioned in September 1939 to train Coastal Forces' officers. This book and the *Royal Navy Research Archive* website both provide insight into the environment in which potential officers would have found themselves. After their basic training, recruits would be drafted to a ship; in Don's case *HMS Mauritius*. Some would already be under observation for officer training and, after serving a minimum of three months at sea, with the recommendation of their CO, those with OLQ would be put forward as commission and warrant (CW) candidates. All Royal Naval Volunteer Reserve (RNVR) officers worked their way through *HMS King Alfred* before completing their training at *HMS St Christopher*.

At *HMS King Alfred* they were taught something about gunnery, navigation, seamanship, torpedoes, knots, chart-work, boat drill, general administration, code books and rules of the road. Boat handling would be practised in Shoreham Harbour. The two-month course was intensive and the incentive was not just to pass but also to achieve really good results. In a typical intake of 40 candidates around a quarter would drop out in ones and twos and be returned to their ships. Those with the top marks were destined for Coastal Forces or Destroyers, whereas those at the bottom of the heap would finish up on landing craft.

On 11th September 1941, Don was granted the temporary commission of Sub-Lieutenant:

CONFIDENTIAL.

C.W.

By Command of the Commissioners for Executing the Office of Lord High Admiral of the United Kingdom, &c.

To Sub-Lieutenant *F. D. BICKERTON, R.N.V.R.*

THE Lords Commissioners of the Admiralty hereby appoint you *Temporary Sub-Lieutenant, R.N.V.R.* of His Majesty's Ship *King Alfred addl.*

~~and direct you to repair on board that Ship at~~ ~~on~~ *11th Sept. 1941*

Your appointment is to take effect from ~~that date.~~

You are to acknowledge the receipt of ~~this~~ Appointment *forthwith*, addressing ~~your letter~~ to the Commanding Officer,
H.M.S.
~~taking~~ care to furnish your address.

By Command of their Lordships,

H. V. Markham

17 SEP 1941

Admiralty, S.W.1.

(18/10/40) (282) Wt 43162/3936 10M 2/41 S.E.R. Ltd; Gp. 671.

Don's Letter of Appointment

His "Passing Out" certificate showed that he scored 740 marks out of 1000:

H.M.S "KING ALFRED"

"PASSING OUT" CERTIFICATE

of a SPECIALLY SELECTED RATING examined for the rank of

~~ACTING SUB. LIEUTENANT~~
TEMPORARY SUB. LIEUTENANT   } R.N.V.R.
~~MIDSHIPMAN~~

This is to Certify

that at an Examination held in

H.M.S. "KING ALFRED"

FRANK DONALD BICKERTON

O/SEA   O/JX 203168

[NAME, RATING AND OFFICIAL NO.]

obtained   740   marks out of a maximum of a 1000

~~and is awarded a~~

~~CLASS CERTIFICATE~~

COMMANDER   INSTRUCTOR COMMANDER

Approved

11th september 19 41

CAPTAIN

Don's "Passing Out" Certificate

Don's service history (see page 12) records that, after 'passing out' from *HMS King Alfred* on 11th September 1941, he remained officially attached to this training establishment until 3rd October 1941. This would have included a period of leave before he was transferred to *HMS St Christopher* in Fort William on 4th October 1941 (see **Map A**, on page 4) in the Scottish Highlands to complete his training. Newly appointed officers would attend lectures on types of ships, their engines and aircraft recognition. They would also learn about Morse signalling. There were two Motor Launches (MLs) attached to the base at Fort William for the purpose of training newly appointed officers. Over 30 full-time officers ran the base and around 50,000 personnel passed through. As Don was to serve on MLs, it is possible that he would have attended the anti-submarine school at Ardrishaig (see **Map A**) on Loch Fyne, at the entrance to the Crinan Canal, 60 miles south of Fort William.

To cope with the influx of Coastal Forces between October 1940 and December 1944, four hotels were taken over by the Navy. The administrative base *HMS St Christopher* was established in the resort's main hotel, the Highland; senior naval officers were in the Grand; and the Women's Royal Naval Service (WRNS) occupied the Waverley, the Station Hotel and an annexe to the Palace Hotel. However, many of those who arrived for Coastal Forces training were billeted with families in the town. There was also the inevitable sprawl of Nissen Huts, which provided additional sleeping accommodation and classrooms.

Returning to *Coastal Forces at War* by David Jefferson, the social life of Fort William was enlivened by the arrival of the Navy and the Army. The Playhouse Cinema was reopened and there were frequent dances at the Town Hall and at the Braxy at Inverlocky. The Garrison Theatre, which was a large Nissen Hut put up by the Army, was primarily used by both services for concerts and tombola evenings but also held occasional dances to which the locals would be invited.

With his formal training at *HMS St Christopher* completed on 2nd November 1941, Don is recorded as serving as second-in-command under Richard Vick on *ML 280*. From 3rd November 1941, they were on patrols and manoeuvres off the west coasts of England and Wales, in preparation for being sent into action in the Mediterranean. In one of his letters he mentions operating in the Bristol Channel during this period.

HMS Skirmisher II, Milford Haven 23rd March 1942
Medmenham Collection M2262 (Welsh Government)
Courtesy *Dyfed Archaelogical Trust*

Between November 1940 and November 1941, Coastal Forces bases had increased from 5 to 20 and the number of MLs in service from 22 to 174. One of these bases was *HMS Skirmisher II* at Pembroke Dock on Milford Haven (see **Map A**). Don mentioned being there when he met his future wife, Linda (see Chapter Four).

The document *Royal Navy Ship Dispositions, Home Waters, January 1942* (published on the *Naval History* website) shows that MLs *280* and *338* were attached to the 25th ML Flotilla, based at *HMS Skirmisher II*, Pembroke Dock, but that they also berthed at Tobermory on the Isle of Mull (see **Map A**).

The period when Don was serving on *ML 280* and, from October 1942, on *ML 338* is covered from Chapter Four onwards.

Don on the bridge of *ML 338*

Returning to Don's service history (on page 12), there are some comments and anomalies that should be noted:

- *HMS St Angelo (Gregale)* was the naval base on Malta used by Coastal Forces.
- The reference to "Guliet" is unclear; there was an *HMS Juliet*, described as a minesweeping trawler.
- Not totally explained are the brief entries for CFB (Coastal Forces Base) Ischia and MLs *1234* and *462*. Don does report on several occasions staying at a rest camp on Ischia, although they are not all recorded in his service history.
- The period 5th-25th June 1945 was when he was awaiting transport to return to UK.
- *ML 462* was commanded by Don's friend, Hugh Gwynn (see page 231).
- Don was attached to *HMS Drake*, Plymouth after the war and before he was demobbed.

Navy Command

FULL NAME: FRANK DONALD BICKERTON   OFFICIAL NO: JX203168

Listed below is a record of Frank Donald Bickerton's service history between 11 September 1941 and 28 December 1945. This information has been extracted from Payment and Victual (P & V) Ledgers as it was not recorded on the attached service record card.

Ship/Shore Establishment	Rank/Rating Held	From	To
HMS King Alfred	Temporary Sub Lieutenant	11 Sep 1941	03 Oct 1941
HMS St Christopher	Temporary Sub Lieutenant	04 Oct 1941	02 Nov 1941
ML 280	Temporary Sub Lieutenant	03 Nov 1941	03 Jul 1942
ML 338	Temporary Sub Lieutenant	04 Jul 1942	08 Jul 1942
ML 280	Temporary Sub Lieutenant	09 Jul 1942	10 Sep 1942
ML 280	Temporary Lieutenant	11 Sep 1942	06 Oct 1942
ML 338	Temporary Lieutenant	07 Oct 1942	03 Oct 1943
HMS St Angelo (Gregale)	Temporary Lieutenant	04 Oct 1943	17 Oct 1943
ML 338	Temporary Lieutenant	18 Oct 1943	19 Nov 1943
Lent: "Guliet"	Temporary Lieutenant	20 Nov 1943	20 Nov 1943
Lent: CFB (Coastal Forces Base)	Temporary Lieutenant	21 Nov 1943	25 Nov 1943
ML 1234	Temporary Lieutenant	26 Nov 1943	27 Nov 1943
ML 338	Temporary Lieutenant	28 Nov 1943	11 Apr 1945
Lent: CFB Ischia	Temporary Lieutenant	12 Apr 1945	16 Apr 1945
ML 338	Temporary Lieutenant	17 Apr 1945	31 May 1945
ML 462	Temporary Lieutenant	01 Jun 1945	04 Jun 1945
Lent: CFB Ischia	Temporary Lieutenant	05 Jun 1945	25 Jun 1945
Passage	Temporary Lieutenant	26 Jun 1945	03 Jul 1945
HMS Drake	Temporary Lieutenant	04 Jul 1945	28 Dec 1945

Frank Donald Bickerton was released to shore in Class B on the 28 December 1945.

Don's service history as an officer

Chapter Two

LINDA RUSSELL

Linda Ruby Russell was born at 138 High Street, Newport, Isle of Wight on 22nd May 1920. Her father, Stanley Russell, was a motor and cycle engineer with his own business and was a well-known figure on the island. Her mother, also Linda, helped in the business and brought up their three children. Because mother and daughter shared the same first name, Linda junior was known as Ruby. She had an older sister, Peggy (to whom she was particularly close) and a younger brother, Gordon.

Between the ages of 5 and 15 she attended Braunstone House School in Newport. This was a small private school which is now a restaurant. She was a popular girl and formed close relationships with two girls in particular, Berrie and Olga. They were typically friendly and giggly girls, full of fun. When they were older they took advantage of the fact that the boys' grammar school was opposite and used to meet some of the lads in town.

Linda Ruby was blonde and attractive and excelled, in particular, at dancing. She was a pupil of Nellie Furmage who taught dancing and ballet at schools all over the island. She was such an acrobatic dancer that she would bring handstands and flying splits into her routines.

Academically she was of above average ability but, although she stayed at school a year longer than the then national leaving age of 14, she did not have any opportunity to further her education. Her father's business had run into difficulties during the 1930s depression and he sold up and moved to Freshwater, where he managed Starks Hotel. Ruby found a job at the nearby Freshwater Bay Hotel, where she was employed as a secretary. Having left school, she reverted her name to Linda (she hated being known as Ruby).

Conscription for women was not introduced until December 1941 so, like her future husband, Don, she too volunteered.

Authy. C. Form	Description.	Date of Effect.
	Enrolled ACW2	3/4/41
649/42	L.A.C.W.	1·11·42
	T/CPL	

Linda's service record

From her service record (see above), it appears that she joined the Women's Auxiliary Air Force (WAAF) on 3rd April 1941 as an Aircraftwoman Second Class (ACS2) in Gloucester, where her role was a Clerk, General Duties.

The *RAF Museum* website contains memories of women recruited at that time. One, who joined a month later than Linda, was also sent to Gloucester from the recruiting office. There, she recalled, new recruits were housed in huts containing about 20 beds. She remembered that, on each bed, were three square mattresses known as 'biscuits', three hairy air force blue blankets, two unbleached sheets and a roly-poly pillow filled with hay. They had to adjust quickly to service life, with its strict rules and discipline. The first few days at Gloucester were a test on recruits' stamina. After being fitted with uniforms and given vaccinations they were drilled and marched until their heels blistered. From Gloucester, recruits were transferred to RAF bases and trained in particular skills.

The service record is difficult for the uninitiated to decipher but it appears that, on 1st August 1941, Linda was sent to 'Radio School'. On 29th August 1941 she started as a Radio Operator at *RAF Branscombe*, near Sidmouth, Devon (see **Map B**, over the page).

During the 1930s the Air Ministry conducted experiments on the new technology of radio aircraft detection, some jointly with the BBC who had the necessary radio transmitters together with the electronic equipment trialled with Government scientists. They were able to detect aircraft up to 40 miles away and identify their direction of travel. They were also able to distinguish between friend and foe. Experiments on airborne radar proved problematic as the equipment, in order to be effective, proved too heavy. A decision was made in the late 1930s to proceed with the construction of radar sites along the east and south coasts. By the start of the war in September 1939, twenty such sites were operational. They played a prominent part in the defeat of the German plans to invade Britain, both through the 'Battle of Britain' between July and October 1940, and the subsequent night-time 'Blitz' which lasted until June 1941. *RAF Branscombe* was one of these sites as was *RAF Worth Matravers*, near Swanage (see **Map B**), where Linda later served.

MAP B

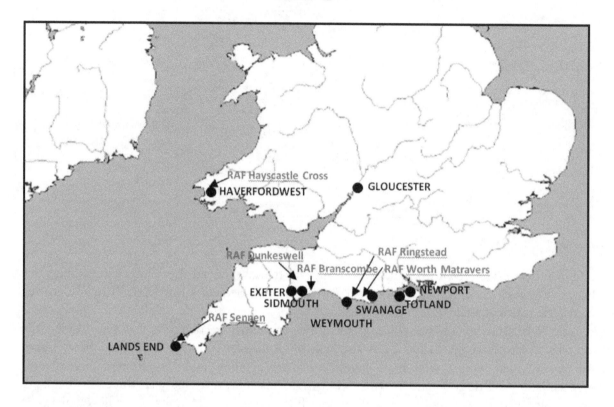

With the overrun of France by the Germans in 1940 and the war of the Atlantic, with British merchant shipping being destroyed by U-boats, a second wave of radar stations was constructed to the west of Branscombe and along the west coast. One of these was at Hayscastle Cross, near Haverfordwest, Pembrokeshire (see **Map B**) and was established in July 1940, although it was several months before it was fully operational. After just a month at *RAF Branscombe*, Linda transferred to *RAF Hayscastle* on 22nd September 1941. It was whilst there in July 1942 that she met Don. In her service record (see previous page) *RAF Branscombe* was described as '78 Wing AMES' (Air Ministry Experimental Station) and *RAF Hayscastle* as '76 Sigs AMES'. It was whilst at the latter in July 1942 that she and Don met.

Information on this establishment is available on the *Subterranea Britannica* and *Hayscastle* websites. *RAF Hayscastle* had two main receiving towers, which were 325 feet high with supports constructed of timber. The four steel transmitting towers were 240 feet high. Linda used to relate that she spent much time sitting in front of a radar screen. She would have identified each 'dot' as either friend or foe and passed the data on to the plotters. The information would then be transmitted on to Fighter Command. If a threat was identified, then fighters would be scrambled to intercept intruders.

The technology was not exclusively British, although the Germans were more intent on radar's offensive possibilities, such as developing radar-assisted guns and searchlights. Furthermore, there was much less coordination between the German services and the scientists. They were unable to distinguish between friend and foe or estimate the altitude of aircraft.

After her stint at *RAF Hayscastle*, Linda's location can be traced through her correspondence with Don. She was transferred to *RAF Ringstead*, near Weymouth, Dorset (see **Map B**, on previous page), in September 1942, around the time that they were planning to marry. This scuppered their marriage plans as, in those days, one partner was required to be resident in a district for a minimum of two weeks. As a result, it became difficult to marry prior to Don's ship leaving for the Mediterranean in October 1942, although, from Don's later correspondence, it seems that anyway he had cold feet at the last moment.

Whilst at *RAF Ringstead* and, with effect from 1st November 1942, Linda was promoted to Leading Aircraftwoman Second Class (LACW).

Linda's next posting was to *RAF Worth Matravers* in January 1943. Whilst there, she seems to have lived in lodgings at Swanage, whereas at the other establishments she was housed in on-site barracks.

In April 1943, she returned to *RAF Ringstead*. In her service record she is shown as being attached to 78 Wing on 30th June 1943. From November 1943 to November 1944, she was again located at *RAF Branscombe*. On her service record she is shown as having been attached to Exeter on 4th September 1944 (possibly for training) with another two entries enscribed '78 Wing' on 30th June 1943 and 8th September 1944. *RAF Branscombe* worked in conjunction with

Radar development site near Renscombe Farm, Worth Matravers around 1941
(photograph from *Purbeck Radar Museum Trust*)

Dunkeswell Airfield, home to the American 7th Fleet Air Wing. It was whilst Linda was at *RAF Branscombe* on 12th August 1944 that Joe Kennedy (John F Kennedy's eldest brother) was killed flying on a mission from Dunkeswell Airfield.

The *RAF Museum* website shares memories of women recruited at that time. One recruit, who volunteered to go to Exeter, related that transport from Exeter Central Station took WAAFs about 6-7 miles the other side of Exeter City to a pretty village called Pinhoe. She said that Pinhoe was small, with two pubs. The Poltimore Arms was the one the Army favoured and the Hearth of Oak was frequented by the RAF – one never found a mix in either pub. A large house and park was their destination, a few huts nestled in this park, which became their temporary new home, and in each hut there were about 20 beds, ten on each side. The most coveted beds were the end ones, under the small windows. The WAAF leaving the hut would say who was to occupy her bed! WAAFs took pride in their huts, with each keeping the floor space under their bed polished and stacking their bedding neatly, kitbags with everything they owned standing like sentries to the left and head of each bed. They put their shoes on outside, or walked on dusters, so that the floor shone like a sheet of glass. Airfields, especially "Ops" buildings, were a target. The enemy bombers did get some, and some WAAFs lost their lives.

Although there is no mention on her service record, Linda transferred to *RAF Sennen*, near Lands End, Cornwall (see **Map B**, on page 16), where she served from November 1944 until July 1945. *Wikipedia* records that *RAF Sennen* was sited in 1942 on a plot of land in Cornwall about 1.5 miles east of Land's End, adjacent to the B3315 between Screwjack and Trebehor Farms. The base was just one mile from Sennen Village and two miles from Sennen Cove. Several radar masts were erected, some over 300 feet high.

Linda married Don in Penzance, on his return from the Mediterranean, on 14th July 1945. As there were no further letters kept until 1946, it is not known whether she returned to *RAF Sennen*. The final entry in her service record is dated 17th September 1945 and reads "78 Wing, 105 PDC (Personnel Despatch Centre) – Release", so this is presumably her date of discharge.

After the war the radar stations were soon abandoned. For a while *RAF Sennen* was converted into a holiday camp. *RAF Hayscastle* was returned to agriculture, although various buildings remained for some time and photographs of these have been posted on the *Subterranea Britannica* website. Some buildings also remain at *RAF Ringstead*, where there is now a caravan site. *RAF Branscombe* has been transformed into a business park, a farm and a caravan park.

From May 1940 – May 1942, *RAF Worth Matravers* was the nerve centre for development of radar in Britain although, owing to its proximity to the coast and vulnerability to attack, Churchill ordered its work to be transferred to a more secure location. Little of *RAF Worth Matravers* has survived but there is a Radar Memorial.

Radar Memorial at Worth Matravers (by kind permission of *Purbeck Radar Museum Trust*)

The plaque on the memorial reads: "THIS MEMORIAL COMMEMORATES THE RADAR RESEARCH CARRIED OUT AT WORTH MATRAVERS FROM 1940-1942 WHICH WAS CRUCIAL TO THE WINNING OF THE WAR AND THE BIRTH OF MODERN TELECOMMUNICATIONS"

Chapter Three

THE FAIRMILE

As mentioned in Chapter One, after Don received his commission and transferred to Coastal Forces, he served on two minesweeping Motor Launches: *ML 280* as Sub-Lieutenant, and *ML 338* as Lieutenant. The boats were Fairmile B Motor Launches. (Interestingly, until 2007 a converted ML was used for the *Western Lady Ferry Service* in Torbay.)

The publications *Allied Coastal Forces of World War II* by John Lambert and Al Ross and *Flag 4* by Dudley Pope provide some useful information on the history of these craft. The idea behind building wooden MLs as anti-submarine ships sprang from the German submarine menace of the First World War. In 1915, the Admiralty selected Elco of Bayonne, New Jersey, USA, to construct 550 MLs, the first few being 75 feet long. The remainder were 80 feet long and had a displacement of 42 tons. However, they afforded a bumpy ride and, in hindsight, it was considered that they should have been designed with a hull of 100-120 feet long.

Having served on one of these early MLs between 1916 and 1918, as war approached in the late 1930s Noel Macklin considered that he might be able to interest the Royal Navy in such vessels. He founded the Fairmile organisation from his house in Fairmile, Cobham, Surrey. His first design was the 110 feet long Fairmile A which displaced around 55 tons and, when the Admiralty showed reluctance to embrace his idea, he arranged for and self-funded a prototype (*ML 100*) to be built at Woodnutt's Yard at St Helens, Bembridge, on the Isle of Wight.

Macklin's Fairmile prototypes were clearly successful as, less than two months before the outbreak of war, the Admiralty ordered 11 type A's and 13 type B's, the latter being an Admiralty-designed variant. Kits were manufactured in Brentford and assembled at various boatyards (43 in total) around the UK. In fact MLs were built around the world. Those in Egypt were assembled by Thomas Cook & Son (the travel business), others were constructed in Canada and India. They were also built under licence in the USA by Elco and others (where they were known as PT (Patrol Torpedo) boats. John F Kennedy, who later became President of the USA, was skipper of *PT 109*. Over 600 MLs were constructed and put into service during the war.

Of the two MLs on which Don served, *ML 280* was ordered in May 1940 and completed in September 1941 by Frank Curtis Limited of Looe, Cornwall; while *ML 338* was built the following year by Risdon Beazley Limited at Northam Bridge, Southampton.

Fortuitously, both a 1945 photograph and a naval architect's impressions of *ML 338*, which was employed as a minesweeper, appear in the book *Allied Coastal Forces of World War II*:

ML 338 **as a minesweeper in 1945 from** *Allied Coastal Forces,* **Volume I (Courtesy F Kennedy)**

Typically, *ML 338* would be fitted with a 40mm Borfors Mark III gun (forward), two single 20mm Oerlikon guns, Oropesa sweep gear (for mine clearance) and a minimum of six anti-submarine depth charges. Sonar equipment would assist in the detection of submarines.

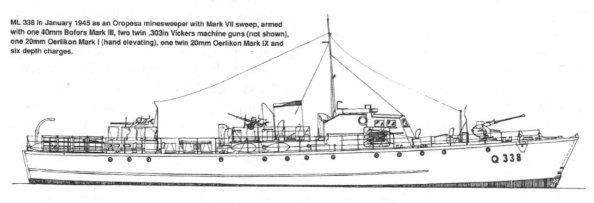

ML 338 **as a minesweeper in 1945**
Drawing by John Lambert
From *Allied Coastal Forces,* **Volume I © *Seaforth Publishing* 2018**

The Fairmile B was 112 feet long, overall, with a waterline length of over 105 feet, and a beam of 17 feet 10 inches. Its 4 feet 10 inches deep draught enabled it to access shallow waters. She displaced 80 tons and was powered by twin 600 horsepower Hall-Scott petrol engines. Her fuel capacity was 2,305 gallons. Her top speed was around 20 knots but a typical cruising speed would be around 15 knots, and to achieve her 1,500-mile range she would need to reduce her speed to 12 knots. Her range could be increased as she had the space to stow an additional 345 gallons of fuel on the upper deck.

In his book, *Flag 4*, Dudley Pope provides a considerable amount of information that makes compelling reading. Unfortunately, although *ML 280* gets a brief mention, *ML 338* does not feature. The book tends to concentrate on the more glamorous roles of Motor Torpedo Boats (MTBs) and Motor Gun Boats (MGBs). However, the MLs were recognised to possess a multi-role capability including minelaying, minesweeping, anti-aircraft and anti-submarine duties, rescue ship, convoy duties and escorting landing craft to the beaches.

Don became very fond of *ML 338* and, in his later letters, expressed a desire to sail her back to England but acknowledged that this would not be possible. Although he spoke little of the war, in later years he would sometimes spot a decommissioned Fairmile around the British coastline and was heard to comment: "There's a converted ML."

In addition to the ship's commander (a Lieutenant) and his No. 1 (a Sub-Lieutenant) whose quarters were the wardroom, there would be a crew of 15. The coxswain and motor mechanic would occupy a separate cabin. The remaining complement, comprising a telegraphist, two stokers and ten seamen, would be accommodated in the large open forecastle. Some MLs had the benefit of a paraffin-operated refrigerator.

ML 338 in action

H.M.M.L. 280
c/o G.P.O.,
London
31st July 1942

2
... return from leave.

My dear Linda

[...] angry with me [...] yesterday, it was [...] point of fact we will [...] since I spoke to [...] and at the m[...] hoping that no [...] up [...] Just [...] not shirking [...]

I was spending [...] at sea — only [...] like this [...] working hard in [...]

I haven't seen John or Max but I'm expecting to catch up with them within the next few days and then I suppose there will be one of the usual parties — still I'm in good training as I've been off the scotch for over a week, even without a shortage of beer!

The weather is ideal for spending the whole of one's time [...] only wish it had been [...] while we were [...] the winter.

Must finish, my darling, I really am only snatching a moment from duty, but need I add that [...] I am missing you badly [...] that I do love you rather a lot and feel at the moment very lonely

Don

Don's letter 31st July 1942

Chapter Four

JULY 1942 – OCTOBER 1942

In Chapter One, I established that Sub-Lieutenant Don Bickerton 'passed out' from *HMS King Alfred* in September 1941 and was then attached to *HMS St Christopher* at Fort William in Scotland, specifically to train in the skills required to manage an ML (Motor Launch) in action. These skills were put into practice when he served as second-in-command on *ML 280* on manoeuvres and patrols in the Bristol Channel in preparation for action in the Mediterranean. During this period, *ML 280* was sometimes based at *HMS Skirmisher II*, Pembroke Dock. It is apparent that the 25th ML Flotilla was in the process of being assembled. Many of the other officers, and probably crews, were attached to *HMS St Christopher* during the period between autumn 1941 and summer 1942.

Many years later, when I was living and working in Pembrokeshire, I told my father that I often moored my boat in Milford Haven alongside the hulk of *HMS Warrior* as it was a favoured spot for catching conger eels. He recalled mooring *ML 280* at the same spot when attached to *HMS Skirmisher II*. In 1979, *HMS Warrior* was towed to Hartlepool where she was refurbished and now she graces the Portsmouth Historic Museum.

In Chapter Two, I described how ACW Linda Russell had been posted to *RAF Hayscastle* (near Haverfordwest) also in September 1941, where she was a radar operator.

On 1st July 1942, Don and a fellow Sub-Lieutenant, John Bick travelled some 10 miles from Pembroke Dock to Haverfordwest to discover whether it was a place of interest. Whilst having a drink in the County Hotel they met Linda and her WAAF (Women's Auxiliary Air Force) colleague, a female named Johnnie. After a few drinks and, one speculates, a meal, they visited the local cinema. It is apparent that there was already quite a bit of social interaction between the WAAF at *RAF Hayscastle* and the RNVR (Royal Naval Volunteer Reserve) personnel at *HMS Skirmisher II*. As we discover, from the correspondence, they had many mutual friends. On this occasion two friendships were born, one to last a lifetime and the other but a few months.

Some years after my parents died, I was sorting through their papers and documents, which had been residing in my loft, and discovered nearly 150 letters written between 1942 and 1945.

The earliest letter found is one sent to Linda whilst on home leave with her parents at Amos House, Totland Bay, Isle of Wight. In this letter of **31st July 1942** from Don, addressed from *HMML 280*, his ship is at anchor, presumably in Milford Haven, the Bristol Channel or the Irish Sea. Considering they had only known each other for a month, from Don's tone, it is clear they are already in an intense relationship. He tells her that he is missing her "rather badly" and that he loves her "rather a lot".

He admits, in his communication **two days later,** that it may not be possible to keep his promise to write every day. Owing to censorship, he cannot say where he is located or the nature of his ship's exercises. Instead, he concentrates on the social side, which seems to involve partying and drinking. He mentions colleagues – namely John, Richard, Max and Gibby – as though Linda has already met them. He talks about "Max's ship", implying that it is part of a flotilla. References to "near-civilisation" and a "horse show" suggest that the flotilla is in a small port, presumably somewhere on the west coast of England, Wales or Scotland, or possibly on the Ulster coastline.

Johnnie, Peggy and Linda in WAAF uniform, July 1942

In Chapter Five, I list the characters that feature in their correspondence and what I have managed to discern about them. Frustratingly, more questions remain than are answered.

In his letter of **7ᵗʰ August 1942**, Don thanks Linda for hers of the previous Friday, 31st July 1942 (which has not survived). He again says that he is not allowed to communicate his whereabouts. It seems that they had also been able to talk on the telephone. He refers to a party being "a washout" and assures Linda that she should therefore have no fears about Stephanie (possibly the woman to whom he was engaged when he met Linda – see his letter dated 22nd September 1942) and that he is behaving himself. He promises to ring Linda on the following Sunday.

His next mailing is dated **10ᵗʰ August 1942**. He has been moving from place to place and experiencing stormy weather. He again mentions the partying and several mutual friends, namely Gibby, Vick and also 'Spotless' (who must be the ship's dog as Don surmises that he is chasing rabbits in his slumbers – and it is unlikely that any of his colleagues would have such fantasies!).

There is some ambiguity surrounding Don's letter of **3ʳᵈ September 1942**, in which he notes that the war is entering its fourth year. He talks about standing on a jetty waiting for Linda, 24 hours earlier, and feeling equally miserable now that she has gone again. It sounds as though she had travelled by train to meet him but then had to return to Haverfordwest the following day.

The next communication in the collection is also from Don, dated **22nd September 1942**. It is sent from Fairfield, 93 Thomas Lane, Broadgreen, Liverpool 14, his parents' house where he must have been spending his leave. He mentions having received a letter from Linda, but many of hers have been lost. They had just spent a week of their leave in Tenby and Linda was probably returning to Haverfordwest, so she would have alighted at Whitland. Don describes watching the platform at Whitland departing as he speeds on to Paddington.

This week that they spent together in Tenby at the Lion Hotel, in September 1942, just over two months into their relationship, crops up time and again in their future correspondence. Don talks about that "heavenly week" and says he will never forget it, "even when I dodder along tripping over my ancient beard at every other step". They joke about being disturbed by Alice.

Continuing with his letter of 22nd September: he tells how, after spending a day and night in London with Len (probably a Civil Service colleague; Don returned to his job there after being demobbed in 1945) and another unnamed person, he had caught the Liverpool train from Euston the next morning. Don had travelled to his parents to confess that he had broken off his engagement to a Liverpool girl because he had met Linda. He admits that his mother could not be mollified but predicts that she will come round within two days. The girl in question may have been the previously named Stephanie. Don promises to investigate all the necessary marriage formalities, presumably so that they could tie the knot before he is sent to the Mediterranean.

Don sends another letter from Liverpool **three days later**. Again, he confirms having received one from Linda. He addresses this letter to *RAF Camp, Ringstead* near Weymouth as she has just been transferred there. As he points out, this creates an unforeseen problem regarding their plans to marry before he is sent to the Mediterranean. One partner must be resident in the district in which the ceremony is to be performed for at least two weeks. He asks her to write to him at *HMS Forte N* at Falmouth, to which he will be travelling the next day. That is the location at which the ships of the flotilla are assembling. In the same letter he talks about meeting friends, seeing a film entitled *Ladies in Retirement* and going to "the local". He has also been to Middlesborough to visit friends and seen the film *Pardon My Sarong*.

Don mentions seeing his maiden aunts, Bertha and Margaret. (They lived at 166 Bowring Park Road, in the Childwall district of Liverpool, in a three-bedroomed semi-detached property they had purchased for around £750 in 1939. Margaret, who was a telephonist, died in 1977 at the age of 91. Bertha, the elder of the two and a teacher, passed away in 1991 when she was 108.) Don also notes that his younger brother, Leslie (who would have been aged 21 at the time) looked resplendent in his Home Guard uniform. He ends his letter by reminiscing about their heavenly week in Tenby. In addition he sends a second, this time brief, note with an enclosure (possibly a cartoon) later the same day.

He writes from *HMML 280*, now in Falmouth Harbour, on **29th September 1942** confirming that he has received another letter (not found) from Linda saying that she has some leave available. Unfortunately he does not have any (the flotilla is preparing to sail) and he suggests that she will have to travel to Falmouth if she wants to see him before he leaves. He describes his journey from Liverpool to Falmouth, having stayed overnight in London again with Len in Hampstead. He speaks of his dismay at finding *HMML 280* in a mess and of Dick arriving with Spotless and a "wench". He is to have an inoculation that afternoon. This is the last remaining letter that Don wrote before sailing to the Mediterranean. His next is a month later from Gibraltar.

There is one other letter of note and that is from Rear Admiral Piers Kekewich, dated **17th October 1942**, congratulating Don on his promotion to Lieutenant and his appointment to command *ML 338*. In fact, Don's promotion to Lieutenant had taken effect from 11th September 1942 and he had assumed command of *ML 338* on 7th October 1942.

Telephone
HAMpstead 7661-4

Office of Rear Admiral, Coastal Forces,
Wendover Court,
Finchley Road,
London, N.W.2

My dear Buckerton,

My congratulation
on your getting Command
of ML 338 –

I am sorry I
couldn't get to Milford
Haven to see you all
before you sailed.

To Command one of
H.M. Ships is a proud
Position – however small
the ship the responsibilities
are the same. The
success of the duties you
may be called upon to
carry out depend on many

little details - the
training & the welfare
of your men. They must
be able to look to you to
give the right answer.
in whatever situation you
may find yourself placed -
It needs imagination,
energy & skill.
I am sure you will
not be found wanting -
May the opportunity soon
come your way -
Good luck
Yours very Sincerely,
Piers Kekewich

17.10.42.

Letter from Rear Admiral Piers Kekewich

27

It reads: *My dear Bickerton,*

My congratulations on your getting command of ML 338.

I am sorry I couldn't get to Milford Haven to see you all before you sailed.

To command one of HM Ships is a proud privilege – however small the ships the responsibilities are the same – the success of the duties you may be called upon to carry out depends on many little details – the training and the welfare of your crew. They must be able to look to you to give the right answer in whatever situation you may find yourself faced.

It needs imagination, energy and skill.

I am sure you will not be found wanting – may the opportunity soon come your way.

Good luck

Yours very sincerely

Piers Kekewich

Thus, instead of being a Sub-Lieutenant and second-in-command of *ML 280*, he is a Lieutenant with his own command at the age 25. In an upcoming letter, Don will reveal that several of his colleagues are none too pleased that he has got a command despite being junior to a number of them.

Evidence points to the sequence and dates of events leading to Don's departure from UK as follows:

- September 1942 – construction of *ML 338* completed at Northam Bridge, Southampton. It is probable that she sailed along the south coast to Falmouth where the new crew would have taken delivery and undertaken trials.
- 28th September 1942 – Don arrives in Falmouth from leave taken in Liverpool (see his letter of 29th September appended to this chapter).
- 29th September 1942 – Don given inoculations and reports that *ML 280* was in a mess but states: "no doubt things will get straightened out over the next few days" (see same letter).
- 7th October 1942 – Don assumes command of *ML 338*, having been informed of his promotion.
- 8th October 1942 – Don waves goodbye to Linda in her taxi at Falmouth. Don's letters of 25th October and 29th December (appended to Chapter Five) and Linda's of 24th September 1944 (appended to Chapter Twelve) refer to this.
- 8th October 1942 or soon thereafter – MLs *280* and *338* (and possibly others) sail for Milford Haven where the 25th ML Flotilla assembles. *ML 338* is holed by *ML 280* when the latter's steering gear packs in. In his letter of 25th October, Don reports that his ship was "repaired elsewhere".
- 14th October 1942 – The flotilla sails from Milford Haven. There was talk of leaving *ML 338* behind, but it seems that Don sails her alone from the port where she has undergone repairs and meets the flotilla en route. In his letter of 25th October, Don jokes that he was "lucky" with his navigation.
- 17th October 1942 – Letter from Rear Admiral Kekewich confirming Don's appointment.

The BBC Website *WW2 People's War*, an archive of wartime memories, gives useful insight to the times. George Wishart, who was a petty officer and motor mechanic on *ML 238* (commanded by Lieutenant Commander Dudley Arnaud – the flotilla leader), recalls that he sailed from Milford Haven to Gibraltar in October 1942 and that there were eight ships within the 25th ML Flotilla. It was necessary to take a route well out into the Atlantic to avoid being within range of enemy aircraft operating off the French coast. To this end, each ship carried extra fuel tanks to increase its range.

So, after just a 14-week friendship, Don and Linda were to be parted for nearly three years. With the exception of their "heavenly week" in Tenby, one wonders on how many other occasions they could have been together during this period. After all, they had serious commitments to their respective services, and periods of leave were probably quite short and intermittent and would not always coincide. Certainly, after the first four weeks, they were already communicating by letter and had also spoken on the telephone. This was in the days when the cost of calls was pricey and mobiles were devices of science fiction. Some of Don's leave was taken up in London, Liverpool and Middlesborough. Meanwhile, Linda spent part of hers with her parents on the Isle of Wight. They could hardly have known each other, yet the love between them is palpable. For their final liaison, Linda had travelled by train from *RAF Ringstead*, near Weymouth, to *HMS Forte* at Falmouth.

More of their relationship is revealed in the correspondence that follows. As we have already discovered, there is serious talk of marriage before Don leaves for the Mediterranean but matters are complicated by Linda's transfer from *RAF Haverfordwest* to *RAF Ringstead*. Then, it seems, Don gets cold feet at the last moment saying that he is too hard up to marry. He soon regrets not having taken the oath and admits that he had been "a rat". His excuse is "pressure of work", which must have been genuine – he had been promoted, at the age of just 25, to skipper an ML. He was responsible for a complement of 17 sailors, and for navigating his new ship to Milford Haven, then Gibraltar, and on into unknown action in the Mediterranean – these must have been daunting prospects.

Their emotions pour out in the correspondence that follows. As few of Linda's letters remain, we hear mostly of Don's feelings. He becomes more and more agitated the longer the gap between Linda's letters, exacerbated by an unreliable, wartime postal service. He expresses doubts about her sincerity and says he would rather know if she has changed her mind. When he receives post from her, the reader can feel his mood lift. Don often refers to his "reputation" with the girls but insists that, since meeting her, he is a reformed character. He promises to kerb his drinking, although he then proceeds to describe all the parties and hangovers! They both reminisce about the week in Tenby and Don insists that, on his return, they will marry without delay and make up for lost time and he will never leave her again.

In Chapter Thirteen we discover that, at last, they were able to marry ten days after his return to Liverpool from the Mediterranean. One hopes they found opportunities to make up for lost time but they were still committed to their respective services. How much time they could spend together in the first few months of their marriage, we can only surmise. We learn, in Chapter Fourteen, that as soon as Don receives his discharge from the Navy (in December 1945) he has to move away from his pregnant wife to take up his post in the Civil Service, initially in Blackpool and then in London. London suffered such devastation that housing was in short supply. It would take right up until August 1947 before Don could arrange for Linda and me, his new young son, to join him in lodgings, and it would be yet another year before he could finally find a flat.

Letters: July – October 1942

H.M.M.L. 280
C/o G.P.O.,
London
31st July 1942

My dear Linda

Don't be too angry with me for not writing yesterday, it wasn't... In point of fact ... since I spoke to you ... and at ... hoping that ... up ... not shirking ...!

I was rather hoping that you might be able to spend the first day of your leave with me but you've been spared that again...

"FAIRFIELD"
Thomas Lane
Broad Green
LIVERPOOL
25th Sept 1942

... Just received your ... what filthy luck to get ... before I go away — I ... if I can manage to ... Weymouth ...

... marriage business. ... the position. One of ... acting parties (not ... ideology, I may say!) ... resident in the ... in which the ceremony ... performed for a period ... two weeks before ... mentioned ceremony. ...! But that doesn't ... particularly. I suppose ...

... knows how many ... I do love you would ... simply must see you ... All my love angel ... as ever

Don

2.C.W. Russell W.Q...,
R.A.F. Camp,
Ringstead,
N' Dorchester,
Dorset

H.M.M.L. 280
c/o G.P.O.,
London

31st July 1942

Miss Linda Russell,
Amos House,
Totland Bay,
Isle of Wight

My dear Linda

Don't be too angry with me for not writing yesterday, it wasn't choice. In point of fact we've been on duty since I spoke to you on the phone and at the moment are anchored, hoping that nothing will turn up. Just tired, my sweet, not shirking – much!

I was rather hoping that you might be able to spend the first day of your leave with me but you've been spared that agony. Believe it or not I'm missing you rather a lot and, rather meanly, awaiting your return from leave.

I haven't seen John or Max but I'm expecting to catch up with them within the next few days and then I suppose there will be one of the usual parties – still I'm in good training as I've been off the hootch for over a week, even without a shortage of beer!

The weather is ideal for spending the whole of one's time at sea – only wish it had been like this while we were working hard in the winter.

Must finish, my darling, as I really am only snatching a moment from duty, but need I add that I am missing you badly, that I do love you rather a lot and feel at the moment very lonely.

Yours Don

H.M.M.L. 280
c/o G.P.O.,
London

2nd August 1942

A.C.W. Russell W.A.A.F.,
R.A.F. Camp,
Hayes Castle Cross,
Wolf's Castle,
Pembrokeshire

My dear Linda

I don't appear to be keeping my promise to write every day but yesterday really was an impossibility – for reasons that you can probably guess.

I saw John and Max last night and they appear to have been enjoying life in these 'ere parts. John is as full of flannel as ever and still attempting to "get things organised" in his usual manner. I haven't been ashore since our arrival but Richard and I stooged across to Max's ship as soon as we had secured alongside and made ourselves unpopular by interrupting a party, drinking their whisky, completely ignoring all hints to remove our unwelcome bodies until in the end the others stooged off leaving us with the bottles as consolation. No doubt they will try to take it out of us as soon as an opportunity occurs.

This is one of the filthiest places I have yet struck but there are signs of near-civilisation and I think we should be able to enjoy ourselves. Tomorrow we propose going to the Horse Show which is apparently one of the big events of [the] year. More about that when we come back.

And how are you enjoying your leave? I'm missing you quite as much as I feared I should and looking forward to receiving your first letter. Incidentally I can find no confirmation that I snore and any comments you make on the subject will be considered libellous!

Haven't run across Gibby to date but I hope to see him within the next few days and then we really will have a party. From all accounts Gibby has been enjoying himself and fully living up to his reputation – just one of those things he can't help.

Must finish my sweet – do write soon and tell me that you still love me as much as I do you and console a rather lonely and dejected

Don

H.M.M.L. 280
c/o G.P.O.,
London

7th August 1942

My sweet

Just received your letter of last Friday – a whole week to catch up with me, I really thought you had seen the light and decided that I was that which everyone had told you I was (sounds complicated!) And, in any case, I know exactly what you must be thinking about me. Honestly, wretch, this is the first opportunity I've had to write since my last letter and (says he pitifully) it's even after 1.00 a.m. now.

Do you find it very hard to believe that I was very thrilled to receive your letters tonight and to know that I have a fair chance of seeing you within the next week?

You know, as well as I, that it is impossible for me to tell you my whereabouts at the moment but suffice it to say that it is, at any rate, within reach of civilisation – and that is a very pleasant change.

My darling, of course you weren't a nuisance t'other Wednesday. Didn't I sound thrilled to receive your phone call? If I didn't, put it down to some G.P.O. defect – it certainly had nothing to do with me. As if I'm ever busy!

I'm afraid the party was a washout as none of us was anywhere near the rendezvous. Thus you need have no fears about Stephanie – and isn't it already quite clear that I always behave myself?

Haven't done a thing worthy of report (that would pass the censor) since my last letter. Just stoogeing as usual.

I do so want to see you again very soon my dear and I intend phoning you on Sunday. In the meantime suppose you apply your own warnings about behaviour to yourself.

Inevitably all my love,
Yours Don.

H.M.M.L. 280
c/o G.P.O.,
London

10th August 1942

A.C.W. Russell W.A.A.F.,
R.A.F. Camp,
Hayes Castle,
Wolf's Castle Cross,
Pembrokeshire

My darling

To date I have only received the letter to which I replied last time, but as it's some time since we had any mail I'm expecting a bumper crop when it does arrive. And if it isn't – then look out for trouble my sweet! I know that I haven't kept my promise and written every day but I have <u>the</u> perfect alibi – we've been working. Anyway pet should you have recovered from your surprise I'll phone you tomorrow.

We've been to several other places since my last letter and although I can naturally give you little information I'll do what I can.

I believe I last wrote on Friday. On Saturday I found Gibby and naturally that called for a celebration. So quite a crowd of us had numerous drinks and then went on to a dance where we behaved ourselves as officers although not necessary as gentlemen – if you know what I mean. On second thoughts that sounds very much worse than the truth; therefore let me leave it at that – we did behave ourselves!

On Sunday we pushed on our way in fairly bad weather and lay to a buoy rolling our guts out (naval expression). It was most unpleasant and we were all very thankful to leave this morning.

And now we are in another dump and so far as it is possible to foresee at the moment, stuck here until the weather improves.

Poor old Vick is looking very miserable with something I imagine to be a dose of the 'flu'. Even Spotless has his head down and appears to be chasing rabbits in his slumbers.

Linda my darling do write again soon as I am missing you a hell of a lot and, for the present, your letters are the only consolation for your absence. Need I add that, peculiar as it may seem to the uninitiated, I do love you rather a lot and only wish you were here to comfort an otherwise very lonely

Don

H.M.M.L. 280
c/o G.P.O.,
London

3rd September 1942

A.C.W. Russell W.A.A.F.,
R.A.F. Camp,
Hayscastle Cross,
Wolf's Castle,
Pembrokeshire

My dear Linda

Exactly 24 hours ago I was standing on a jetty waiting for you and feeling pretty fed up with life. Now I'm feeling equally fed up. The reason is not quite the same, but the fact remains that you are some distance away and, frankly, I don't like it at all. Last night was complete bliss but, unfortunately, that only accentuates your absence - because, as you may have guessed, I do love you rather a lot.

Wretch, all I want to write and keep on writing is that I love you and that I just daren't let you go.

About this leave business. I hope to be able to tell you more about that when we arrive and as soon as everything, including my own leave, is settled, then I shall send off a frantic telegram.

I felt pretty miserable when the train steamed out this morning and it struck me as no method of celebrating the commencement of our fourth year of war.

Must finish angel as I'm desperately tired (I fully realise that this letter is quite incoherent) but I simply had to write to you.

All my love pet, [not legible]
Don

"Fairfield"
Thomas Lane
Broad Green
LIVERPOOL

22nd Sept 1942

My darling

Many thanks for your letter which I received this morning. I know I promised to write yesterday but it was just impossible by the time I arrived home.

Would you like to hear (beg pardon – read) of my activities from the time I left you at Whitland. Well I just stared at the departing platform until it was long ago out of sight and then I returned to my compartment feeling pretty fed up with life. I tried to go to sleep but all I could do was think about you and the past week and the marvellous time we had together, and sleep was clearly impossible. I tried to carry on with the "Loom of Youth" but my mind was weaving other thoughts and I was rescued when the steward came in to ask me at what time I should like some tea. "Right Away" said I very hopefully and was quite shattered when it actually arrived within two minutes.

A peculiar old boy in the opposite corner insisted upon discussing present day difficulties in travel and refused to be quietened when I abruptly informed him that I was well aware of these difficulties, that I had more travelling to do over the next few days and that I therefore desired to sleep. I am afraid he was very thick skinned and it had not the slightest effect upon him. I was thankful when he got out at Swansea.

The train arrived at Paddington at 0630 and after a welcome bath I had breakfast and lazed about until 0830, which seemed a reasonable time to call on Len.

We went to town after some little argument (he wanted to spend the afternoon working at the office!) and after lunch and odd drinks decided to go back to Hampstead and laze. In the evening the three of us went across the Heath to the Freemasons and consumed as much beer as we could, argued the whole time – chiefly on classical music about which I know nothing – and then returned to have a night cap & turn in.

Yesterday I caught the 1035 from Euston (two minutes to spare) and arrived in L'pool at 1515. I went over to my Father's place and broke the sad news to him. Then I loafed about looking up odd people until about 1800 – then home.

At the moment Mother is more than a little annoyed with me for breaking my engagement and she refuses to be mollified even when I point out how much I happen to love a nasty little wretch by the name of Linda. Still, she'll come round within two days.

I don't know what I shall do with the rest of my leave. I feel completely lost without you. Angel I've never been so blissfully happy in my life as I was last week and I shouldn't need to tell you that I love you far more than any words of mine can adequately convey. It is something which I have never before experienced – and I thought I knew all the answers. I hope to make all the inquiries by the necessary marriage formalities this afternoon and I'll let you know the result as soon as I can. In the meantime don't you dare use that last 48 of yours.

Seem to have picked up a filthy cold from somewhere so I guess I'll wander down to the post and take a little nourishment at the local.

I do love you such a hell of a lot, sweet, so write soon and cheer up your rather miserable and very lonely.

Don

P.S. Do take care of that cold of yours otherwise there'll be trouble when I next see you.

"Fairfield", Thomas Lane
Broad Green, LIVERPOOL

25th Sept 1942

A.C.W. Russell W.A.A.F.,
R.A.F. Camp, Ringstead,
Nr Dorchester, Dorset.

My sweet

Just received your letter. What filthy luck to get posted just before I go away – I must see if I can manage to get to Weymouth.

This marriage business. This is the position. One of the contracting parties (not my phraseology, I may say!) must be resident in the district in which the ceremony is to be performed for a period of at least two weeks before the aforementioned ceremony. Quite clear? But that doesn't help us particularly. I suppose I am correct in the assumption that although you have changed your base, it will make no difference to the leave position? Do let me know and write to me at H.M.S. FORTE N, FALMOUTH as I return tomorrow.

You seem to have had a pretty miserable journey to Bristol – the only thing which surprises me is that you didn't find a comfortable knee on which to sit – or am I being catty?

I suppose I'd better avoid cross examination and tell you just what I've been up to since I last wrote.

Not very much. On Tuesday I went into town to meet my people and we went to a flic "Ladies in Retirement" (Ida Lupino) – it's worth seeing and then into the local (with Mother's too evident disapproval) when I got back.

On Wednesday I went up to Middlesborough to see some people – this is what I so adore about leave, nowt but travel – and saw another film "Pardon My Sarong" – also quite good. Back again on Thursday morning and in the evening I attempted not to look bored while I listened to the platitudes of two maiden aunts. I eventually escaped and went with my brother, resplendent in his Home Guard uniform, to consume as much beer as I could in half an hour. All things considered we did quite well but unfortunately the aunts were still there when we returned. So we treated them to a jazz session – they just adore swing – until they were pleased to retire hurt.

Today has been uneventful. I was stung for an expensive lunch but it was worth it to see Mother behind a pint pot of lager. Useful blackmailing material for the future.

Well all good things come to an end and tomorrow I go back but spend the night at Len's place at Hampstead and on to Falmouth on Sunday morning.

Angel you've no idea how fed up I've been this week without you. I suppose its reaction after such a heavenly week in Tenby – I shan't ever forget it not even when I dodder along tripping over my ancient beard at every other step. We simply must get married before I leave – being away from you has shown me how essential it is. And anyway I can't go away for Lord knows how long without seeing you again. You should know by now that I did and always will mean all the things I told you. In three words – I love you. My only fear is that, if I am away for a long time, you will get bored and eventually forget all about me. However I don't altogether advise it – no! Not really a threat!

Must finish my darling. Write soon and let me know if you can get away.

All my love always
Ever Thine,
Don

"Fairfield"
Thomas Lane
Broad Green
LIVERPOOL

25th Sept 1942

A.C.W. Russell
W.A.A.F.,
R.A.F. Camp,
Ringstead,
Nr Dorchester,
Dorset.

My Dear Linda

I saw the enclosed and it struck such a familiar note that I couldn't resist sending it to you. Although I don't remember you wearing your cap!

All my love, pet,
Yrs
Don.

H.M.M.L. 280
c/o G.P.O.,
London

29th Sept 1942

My darling

As you can see I managed to get back to the ship on time although I must admit that I didn't enjoy it at all.

I've just received your letter from Ringstead and I shall reply to that before I give you any news. As you may guess I was more than a little shattered to learn that you had been posted to Weymouth – especially after my cosy dreams of seeing you at P.D. It must have been a miserable journey but I should have thought Weymouth would suit you far better than Hayscastle. I appreciate that changes are invariably unpleasant but I'm sure you'll enjoy it once you settle down.

So you think you can manage a few days leave. I propose wiring you this afternoon but I can't get away and it will mean you coming down here. Do try and make it my sweet – I don't know what I shall do if I can't see you before I go. I'd no idea that I could fall so irrevocably in love – but it has happened just the same.

Would you like to know how I've spent (or misspent if you prefer it that way!) my time since I last wrote to you? You can't help yourself anyway.

I caught the 10.00 train from L'pool and went over to Len's place at Hampstead when I arrived. I was overjoyed to find a little whisky left and it helped to banish thoughts of the journey. After dinner we crawled over the Heath to the Freemasons and met some people I know - awful bores - and made small talk for several hours. It was almost a relief to get away from the pub and that (let me say it for you) is quite a change.

On Sunday I was up bright and early (09.30) but the other slackers stayed in bed until noon when we dashed across the Heath once more. After lunch Len was still tired so while he slept Hazel and I went for a walk round the Heath. I think I must be out of training as I nearly finished on my knees.

I caught the 21.50 from Paddington and arrived here yesterday morning only to learn that a telegram had been sent extending my leave until today. The ship was in a hell of a mess – nearly burst into tears when I saw it – but no doubt things will get straightened out over the next few days.

Dick arrived back with Spotless and a wench last night – and everyone gives me the bad reputation! We had quite a party last night and as the beer ran out at 22.00 I had a very early night.

This afternoon I'm due for inoculation so I'm having my last alcoholic fling this lunch time – probably just pass out anyway after the inoculation.

Anyway darling I'll send the wire this afternoon – do try and get down here as it will be the last time for Lord knows how many years. I do love you wretch and I simply must see you.

All my love Angel
As ever
Don

Chapter Five

OCTOBER – DECEMBER 1942

At this point it is worth examining the state of the war in the Mediterranean and the growing role of Coastal Forces.

The situation when war broke out was that North Africa, like most of the continent, was colonised by European powers: the British ruled Egypt; the French, Algeria; and the Italians, Libya. The Italians made the first move in September 1940 and invaded Egypt. However, two months later, the British counter-attacked and pushed the Italians back into Libya, taking over part of the country. Mussolini sought Hitler's help, and a small German force landed in Tripoli and set up a defensive line. As the Germans were also threatening Greece, which they attacked in April 1941 followed by Crete in May 1941, the British withdrew most of their forces from Libya but a rearguard stood firm in Tobruk. Under their new commander, Rommel, the German and Italian Armies went on the offensive again and Tobruk was besieged by the Axis forces for 241 days. Eventually they withdrew, and Tobruk was relieved by the British on 9th December 1941. Two days earlier, on 7th December 1941, Japan had attacked Pearl Harbour, bringing the USA into the war.

Coastal Forces mostly comprised RNVR (Royal Naval Volunteer Reserve) personnel. One ship in the 3rd Flotilla of Motor Launches, to which Don's *ML 338* was later transferred, was *ML 126* commanded by Gordon Stead, a Canadian on loan to the Royal Navy. In his book *A Leaf Upon the Sea*, Stead describes being in the vanguard of small ships sent to Malta. In June 1941 his ship joined seven vessels from the 9th Flotilla of Motor Launches in Plymouth. The plan was for the MLs to travel initially to the British base in Gibraltar, where they would join the remainder of the 3rd Flotilla, by taking a route 1,800 miles long and 300 miles beyond the ML's fuel range. This was far out into the Atlantic and out of range of enemy aircraft. Despite the fact that *ML 126* had an extra fuel tank, it was decided that four destroyers of the 8th Flotilla would tow two MLs each. Although bad weather hampered the operation, all ships arrived safely in Gibraltar. Their tasks there included undertaking patrols (usually singly) to deter sabotage raids, boarding and checking neutral ships, etc.

Early in 1942, plans were made to dispatch the 3rd Flotilla to Tobruk. Two ships, MLs *126* and *130* would be sent first to Malta. The 1,000-mile journey was undertaken by these petrol-driven wooden ships, which were disguised in Italian grey camouflage and flying the Italian flag. By the rules of war, this was legal for the purpose of infiltrating a hostile area, provided they did not open fire without first displaying their own national colours. The two ships succeeded, although not without incident, completing the journey between 12th and 17th March 1942. Despite Lieutenant Stead's advice to the contrary, two more MLs followed. They ran into trouble and their personnel spent much of the rest of the war as prisoners.

It was between mid-March and mid-June 1942 that Malta came under the heaviest Axis bombardment. On one patrol in May 1942, *ML 130* was attacked by six E-boats and their crew were also taken prisoner.

E-boat was the Allies' designation for the German fast attack craft (Schnellboot or S-Boot). The most popular, the S-100 class, were very seaworthy, heavily armed and fast – capable of sustaining 43.8 knots. They were 107 feet 6 inches long with a beam of 16 feet 7 inches. Their diesel engines had a longer range than the American and British alternatives. As a result, the Royal Navy later developed a better matched version of the Motor Torpedo Boat (MTB), using the Fairmile 'D' design.

E-Boat by Lt. J.E. Russell, *Royal Navy* **official photographer**
[**public domain**], via *Wikimedia Commons*

It was not until June 1942 that the remainder of the 3rd ML Flotilla arrived in Malta. By then, much of the Luftwaffe had been diverted elsewhere, in particular to Stalingrad, and the RAF's strength had increased considerably. However, in July 1942, Tobruk fell, and it was not until the 1st Battle of El Alamein, in July 1942, that the British were able to blunt Rommel's advance. The 2nd Battle of El Alamein would accomplish a decisive victory for the British. It would commence on 23rd October and end on 11th November 1942. This Allied victory coincided with Operation Torch – the Allied sea-borne invasion of French North Africa which would commence on 8th November 1942.

MAP C

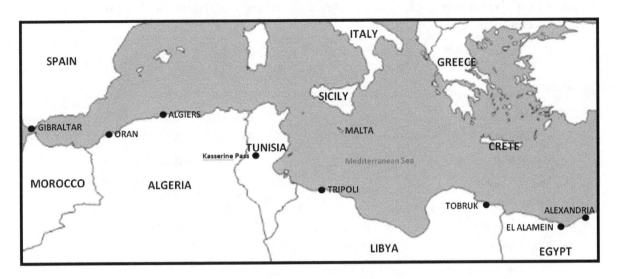

It is probable that the timing of Don's 25th ML Flotilla transfer in mid-October 1942 from Southern England to Gibraltar was directly linked to the planned Operation Torch. The first letter he sends (briefly mentioned in Chapter Four) is dated **25th October 1942**. He declares that life has been hectic since he saw Linda off in the car. He says that they sailed for 'this dump' (Gibraltar) in filthy weather and, because of the damage incurred (between Falmouth and Milford Haven when *ML 280* collided with him), there was talk of leaving *ML 338* behind. In the event, repairs were undertaken and *ML 338* left later than the remainder of the flotilla. Don had joined them in fog, and is clearly pleased with his navigational skills. He says that, after a couple of days, the fog cleared and the sea was like a mirror. However there had been an air raid during their first night in Gibraltar, which he reports was noisy but nothing was dropped.

In the same letter he thanks Linda for hers (which has not survived), together with her enclosure of £2. (The first communication found from Linda is a telegram dated November 1942, and her first remaining letter is from December 1942 – see later in this Chapter.) Don tells Linda how much he is already missing her and apologises for "F-------". This is probably a reference to Falmouth (all his letters are subject to censorship; he would have censored his crew's letters and self-censored his own). He reveals that, despite his talk of marriage, it had been his decision not to proceed before he left for the Mediterranean because he was so hard up. He acknowledges his reputation and promises to lead a sober life and not "stooge around with any women at all". He says his love for her will never change. He asks her to send a photograph (repeated in letter after letter) of herself and to use airmail, which takes one week rather than four weeks by ship. He also says that Dick and Alan send their love.

Two days later, on **27th October 1942**, he writes again, addressing his letter from Mess 45, Coastal Force Base, Gibraltar. He reports that there is not much to do except drink, either on board or at the Capitol (presumably an officers' club or hotel), which closes at 9pm. While there, they drank John Collins (a gin-based cocktail dating back to the 18th century and named after a head waiter who worked at Limmer's Old House in Conduit Street, Mayfair).

On 29th October 1942 there had been a Flotilla Dinner at the Rock-Hotel, Gibraltar, and in his letter of 4th November 1942, Don encloses a signed copy of the menu. An attempt has been made to decipher the signatures:

Signatories:

F D Bickerton

E C Denton

Richard Vick

Peter W Sanson

Dudley Arnaud

Donald E Beswick

D Venning

[signature illegible]

Alan [surname not legible]

Max Johnson

Leo A Clegg "The Lout"

A H Paul

R Sheppard

[signature illegible]

F D

H J Ayres

Each ML would have had two officers, a Lieutenant commanding and a Sub-Lieutenant as his No. 1 (plus a crew of 15). Therefore 16 officers' signatures, would imply there being eight ships in the flotilla, which is borne out by other evidence (see Chapter Four).

After the dinner, it appears that drinking had resumed once they returned to their ships, and that there had been a number of hangovers the next morning. In his 4th November letter, Don also mentions drinking the following evening at the Capitol with Alan, Dudley, Max, John and Shep.

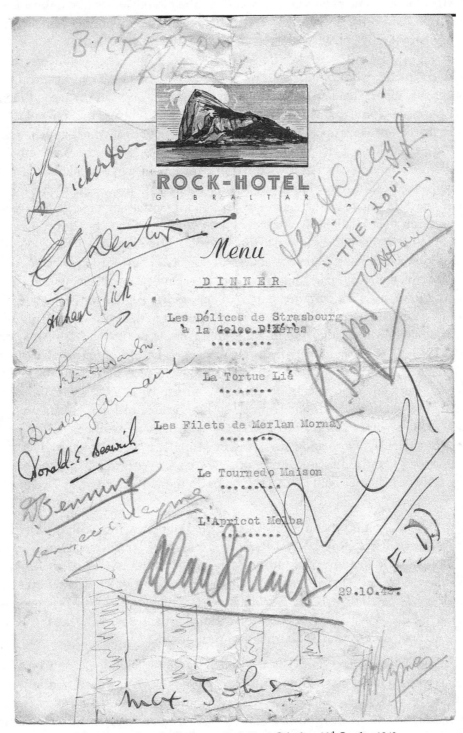

Signed menu from flotilla dinner, *Rock-Hotel***, Gibraltar. 29th October 1942**

In his letters over the ensuing months (and years), Don frequently refers to his fellow officers of the 25th ML Flotilla, some of whom Linda knows. She has obviously met quite a few of them, probably at parties and other social events. Although there is only limited evidence available, I now examine what is known of the characters that feature.

Dudley W S Arnaud, who commanded *ML 238*, seems to be Don's closest friend with whom he has a special rapport. Dudley had been granted his commission in the second month of the war on 29th October 1939, implying that he joined the reserves before the war and is quite a few years older than Don. He is appointed senior officer of the flotilla, which initially assembled at *HMS St Christopher* at Fort William in Scotland, and holds the rank of Lieutenant Commander. After the invasion of French North Africa, Don suggests that Linda should write to Dudley's wife, Eda, in Kent. However, Dudley is having serious extra marital affairs whilst away from home. In one of his letters in January 1943, Don tells of a tearful Dudley writing to 'Jane' to break off their relationship as he does not wish to go through a divorce with Eda and, in Don's opinion, is "genuinely attached" to his wife. Three months later, Don relates that Dudley has now fallen for a "French female" in Algiers. They are together in August 1943 when another of their colleagues informs Don that Dudley is still living with that "awful" French girl. However, in the summer of 1943, Don has left Algiers for Malta and transfers to Gordon Stead's 3rd ML Flotilla. Both flotillas are involved in the invasion of Sicily, after which Don meets up again with Dudley and his other colleagues of the 25th in Malta. However, in the autumn of 1943, there are a number of personnel changes. Dudley is to leave Coastal Forces to take command of a corvette in the Mediterranean but, in fact, he returns to the UK for six weeks leave before taking a posting as training commander at *HMS St Christopher* at Fort William. They correspond with one another, so Don is able to follow Dudley's progress. In June 1944, Dudley takes command of *ML 147* and, as senior officer, leads the 20th ML Flotilla in the D-Day Normandy invasion for which he receives an MID (Mention in Despatches) for gallantry. In the autumn of 1944, he is then given a shore job in London. We never discover whether Dudley and Eda went on to have a happy marriage but I do hope that was the case.

If Dudley receives the most mentions in Don's correspondence, then Gibby is not far behind. **W Gibson** was an RNR (Royal Naval Reserve) Lieutenant. Whenever Don is involved in a party, Gibby and Dudley invariably feature and consequently suffer competing hangovers. When Dudley leaves the Mediterranean in the autumn of 1943, Gibby takes over *ML 238* as senior officer of the flotilla. RNR personnel were generally merchant seamen, who were called upon by the Royal Navy in times of national emergency, whereas the RNVR were volunteers without a professional seafaring qualification.

Richard W Vick (known as **Dick**) is a Lieutenant commanding *ML 280* and the third colleague to whom Don is close. In the summer of 1943, when Don had transferred to the 3rd ML Flotilla, it is Dudley, Gibby and Richard whom he misses the most. Initially, after training at *HMS St Christopher*, Don is Dick's No. 1 before getting his own command. A month after Operation Torch in December 1942, Don says that he misses Dick and Spotless (the *ML 280* ship's dog). Perhaps he sails to Gibraltar or Malta for a refit because, at the end of January 1943, Don reports that Dick has "rejoined the fold".

Dennis Max Johnson (referred to as **Max**), another of the Rock-Hotel signatories, is also a Lieutenant but the ML under his command has not been identified. Max is in a relationship with Louise, another WAAF. In January 1943, Linda tells Don that Louise has not heard from Max but there is no further information on the relationship in any of the correspondence. There is a farewell party for Max in April 1943, but then in August and November 1943 Don mentions coming across Max, and that both are missing their friends from the 25th ML Flotilla.

Dennis Venning is a Lieutenant commanding *ML 336*. In November 1943, Don reports that Richard and Dennis are transferring to bigger ships.

Reginald S Sheppard (Shep) is a Sub-Lieutenant but his ML has not been identified. In August 1943, Don mentions that he has met MacInnes, whom he had known from Falmouth and that Shep is his No. 1.

H John Bick is with Don on 1st July 1942, that fateful day when they venture to Haverfordwest and meet Johnnie and Linda in the County Hotel. However, John and Johnnie's relationship does not last. When Don receives his promotion to Lieutenant and takes command of his own ship, he reveals that some of the other Sub-Lieutenants are none too pleased that he has been promoted when he is the most junior (he was 25 years of age). He says that John, in particular, was not impressed. John develops pneumonia in November 1942, and the following month he returns to the UK. On 5th December 1942, Linda tells Don that Johnnie has terminated their relationship, which John discovers for himself when he contacts her. In fact, she is now engaged to another. John does return to the Mediterranean, after a spell at *HMS Midge*, Great Yarmouth, taking command of *ML 596*.

Alan is Don's No. 1; his surname has not been identified. At the end of 1942 it is decided that he should swap places with Gibby's No. 1, **Eric C Denton** (known as **Phyllis**) as they were always quarrelling. Don does not seem to hold too high an opinion of either of them, although he says that Phyllis is annoying him rather less than Alan – but Gibby is regretting the change! In April 1943, Phyllis is hospitalised with jaundice and, during the following month, Alan is sent home for leave and a shore job because of "anxiety neurosis". No more is heard of Alan, but Phyllis returns to *ML 338* to be Don's No. 1 again until he receives his own command in November 1943 and **Ken J Hall** takes his place. Don does not reveal how he rates Ken who remains his No. 1 until June 1944.

Stan G Munns replaces Ken as Don's No. 1 in June 1944. Initially Don thought him very green but warms to him and, in February 1945, reports that Stan is turning out very well. They kept in touch all their lives, meeting at flotilla reunions and exchanging Christmas cards. When my father died in 2008, at the age of 90, I rang Stan who was a few years younger. I spoke to his wife, who explained that he had dementia and, sadly, would not be able to hold a coherent conversation with me.

Peter W Sanson is briefly mentioned in November 1943, when all the changes are taking place. He transfers from MLs to MTBs (Motor Torpedo Boats).

Leo A Clegg, DSC, who is a Lieutenant commanding *ML 307* signs himself "The Lout" on Don's Rock-Hotel menu but is not mentioned in Don's letters.

It has not been possible to expand on the remaining names.

As mentioned earlier in this chapter, Operation Torch, which was the Allied invasion of French North Africa, commenced on 8th November 1942. It would finish three days later. Fortunately for Don, his ship is sent to Algiers where the French Resistance stages a coup, on that same day, against the Vichy authorities. They arrest the Vichy commanders of the French XIX Corps just before the Allied landings. The Allies are not so fortunate further along the coast in Oran and Morocco, where the Vichy French troops put up strong and bloody resistance. However, after high level talks, they cease operations there by 11th November and a Free French Administration takes over and the French forces join the Allies. This prompts the Axis occupation of Vichy France, and the French fleet is captured at Toulon by the Italians, although the bulk of the fleet has been scuttled.

A DVD is available from the Imperial War Museum showing Convoy KMF(A)1 sailing from Gibraltar to Algiers at the commencement of Operation Torch. *ML 338* is part of this convoy and on Reel One, Scene II, she can be observed steaming between *HMS Orontes* (a liner converted to a troopship) and *HMS Marne* (an 'M' class destroyer). The official synopsis of **Reel One, Scene II** reads:

Convoy KMF(A)1 at sea. LS of HMS Biter amidst the convoy, and MS of the aircraft ranged aft – Sea Hurricanes of 800 Squadron and Swordfish of 833A Flight, one of which is running up. Shots of the LSIs in the convoy, including Orontes, Strathnaver, Sobieski. A Fairmile B **ML 338** steams between Orontes and Marnix. Three Fairmiles pass in line abreast through the convoy.

Author's note: On the above details of this film, it seems that the title should read 'from Gibraltar' and not 'for Gibraltar'. Also in the synopsis, Scene II, 'Marnix' should read 'Marne'.

In his letter of **15th November 1942**, Don reveals that he has been successfully involved in action and that there have been no casualties on his ship. Censorship rules would have prevented him from adding any further details. He discloses more in later correspondence, saying, on 6th January 1943, that their craft had been "first in" and that the experience was "good fun and thrilling". The fact that his ship was first in lends more understanding to his admission, on 8th November 1943, that they had been "scared stiff" during the invasion. Whilst he does not reveal his whereabouts, he divulges that he has been ashore (presumably in Algiers) and that the local populace is mostly friendly and welcoming. One resident has invited Don and his colleagues into his house for drinks and wishes to arrange a dinner party. He has introduced them to a crowd of his friends. The tone of this letter must have put Linda's mind at ease after discovering that her fiancé has been in action. Don ends his letter with his usual expression of his love for Linda. He admits his mistake in not marrying her before his departure and vows to rectify matters as soon as possible on his return. He suggests that Tenby might be a good spot for a honeymoon as the town holds happy memories. In a postscript he asks whether he should address her as Corporal rather than ACW (Aircraft Woman). She perhaps announced that she had received promotion, and he is making the incorrect assumption that she is now a Corporal. From her service record, it can be gleaned that she was promoted to LACW (Leading Aircraft Woman) with effect from 1st November 1942. It is not until later that she will become a Corporal.

The first surviving communication from Linda is a telegram, dated **19th November 1942** and transmitted through Cable and Wireless Limited. Linda sends it from Warmwell, which is presumably the nearest post office to Ringstead.

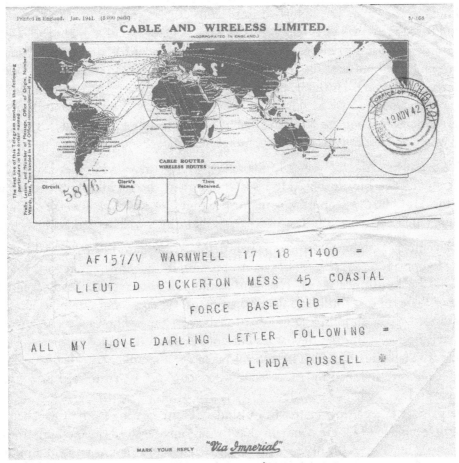

Telegram from Linda dated 19th November 1942

The paralysis of the postal system in wartime is highlighted in Don's mailing of **26th November 1942,** in which he acknowledges receipt of Linda's letter of 6th October 1942 (which sadly has been lost). This is the first letter in which he addresses her with the title LACW and, in a postscript, he congratulates her on her promotion. He says that he has just received a cable at the same time, which must be her telegram above, sent on 19th November 1942. She reports that she has not been well. Don informs her that he has watched the film *Holiday Inn* on one of the bigger ships. The navy obviously showed current films to keep up morale. Don appears to reply to a point made in Linda's letter, clarifying that he was not in Tenby (on the occasion in question) because he was in Cardiff undergoing repairs to his ship – although, as her letter has not been found, it cannot be surmised what she said. He then makes the point that, to him, Tenby is a holiday resort where he spent the happiest week of his life. He also responds to a reference she had made regarding photographs and says he has some perfume and "stuff" for her.

Don writes a series of letters to Linda over the next few days, dated **28th and 30th November** and **2nd, 4th, 5th, 7th and 10th December 1942.** In the first, he expresses his annoyance in not receiving any communication from her since her 17th November cable (possibly the one with the 19th November franking, mentioned before). His fears about her continued sincerity emerge, although he gives her the benefit of the doubt by suggesting that there may be good reason why he has not heard. Although these letters are addressed from *HMML 338*, c/o GPO, London, one assumes that he is still based in Algiers or somewhere along the Algerian coastline. He reports that he has had a haircut in a hotel and confesses that, whilst there, he had a few drinks with Alan and some colleagues whom he had not seen for 18 months, although they had to stay sober in case they were called out on a red warning. However, he relates that later he was invited onto one of the bigger ships and had a few more drinks with Max and Gibby, who were also there, and that he had sung *Darktown Strutters' Ball*, a popular jazz song by Shelton Brooks first published in 1917. (Nearly 50 years on, he would enjoy seeing his granddaughter, Julie tap dance to the same tune!)

On **30th November 1942**, he wishes Linda a happy Christmas and invites her to identify any perfume she might like him to buy. He also reports that, the night before, there had been a celebration for Alan's birthday and a viewing of the film *The Reluctant Dragon* on another ship. He also sends, Dudley Arnaud's address in Kent, should Linda wish to contact his wife.

On **2nd December**, Don breaks off from an anti-submarine patrol to write and tell Linda that he has been reading her letter, sent on her return to camp from Tenby. He reports that John is in hospital recovering from pneumonia. He again reminisces about "the most heavenly week" he spent with her there, in more intimate detail than before, and of "that fateful evening" when he went to Haverfordwest with John and met her for the first time. They are on an anti-submarine patrol and have dropped some depth charges but not scored a hit. He jokes that *HMML 338* has fired on a friendly US aircraft, which he had mistaken for a Heinkel III. He also tells of a lucky escape after being dive bombed by a four engine Focke Wulf which missed by 50 yards. That must have shaken Linda when she read it.

Don's despair at not receiving a letter from Linda, despite hearing from others, becomes more frantic on **4th December 1942**. He confirms that he has only received one mailing from her since he left England. He pleads with her to write more frequently, and also to send a photograph of herself. He says he has had several letters from home and that his mother has been rather ill, which he puts down to worry about the war. It must have been a stressful time for the parents and loved ones whose friends and relatives were in action.

He reports that everyone is working fairly hard and that he has been on patrol on four nights out of the last five. In his leisure time he listens to the radio, and an excerpt of the musical comedy running at His Majesty's Theatre has made him feel quite homesick. The *Guide to Musical Theatre* records that *Dubarry Was a Lady* by Cole Porter was running at that time and that, following its success on Broadway, it opened in the West End at His Majesty's Theatre on 22nd October 1942 and ran for 178 performances. It was directed by Richard Bird and the cast featured Arthur Riscoe as Louis Blore, Frances Day as May Daly, Frances Marsden as Alice Barton, Jacky Hunter as Charley, Bruce Trent as Alex Barton and Teddy Beaumont as Harry Norton. The plot is about a washroom attendant (Louis Blore) who wins a sweepstake and subsequently quits his job. In the same letter, Don comments that he enjoys hearing the chimes of Big Ben which, when he was working in London, he sometimes found rather irritating.

Don writes the next day, **5th December 1942**, stating that he is bored, fed up and on duty. He proudly explains that he has worked on cleaning the upper deck and, with Alan's help, is starting on the wardroom. He says he is undecided whether to hang some David Wright prints or original watercolours of Walter Thomas.

David Wright (born 12th December 1912) was a British illustrator who drew a series of 'lovelies' that epitomised female glamour during World War II. He was commissioned in 1941 to draw a number of glamorous women for *The Sketch* magazine, most of whom were modelled on his wife Esme. The illustrations established him as one of the most popular pin-up artists. In the 1950s, he continued drawing in a similar style for *Men Only*. He created the *Carol Day* cartoon strip for the *Daily Mail* in 1956, a soap opera style of comic strip. However, it was his series of 169 illustrations for *The Sketch* magazine (from 1941 to 1951) that made him most popular.

Walter Thomas, on the other hand, produced watercolours not of 'lovelies' but of more mundane subjects, such as Cunard liners. Prints of these were used for advertising posters and were produced by Don's father in the printing business in which he was a manager.

Don declares that he will settle on the David Wright prints.

Returning to his letter: Max again gets a mention, as does John whom Don says will be visiting him the next day. He also admits that he misses Dick and Spotless.

Although he would not have received it for a while, Linda also writes on **5th December 1942**. This is the first letter by her that has survived. She too mentions not having heard from Don for ages, so clearly, at this stage of the war, there is quite a delay in the forces' postal service. She tells him that she is missing him frightfully. She admits that not knowing exactly what is happening is making it more difficult to settle down and write more often. However, she is finding her daily routine fun and is thankful that she is busy. She too reminisces about Tenby and about their short time together. She mentions Johnnie and John, whose relationship appears to have ended now they are apart. She also tells of camp dances and three films she has seen: *The Men in Her Life*, *Holiday Inn* (which Don reported having seen in his earlier letter – see page 49) and *First of the Few*.

On **7th December 1942**, Don again chastises Linda for the lack of correspondence saying that he writes five times a week. Don says he is whiling away the time in Algeria in glorious sunshine. He reports that the food leaves a lot to be desired but there is an abundance of fruit and wine. He had gone ashore for the first time in a week and had lunch with Gibby and others and went on to a music hall where he found his "long neglected French" was improving. He refers to Linda's letter (that has not survived) in which she tells of her leave in Bournemouth. That would have been with her sister, Peggy, and husband, Herbert. Don again expresses his regret at not marrying her before he left and vows that a "beeline for the nearest Registrar" will be his first mission on his return. He asks Linda if she has received the perfume, etc, and there's the usual reminder of the photograph he has requested.

Don's next letter, dated **10th December 1942**, although quite long does not have a great deal of content. He pointedly stresses the importance attached by the crews to post and the fact that the last batch of mail had not been for the MLs. He has been spending more time on sea patrols and finds it some consolation that they are considered to be doing a good job. John is recovering from pneumonia and will soon be leaving hospital but, by contrast, Don thinks Alan is feigning his illness to get home again. He also expresses an ambition to write poetry or a novel to while away the hours. He mentions that he has a young aunt (unnamed, possibly his Aunt Esther) in Bournemouth whom he would like Linda to look up, and he says that he has enclosed the address, although this was not found with the letter; he thinks she might manage a hotel.

On **15th December 1942**, Don reports that the mail still has not arrived but that he has been busy. On Sunday, however, he had briefly gone ashore with Gibby when they had gone to the Aletti Hotel.

Under French occupation, the Aletti was one of the city's chic addresses. The building was grand, the view over the harbour perfect and some of the rooms vast and decorated with character. Anecdotes from contributors to the BBC's *WW2 People's War* website, describe the Aletti as being a better class of hotel, frequented by officers. Afterwards they had gone on to the Paris Hotel with colleagues and "RAF types". His account of the drunken sessions that followed is probably the last thing Linda wishes to read.

Four days later, he advises that the mail has still not arrived and that he has spent six nights of the last eight at sea, mostly in the rain. He also tells of another visit to the Aletti Hotel where he met a person whom he had last seen at Barry Dock. A drinking session had ensued aboard, before visiting a place called Bindles. Later Don had dinner on board ship with their doctor. They were joined by a journalist, and a three-hour political discussion had ensued. Don mentions that at the other end of the wardroom a drunken sing-song, led by Alan, was evident. Don says he heard from Max that John is to go on two months' sick leave.

In the first paragraph of Don's letter of **Christmas Eve,** he makes clear his annoyance at not receiving a letter from Linda. This is despite three mail deliveries and letters from others. His mood is also perhaps affected by the wet, cold weather and the fact that his is the duty boat and that he will be going out on Christmas morning. He says that they are working extraordinarily hard and that everyone is showing signs of strain. He confirms that he has seen John, who is to go home following his dose of pneumonia and will get in touch with Johnnie. He also expresses concern to hear that his mother is ill, and is worrying about the lack of follow-up news, although when he was in Freetown he had not had mail for four months. (That would have been when he was on convoy duty with *HMS Mauritius* - see Chapter One.) He reports that he has been ashore with a friend, drinking champagne cocktails. Don claims only to have had two, whilst his friend drank five. As a consequence, Don had to take him back in a taxi. Don concludes saying that his people are keen to meet Linda. He again expresses regret about his actions in their last week together and promises to marry her as soon as he returns. He pours scorn on rumours that, owing to the excessive strain placed on crews during the initial assault on French North Africa, reliefs will appear sometime in March. On this count he is correct, as he was not to be relieved for another two and a half years!

Don writes again on **Boxing Day** and sends the letter home via John. He reports that on Christmas Day, "in true naval fashion", the officers and three crew members swapped uniforms. He had found it really funny and had a much better time than he had anticipated. Dudley and Gibby had also joined them and entered into the spirit of things. However, in the evening, they did have to undertake "one of these boring patrols", which he does not particularly enjoy. Don also reports that Bob Harrison, who was Secretary of the D Club at Tenby, has turned up in Algiers. He wonders if Linda ever frequents the Crown in Weymouth and, if so, to give old Batty the best wishes from the flotilla. He says there have been a few air raids but nothing on the scale of the first few weeks.

Although Don's letter of **29th December 1942** is addressed to Linda at *RAF Ringstead,* near Dorchester, it was redirected to her at *RAF Worth Matravers,* near Swanage. He says that he has not heard from her for three weeks (this must have been her letter of 5th December, which is summarised on page 51) and again appeals for her to write more frequently. He is not in the best of moods, feeling "a bit seedy" through lack of rest. He had made representations not to go on patrol that night because of the weather and, having been told to give it a go, he quickly returned to harbour much to the pleasure of his crew. He suggests that an official engagement would be a good idea. He says that she should have heard from John Bick, but that he has been informed that Johnnie has got herself engaged and to offer her his most sincere congratulations. Don has decided that the long-awaited photograph has got lost and asks Linda to send another copy.

On **31st December 1942**, Don reports a huge storm which is uncomfortable even in harbour. However, looking on the bright side, although his is the duty boat they cannot be sent out to sea. Forbes, his spare officer, receives his only mention. They had some "quite amusing French types" on board "at gin time" and one brought along two girls, a ballet dancer and a singer, who were to perform at a concert that evening. Gibby and Dudley Arnaud also turned up and arranged to meet at the Patio. When they returned on board, instead of the usual happy session, a quarrel developed. However, Don is able to get unspecified matters off his chest. Being New Year's Eve, he is looking forward and contemplating returning home during 1943 (in fact, he was to wait until July 1945). He reminisces about the heavenly week he spent with Linda in Tenby and the multitudinous subjects they discussed on a walk to nearby Saundersfoot. He debates where they can live after the war – Hampstead or Putney, or maybe further out of London. He assumes the Civil Service will want him back in the capital. His last piece of news is that, because Gibby and his No. 1, Denton, are always quarrelling, there is to be a swap between Don's No. 1, Alan, and Denton (known as Phyllis).

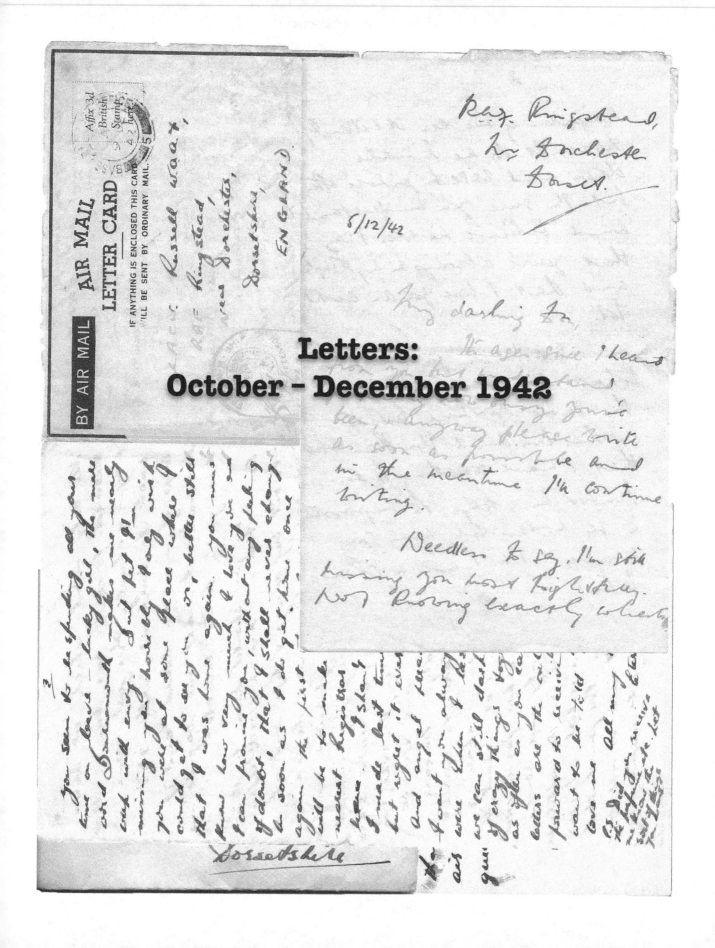

AIR MAIL
LETTER CARD

Affix 3d
British
Stamp
here

IF ANYTHING IS ENCLOSED THIS CARD
WILL BE SENT BY ORDINARY MAIL.

BY AIR MAIL

W/A.C.S. Russell W.A.A.F.
R.A.F. Ringstead,
near Dorchester,
Dorsetshire,
ENGLAND

Dorsetshire

R.A.F. Ringstead,
Nr Dorchester
Dorset.

6/12/42

My darling Jim,

It's ages since I heard from you but I don't know where you've been, anyway please write as soon as possible and in the meantime I'll continue writing.

Needless to say, I'm still missing you most frightfully not knowing exactly where

Mess 45
Coastal Force Base
Gibraltar

25th October 1942

My darling Linda

Am I forgiven for this apparent slackness in writing to you? I haven't really been slack about it – life has been one hectic bustle since I saw you off in the car. Anyway I'll tell you all about it and then reply to your very welcome letter when I have given you all the news.

Gibby & Max arrived but we had a very quiet session as nobody seemed to be feeling as bright as usual (I was very depressed and probably acted as a sort of wet blanket anyway). And of course they weren't any too pleased that I had got command when I was junior to everyone else – particularly John. However I must confess to no loss of sleep on that subject!

We had a filthy 28 hour journey back in a gale; Dick's steering packed up and he put a hole on my side in the night. Still we made it and it was repaired in no time at all, but it did rather make matters a rush before we left as there was some talk about leaving us behind and I had to rather rush things to be ready in time.

We sailed for this dump in filthy weather and I picked them up outside in a fog (we were repaired elsewhere). Apparently no one expected us to find them which just goes to prove that my navigation is as lucky as I've always maintained!

After the first couple of days we struck grand weather and a sea like a mirror – to my intense delight of course – and the whole passage was enjoyable but fortunately quite uneventful (Darling isn't my writing too frightful!)

Our first night here we were caught up in an air raid which sounded terrific but in which nothing was dropped – just the kind I like! Once here the usual frantic rush developed to get things done and as I was away during all the conferences I've been kept pretty busy trying to catch up.

Gibby has gone down with flu and I hope to be able to visit him in hospital tomorrow. He seems to be recovering fairly quickly – takes a lot to keep Gibby down for long.

And that I think brings you up to date for news so I'll reply to the many questions in your letter.

Firstly thanks for the two pounds. Believe me sweet I've never felt so miserable in my life as I have since you went back. The first day was absolute hell and my crew steered well clear of me – I've managed to recover my temper but I'm missing you more than seemed possible in my wildest nightmares. Look wretch I am terribly sorry about F------- but I too felt thoroughly miserable that you still doubted me. What do I have to say or do to convince you that I love you far more than I can possibly tell you and that I shan't change at any time in the future. I want you to marry me as soon as it can be arranged when I get back. The whole point was that I was so filthily hard up that I frankly did not consider it fair to get married before I left. I was, I agree, a fool to talk about marriage so much before I left. Anyway pet I've turned over a new leaf since I met you and I consider that I have sobered down considerably. I won't do any more of the crazy things I used to do (I know my reputation in the flotilla!) and I hope you'll be able to stand an outburst occasionally. One thing I can promise, in the future, I won't stooge around with any women at all. Don't laugh pet, I'm very serious about this business and anybody that knew me six months ago just won't recognise this honest upstanding youth!

One more thing darling. If you do fall for anyone else please tell me – I hope it won't happen – it better not believe you me.

Do send the photograph soon and please write as often as you can. Incidentally air mail takes a week and ship about four weeks.

All my love darling – things will never change – please don't worry about me and when I get back to you, you'll find me completely unchanged.

Don

P.S. No kisses allowed by our SOI – but I do miss them.
P.P.S. Dick & Alan send their love.
P.P.P.S. I just reread my letter and I, too, consider it frightful - especially as I'm supposed to live by writing. Better effort next time I promise. D

Mess 45
Coastal Force Base
Gibraltar

27th October 1942

A.C.W. Russell W.A.A.F.,
~~R.A.F. Ringstead,~~
~~Nr Dorchester,~~
~~Dorsetshire.~~
Amos House
Totland Bay
Isle of Wight

My darling

Having cheerfully announced to Alan that I intended to write to you I now find myself without anything to say – I can almost hear you murmuring "That's a change."

In point of fact I haven't done very much because there just isn't anything to do except the more obvious things such as drink and that is quite impossible for me. Actually much the same thing happens every night here, either stay on board with the danger of a quiet drink developing into a session, or go to the Capitol and drink John Collins. What would you do, chum? Last night Alan and I did go ashore and after the Capitol which closes at 2100 we went on to the place of some friends of his. Need I add that we are all bored to tears and just don't know what to do with ourselves and Alan's question of "What would you give to have Linda here" doesn't bear answering.

Incidentally pet I'm more than looking forward to hearing from you so please write as often as you can. It seems quite clear that your letters will be the one bright spot in this deadly existence. (At the moment we are all rather depressed so please don't take too much notice of these heartrending remarks!)

How are things in Weymouth and how is that photograph coming along – I do hope you are wearing your cap, it doesn't suit you at all. I must say that I think you damned lucky to be based where you are and at the moment there isn't a soul here who wouldn't give his fortune to be there – and that goes double for me.

I am missing you wretch and I'm rather clinging to the hope that you will be there waiting when I eventually get back. I love you a hell of a lot and even this crowd are pulling my leg for falling so badly after my previous stoogeing. I think Dick is especially amused although he was talking very seriously about marrying Sheila.

Must finish before I burst into tears – write soon and write lots.

All my love angel,
Ever Thine,
Don

Mess 45
Coastal Force Base
Gibraltar

4th November 1942

My darling

At least I don't really know whether you deserve any endearments as I'm still desperately waiting for a letter from you. Anyway wretch I hope you have received my letters and cables, or, at any rate part of them by this time. You see my sweet I am missing you rather horribly and a letter might perhaps ease matters a little.

This place is exactly the same as it was last time I was here and, frankly, I dislike it equally as much this time. I haven't been over the border at all in spite of pressure applied by Alan as I know full well that it is just as dreary. (Sorry chum – not a very cheerful letter is it?).

We had quite an amusing Flotilla Dinner party at the Rock the other night and I enclose the signed menu in case it is of interest. Naturally we all got very drunk but fortunately no one was incapable – I just didn't dare as you weren't about to tuck me safely in bed! The trouble really started when we got back on board and attempted to make up for lost time. I was still fortunate enough to survive but next day —! Suffice it to say that I've rarely met so many people who genuinely desired simultaneous death.

The following night we were ashore once more, ostensibly in order to avoid drinking aboard, and Alan and I were eventually joined by Dudley, Max, John and Shep at the Capitol. There we had the misfortune to consume far too many John Collins and it wasn't until next day that on enquiries I learned that the gin in this place is little more than meths. Now I just don't touch the stuff.

Still we are making the best of things here and although we all grumble steadily it could be a lot worse.

Darling are you quite sure that you do still love me? I have a horrible feeling that you may change and God knows I just couldn't go on without you. You must know by this time just how much I do love you and feel quite confident of your unbreakable hold on me (I wish it were a little more literal than it is at the moment).

All my love angel always
Yours
Don

P.S. Please use air mail and don't forget the photograph.

H.M.M.L. 338
c/o G.P.O.,
London

15th November 1942

A.C.W Russell W.A.A.F.
R.A.F. Ringstead,
Near Dorchester,
Dorsetshire, ENGLAND

My darling Linda

This is I fear another rush note as we have only just learned that a mail is to leave very shortly. The main trouble is that I'm not sure just how much I'm allowed to tell you. Anyway you must know that we were concerned with the N. African operations and managed to get away with it quite successfully without any casualties on the ship.

I have had a look round ashore and the populace are most friendly and welcomed us with open arms (don't take that too literally as I'm still behaving myself!) I met one bloke who invited us to his house gave us drinks and now wishes to arrange a dinner party for us. He seems genuinely pleased to dash around with us and as he seems to know his way around we have met quite a crowd of his friends.

I won't be unkind enough to gloat about the weather we are enjoying (and at this time of the year) but – well we'll leave it at that.

To make this place perfect it only requires you to be here and we really could have a terrific time. I am missing you rather horribly wretch and this lack of mail from you rather worries me – there'd better be a heap when it does catch up. You know my sweet this is just the first time in my life that I have really fallen badly and I have to get myself stuck miles away from you. My main consolation is that I'm very sure that I shan't change and I hope and believe that you will wait until I get home. You'd better have a special licence waiting as soon as possible after my return – I made one bad mistake in not marrying you before I left and I don't want to chance a repetition. I think Tenby would be a good spot to go to – happy memories!

Must finish pet. I do love you a hell of a lot so please write as often as you can.

All my love sweet
Eternally,
Don

P.S. Is it ACW or Corporal?

H.M.M.L. 338
c/o G.P.O.,
London

26th November 1942

L.A.C.W Russell W.A.A.F.
R.A.F. Ringstead,
Near Dorchester,
Dorsetshire, ENGLAND

My darling Linda

Just received your letter of 6/10/42 and you can't imagine how thrilled I feel with life at the moment – only hope a further mail arrives in the near future. Incidently I received your cable at the same time – many thanks.

Sweetest you really must take care of yourself particularly when I'm so far away and I can't possibly get to you quickly. Please get well quickly and do write and let me know that you have recovered.

Your friend's sister must be quite an exception and I can only remark that the scarcity of females is the only reason for her having a good time in that forsaken dump – may I add that the dancing girls story turned out to be a lot of hooey. Satisfied?

I've seen one film recently on board one of the bigger ships, one which I have been trying to see for some time "Holiday Inn" (Bing Crosby, Fred Astair[e]) and although everything looked double I quite enjoyed it. No cracks please!!

The reason, or one reason at any rate, that I wasn't at Tenby was that I was round at Cardiff undergoing repairs. In any case I should have had no desire to go there while you were so far away. To me Tenby is more than a holiday resort, it is the place where I spent by far the happiest week of my life, and when I next go back there I want it to be together. Horribly sloppy but I can assure you that it is a very real feeling.

The photograph hasn't arrived so far and that is an additional reason for looking forward to the next mail. While I don't believe the story of the vacant expression I should hate it not to look natural (not catty, just honest!). And I have no desire to be impressed of the insulting remarks which people choose to make about my photograph, although incidentally, I have no illusions!

I haven't much for you by way of news. Things have been fairly warm and we've been worked fairly hard – still I suppose one must do something occasionally.

My sweet I really do love you so much that I can't believe I will be away from you for any length of time and I can't work up any interest on anyone else (and well you know it).

Just keep on writing and telling me that you love me and that you will wait until I get back home. I won't change.

All my love my darling
Take care of yourself,
Eternally,
Don

P.S. I've got some perfume & stuff but I don't know how I can get it to you at the moment. D.
P.P.S. Congratulations on the L.A.C.W.

H.M.M.L. 338,
c/o G.P.O., London

28th November 1942

My dear Linda

At the moment I'm feeling very annoyed with you. A large mail arrived yesterday and the sum total from you was your cable of 17th November promising a letter in the near future. My pet if you have become fed up with me already then I'd much rather you told me or, if writing to me is too much trouble again [I would] prefer to be so informed. I may be most unfair and unkind in making such statements - in fact hope sincerely that I am - as there is, no doubt, some very good reason for your lack of correspondence. But wretch please remember that I do love you a hell of a lot and the only things to which I can look forward are your letters. You know quite well that I am perfectly sincere and in spite of your protestations to the contrary, you are quite sure that I shan't change. If I could feel the same thing about you I should be far happier.

And that, I fear, is a most unpleasant start to a letter. Am I forgiven - please? Darling if you would only realise just how much you do mean to me and how miserable I feel not because I'm away from U.K. but simply because I can't be with you. Perhaps I'm in a rather sloppy mood at the moment but after Tenby and Falmouth you can't fail to realise how serious I am about the whole business. You know quite well of my past misdeeds, and that knowledge must surely confirm the sincerity of my feelings towards you. (That sounds Irish but I think you will understand what I mean.)

Alan and I went ashore yesterday afternoon to try and buy some stuff for the Wardroom. That, at any rate, was the primary idea. However I decided that a haircut was a most urgent necessity and remembered that there was a barbers shop in Hotel A-----. On our way through the bar, where we were misguided enough to stop for one ("well just one"!) drink I met some blokes I hadn't seen for about eighteen months and they insisted that it was an occasion for celebration. Well we had a couple and managed to escape with a promise to meet them there later. We had our haircut and returned smelling like an Elizabeth Arden advertisement. We had a very quiet session talking about old so and so ("what in South Africa!") and, feeling horribly sentimental, returned on board. (Have to stay sober because we go out on the red warning - which is rather rough).

The night before last was even more amusing. We were lying alongside a biggish ship and they were so thrilled with M.L.s (we can still flannel!) that they invited us aboard for a gin. That was very nice (slight interruption for red warning) but as I thought unfortunately, and, as it turned out, fortunately I was sent out on a short job so we missed it. When we returned we had supper and then repaired on Max's Bateau to see what went on. Then came the crowd! All quite happy and it wasn't long before Gibby started the singing. And so we went on until I found myself singing "Dark Town Strutters Ball" and decided I had had enough for one night. But it was the best party we'd had since we left home.

Today I'm on duty and expecting to be sent out any minute so perhaps I'd better finish on my usual boozy note.

Please write soon sweet as, believe me, letters are the one thing to which I do look forward. And please take care of yourself and get rid of that cold.

All my love, angel, always
Still the same
Don

P.S. Darling I would so like to spend X'mas with you - but do enjoy it and we'll make up for it next year (I hope).

H.M.M.L. 338
c/o G.P.O.,
London

30th November 1942

Linda Darling

Just a short note to wish you a very happy X'mas. I trust you won't consider my taste in perfume etc to be as bad as I rather fear but I lay no claims to expert knowledge in such matters. Incidentally you might let me know of any stuff you want in this line and let me have the details.

Yesterday was Alan's birthday and it's a sorry looking Alan who is dazedly meandering around this morning. I think the words Champagne Cocktail would be enough to finish him off once more.

I saw the film "Reluctant Dragon" last night and thoroughly enjoyed it – amazing how one forgets the complications of life in a cinema. Incidentally in case you had low thoughts I saw it on another ship – and I am behaving myself.

Darling I am missing you so much and it wasn't till Dudley pointed it out in one of our mutual commiseration get togethers that I realised we had been away less than two months – seems an age already. I do love you such a hell of a lot wretch that I'm certain I just can't be away from you for eighteen months. Something simply must turn up.

Should you wish to get in touch with her at any time I'll give you Mrs Arnaud's address.

MRS DUDLEY ARNAUD,
ST. AUSTELL,
LANCET LANE,
LOOSE,
MAIDSTONE,
KENT.

She seems to be quite fond of you so keep in touch with her.

Do enjoy yourself at X'mas and I hope that the coming year will see one hell of a reunion party for us all.

Write soon my angel I'm so crazy about you.

All my love sweet
Eternally yours
Don.

P.S. Give my love to Johnny when you write.

H.M.M.L. 338
c/o G.P.O.,
London

2nd December 1942

L.A.C.W Russell W.A.A.F.
R.A.F. Ringstead,
Near Dorchester,
Dorsetshire, ENGLAND

My darling Linda

I've just been reading the letter you sent me on your return to camp from our week in Tenby and consequently I'm feeling horribly sentimental. The thought of the many divine (and, on occasional amusing) moments in that week nearly makes me burst into tears. The spectacle of Alice poking an inquisitive head through the doors, our walks to Saundersfoot and the arguments which ensued on the way, sitting in the club wondering why it was such a boring place, running your bath for you in the morning, thinking how perfect you looked and how much I loved you – and many more things. It really was the most heavenly week I have spent up to the present but I hope we will have an even better week as soon as I get home. Believe me, sweet, I do love you more than I think you realise. I little thought when I went with John to Haverfordwest on that fateful evening that I was to fall really badly for the first time. You know you must have a sobering effect on me because I find that when I'm away from you I still do lots of crazy things – but no women, honest chum! I honestly couldn't work up any enthusiasm for any other person but that, I suppose, is only stating the obvious. I still get my leg pulled about it but Dudley & I have quiet get togethers and almost weep in each other's arms on occasions. Bad thing really but it's pleasant to have someone to talk to.

At the moment we are out on anti-submarine patrol but I got chocka and decided I must write to you. We had some excitement this afternoon and when I dropped some depth charges the crew was thrilled to death – no apparent results just the same.

When we were out at dawn t'other morning we opened up on a plane which I took to be a Heinkel III flying straight for us. He swerved hastily away and made his recognitions. But the story has a sequel. Apparently one of the other ships heard about it and told one of my gunners that a very tall American pilot officer wanted to have a word with him on the quay. He swallowed it hook, line and sinker and amid hoots of laughter asked the sentry where this fellow was. Still I suppose we all buy something at sometime.

Things have been very quiet round here (cross my fingers!) recently and I can express no regret at that. I think the most unpleasant thing that has happened to date was being dive bombed by a great four engined Focke Wulf (the bomb fell about fifty yards on the port beam but fortunately sank for about five seconds before exploding – which is why I'm still writing!). Why he should pick on a poor little M.L. I can't imagine – some people have no sense of proportion.

Must finish my angel – I only wish I could enclose myself in an envelope but the censor just won't play.

Linda darling I'll always love you please don't change.

Your very lonely
Don

P.S. John is in hospital with pneumonia but he's well on the road to recovery.
P.P.S. Don't forget to drink a toast at noon on X'mas day – to our reunion.

H.M.M.L. 338
c/o G.P.O.,
London

4th December 1942

Linda my darling

What is the matter? Another mail and still no word from you. I really am starting to get rather worried about it as I have had letters from everyone else so they just haven't been going adrift. Please write more frequently and don't forget that photograph.

Things are going on in much the same old way in this part of the world and they continue to work us fairly hard - been out four nights out of the last five, and that's something which could have shaken me considerably in the old days at P.D! Still I think we are doing a fairly good job of work so I'm not really grumbling - not more than usual anyway.

I've just been listening to a broadcast of an excerpt of the musical comedy now running at His Majesty's and it makes me feel rather homesick. It's amazing the effect that the radio does have on one. In peace time I used to hear Big Ben striking every quarter of an hour and all I used to say was "Damn that noise". Now I glue my ear to the receiver in case I miss even one note! War certainly alters many things.

Haven't been ashore since last Sunday so have no misdeeds to recount - I'm not sure that Arnaud can say the same thing. I gather he had a hell of a party ashore yesterday and was last seen holding a drink in one hand and a French girl's hand in the other. I haven't seen him since so I can supply no details. Gibby was heard to say, at the same time "To hell with this let's get down to some serious drinking" which seems good sense to me!

I've met an engineer out here who travelled to Lpool with me on my return from Tenby. He fondly thought at that time that he was going to America and I certainly didn't expect to meet him out here. He's a good type and he's been down on board before dinner tonight. I think we must arrange a big party for X'mas day - duties permitting, which they probably won't.

Had several letters from home only to learn that Mother has been rather ill but now seems to have recovered. She does get terribly worried about the war and that I suppose was the basic cause of her illness. Personally I'll be glad when the whole bloody business is over and I can get home to you and everyone else once more. I do miss you so much Linda and the only reason that life is even bearable is your promise to wait until I do return - it does mean so much to me. If I thought that you wouldn't I should just wrap up.

But away depression! Even this war can't last forever (yes I've heard of the Hundred Years War!) and I think we can make up for wasted years when we are together again.

But my angel please write soon - I've had only one letter from you since I left England. And I do so want to be told that you still love me.

All my love sweet
Eternally yours
Don.

H.M.M.L. 338
c/o G.P.O.,
London

5th December 1942

My darling Linda

I seem to be becoming a most prolific letter writer but I must confess this letter is written principally because I am bored, fed up and on duty. That sounds most unkind. In point of fact as you know full well I enjoy writing to you and I hope if I write sufficient letters some, at any rate, will get through to you. I suggest you adopt the same maxim!

Since I wrote to you last night nothing has happened and, for the first time, I have been duty boat and yet have not been required – touch wood, the night is yet young. (I like this fellow in the ARP Quiz, to which I am listening, who would stop bleeding from the ear by applying a tourniquet round the neck – nice guy!).

I must say the ship is starting to look very tiddley. I've just about completed the upper deck and Alan and I are starting on the wardroom – I can't decide whether to hang some David Wright prints or some original watercolours of Walter Thomas. Somehow in this dump I think David Wright will win – it reminds me of civilization (but no cracks if you please).

Max has been on board tonight dripping away in his usual manner. One of these days someone will find another ship on which to drink – Alan and I were even discussing making the whole flotilla honorary members and presenting them with a mess bill at the end of the month. Somehow I don't think the humour would be appreciated – especially by Max.

John, I fear, is not at all well and I hope to visit him in hospital tomorrow – I'll let you know how he is progressing.

Still no sign of Dick joining us and I must say that I miss him – and Spotless. I suppose when we eventually return Spotless will recognise neither of us. I think he'd really enjoy this place as all the dogs are muzzled and he could sniff as hard as he liked without any fear of retaliation.

Darling I do wish we were together, I shouldn't care whereabouts it was. I would never have believed that I was capable of missing anyone quite so much, but the horrible truth is that I seem to spend most of my time thinking about you and talking about you. Please don't change sweet and, incidentally, it might be a good idea if you wrote just occasionally – not so frequently that you strained that delicate constitution of yours but just sufficiently to let me know that you are still getting a kick out of life – even (which I don't mean) in Weymouth. How I wish I were back there – we used to have some pretty good sessions in the Crown and the Officers' Club (is that fruit machine still there?).

I seem to have written quite a lot about nothing but, please, darling do write and let me know that you are quite well. I think that Mess 45 C.F.B. by air mail is by far the quickest method of contact.

All my love darling
I'll always love you
As ever
Don.

R.A.F. Ringstead,
Nr Dorchester
Dorset

5/12/42

My darling Don,

Its ages since I heard from you but I understand perfectly how busy you've been, anyway please write as soon as possible and in the meantime I'll continue writing.

Needless to say, I'm still missing you most frightfully not knowing exactly what's happening makes it extremely difficult for me to settle down and write to you more often, but I'm sure you understand and believe me when I say that you're always in my thoughts and that I love you an awful lot.

At least you know what I'm doing – 8-1 etc: the same routine but its rather fun and I'm thankful that I have something to do. Unfortunately, it's impossible to be moderately near you, maybe, I'll have a chance later! Last week I managed to get home on an SOP, where I caught a shocking cold. The nursing orderly has just taken my temperature and it's normal, which means Church tomorrow! Much to everyone's amusement, although I still have an 'acking cough' like I had at Tenby.

Darling I'd give anything to be back there (PS for you, how awful) as I have so many happy memories, even of Haverfordwest walking by the river, and dinner at the Castle (usually smelly fish but never mind!).

Perhaps one day we'll visit the old place, including Saundersfoot, for a good scratch if nothing else! (I still can't understand why John wasn't bitten, the place was alive with them). I heard from Johnnie t'other day, she's heard from John once and at long last knows his type, anyway, she's met someone in Fishguard who appears to be genuine (I wonder).

Darling, I've done very little lately, apart from a few camp dances I've seen these quite good films – 'Men in Her Life' Loretta Young, 'Holiday Inn', Bing Crosby, Fred Astaire, Dorothy Lamore and 'First of the Few' Leslie Howard, by far the best I've seen for some time.

I'm longing to hear from you, just a few words will cheer me. Darling, I do love you terribly, please don't forget me. Goodbye now.

Always, all my love,
Linda
Xx

H.M.M.L. 280
c/o G.P.O.,
London

7th December 1942

L.A.C.W. Russell W.A.A.F.,
R.A.F. Ringstead,
Near Dorchester
Dorsetshire ENGLAND

My darling Linda

Just received your letter of 16th November and I'm feeling pretty hacked with life – I promise not to complain in this letter about your lack of correspondence!

We are allowed one each of these peculiar letter forms and it is alleged that they will be home before X'mas – with how much truth you must be the judge. Honestly sweet I do write to you a hell of a lot – about five letters a week and I should imagine you will be receiving them by this time. Incidentally I think that it would be quicker if you continued to send your letters by air mail to Mess 45 Coastal Force Base etc as before the only mail which we have received to date has been in that way – actually I've just come back to harbour with 157 bags of mail on board and if there isn't at least one bag for me there's going to be trouble!

As you should know by this time I'm in French North Africa I won't say enjoying life but at any rate wiling away the winter months in most glorious sunshine. The food ashore is very poor indeed and we haven't seen a potato since we arrived – there is, however, an abundance of fruit, wine etc. so we don't do too badly. In case your nasty mind turns to horrible thoughts I really am behaving myself – yesterday was in fact the first day I'd been ashore for a week. I had lunch with Gibby and some of the other blokes and in the afternoon went to the local music hall – it was quite amusing and I've found that my long neglected French is improving quite rapidly. It may be useful once more after the war.

You seem to be spending all your time on leave – lucky girl, the mere word Bournemouth makes me nearly weep with envy. But pet I'm missing you horribly I only wish you were at some place where I could get to see you or, better still, that I was home again. You must know how very much I love you and I can promise you, without any feeling of doubt, that I shall never change. As soon as I do get home once again the first thing I shall do will be to make a beeline for the nearest Registrar and get a special licence. I shan't repeat the mistake I made last time – I've done nothing but regret it ever since I left you and angel please don't you change. I want you to be just as you were when I last saw you, and we can still dash about and do lots of crazy things together. Please write as often as you can because your letters are the only thing I can look forward to receiving and I do so want to be told that you still love me.

All my love my darling
Eternally yours
Don

P.S. Did you receive the perfume etc. Let me know the sort of things you want.
P.P.S. Hurry up the photograph and send it air mail but well packed up.
P.P.P.S. Happy X'mas chum.

H.M.M.L. 338
c/o G.P.O.,
London

10th December 1942

Linda my darling

Probably only a short note I haven't anything to write about – except that I love you and miss you most horribly, but I guess you know that by this time!

Big news just came in – a mail will be ready for distribution tomorrow and if there isn't anything from you my sweet look out for squalls. It's amazing the way everyone looks forward to the mail. My ratings come up at every hour of the day to ask permission to go to the mail office and, when I tell them that there is no fresh mail, they just reply "Well they might have overlooked some from the last lot." So life spins on its axis of hope!

<u>12/12/42</u>

Sorry about the delay in completing the letter but there have been numerous flaps and at the moment I'm at sea on patrol. Frankly I hate patrols – they are too boring for words.

Well, the eagerly awaited mail just didn't materialise so I haven't any good reason for telling you off – not yet anyway. I went into the mail office before I sailed tonight (I'm flotilla mail officer incidentally!) and was informed that a mail had arrived but that there was nothing for the M.L.s – so that was that. I heard the crew informing the world at large exactly what they thought about the delivery of mail and I could hardly disagree with them. It's amazing how important mail becomes when you are away from home, I suppose because it represents our only link with the people with whom we all want to be. Anyway I hope some arrives soon – I am especially keen on receiving the photograph and, if it's at all lifelike I'll be happy (almost!) for the duration.

Went ashore for an hour yesterday afternoon principally to get some exercise but finished up with some blokes I know in one of the hotels. Behaved myself – in case you might possibly have thought otherwise – and was back on board by 1800. Then to sea – we seem to be putting in more sea time since I left home than any M.L. has ever done before – still I find it some consolation to know that there are people who do believe in the uses of M.L's.

John is getting better quite rapidly and I expect he will be leaving hospital in the near future. Meanwhile Alan is also ill and away from the ship. I may possess a suspicious mind but I'm not at all sure that Alan isn't trying to pull a fast one and get home again – I sincerely hope not as there is plenty of work to do out here and, much as I want to get home again, I shouldn't care to do it in that way.

Darling you are taking care of yourself, aren't you? I get worried when I hear that you have got a cold and aches and pains especially in the filthy weather I expect you are having. Please take good care of yourself until I can get back to make quite certain that you do behave yourself.

Haven't seen much of Gibby and Arnaud recently, in fact I've hardly seen anyone except Max who seems to stooge on board most evenings we are in harbour. I rather gather he hasn't heard from Louise and that that particular episode is quite finished. And these blighters have the impertinence to talk about me.

Sweet I do love you so terribly that I'm certain the time is not far off when I shall return to writing poetry – if I do I send the worst samples and you'll discover how bad modern verse can really be. Seriously if things quieten down I'm considering doing some writing (no, not verse!) to wile away the hours. If I put together all the novels I've started at one time or another the Board of Trade would no longer worry about paper shortage. I always seem to get so far and get bored with the whole business – they were pretty bloody anyway.

By the way wretch I have an aunt (a young one) in Bournemouth and I should be most grateful if you would look her up at some time – she really is very sweet indeed and I'm sure you would like her very much. Don't forget will you – the address is enclosed – I believe she manages the hotel or something.

It's just about time for me to go on watch so I simply must finish.

Please write lots pet because I do love you so horribly. And don't you dare change while I'm away – we've too much to make up for when I do get back home.

All my love sweet
Eternally yours
Don.

P.S. If that aunt of mine tells you too much about me – don't believe it anyway! – and give her my love – I'll write to her.

H.M.M.L. 338
c/o G.P.O.,
London

15th December 1942

L.A.C.W. Russell W.A.A.F.,
R.A.F. Ringstead,
Near Dorchester,
Dorsetshire, ENGLAND.

Linda darling

This anxiously awaited mail still hasn't materialised so I think I'd better write again in case I get into trouble - anyway it would be difficult to bottle you if I didn't write myself.

Not very much has happened since my last letter - at least not much by way of enjoyment, there's been far too much work to do. Gibby and I had a pretty good run ashore last Sunday. What happened was that Gibby stooged down on board at his usual time together with a rather chastened looking Arnaud (the result of a session the night before, I gathered) and after our usual gnatter we decided to go ashore for a quick one before lunch - that is with the exception of Arnaud who turned quite an attractive shade of green at the mere mention of it. So off we set first to the Aletti, which was deadly, and then on to the Paris where we found the rest of the blokes together with some R.A.F. types. We had a few drinks together becoming happier and more sociable as time passed and, I regret to say, neither Gibby nor I can discover what happened that afternoon. Max saw me come onboard at about 1700, still in apparent possession of my senses, but the next thing I remember is Alan awakening me at 1830. I had promised to have dinner with a cove I know and how I managed to make it I don't honestly know. However I did make it and after dinner and a cinema show we had more 'ootch and eventually a sing song. When we were thrown out we all came down on board and carried on with the good work. In fact as days go in this place it was quite enjoyable.

I saw Gibby next morning looking very pale and not his usual cheery self but after much hard thought we were completely unable to discover just what had happened the previous afternoon - which may be just as well.

Since Sunday I've been on duty and done rather too much sea time for my liking - still it's a change to know that there is a job for M.L's to do.

Must finish wretch as I'm on watch in a few minutes. And darling I do love you so very much - please write as often as you can, your letters mean more than you can possibly imagine. And incidentally don't forget to hurry up that photograph - I can promise it a place of honour in the wardroom.

All my love sweet
I shan't ever change
As ever
Don.

H.M.M.L. 338
c/o G.P.O., London

19th December 1942

My darling Linda

Still no mail has arrived here for us, so at the moment we are all feeling even more chocka (to use a most expressive naval term) than usual. However we still have hopes that something will arrive before X'mas to cheer us on our way.

Not much has happened since my last letter except that we have spent nearly every night at sea – which isn't so good more especially as it has rained the whole time.

Had quite an amusing time on our last off duty day. Stooged ashore in the afternoon (leave ends at 1800) and after a haircut wandered into the Aletti. There the first person I met was a bloke I ran across in Barry Dock (remember when I was there) and with whom I'd had a most colossal (spelling looks phoney!) party. We did a fair amount of drinking on board and then wandered on to a place called Bindles. He tells me that he doesn't even remember leaving the ship let alone going to Bindles and walking about five miles back.

I left fairly early as I had our Doc coming down on board and then I had dinner with the Doc on board his ship. We had some quite interesting arguments (he's a G.P. in Kensington and a most efficient cove) until one of the Paymasters arrived. He, apparently, is a journalist on the Newcastle Evening Chronicle – and so the fun started. The Doc told him that I was in a Govt Press Office and had been in the M of I and we went at it hammer and tongs for about three hours – much to the unconcealed amusement of every one present. Down at the other end of the wardroom someone was playing, although that's only a polite expression, the piano and I could hear Alan, tight as an owl, singing away at the top of his voice. Last time we had been invited to dinner there we'd started one of these vocal sessions and had been politely requested to leave before the evening was up, so I was much interested in the result of this further outbreak. But this time we had apparently been labelled as incurable and they had become resigned to us.

Must say I'm feeling a little tired as we've been out six nights out of the last eight – and to think I used to grumble about Pembroke Dock.

I understand from Max that in all probability John will be sent home and given two months sick leave. He has more or less completely recovered and I gather that there will be no after effects. Some people seem to have all the luck – I'm contemplating standing in the rain and seeing what I can do in the pneumonia line!

Only six days to Christmas but for all the difference it makes it might just as well be six months. I understand that a special cable service has been inaugurated with standard text messages so by the time you receive this letter and the memories of X'mas and New Year celebrations are quite cloudy you will have received my cable.

Sweet, I am missing you so horribly and this complete absence of mail doesn't help matters – my only consolation is that when it does eventually arrive there should be a whole mail bag of it from you – or else chum! I do love you so very much pet that the only thing I'm waiting for is the day on which I hear that this whole business is over – and we will celebrate when I do get home once more.

Please don't ever change Linda – I promise you that I never shall.
Write lots angel

All my love
Eternally yours
Don.

P.S. How's that photograph progressing?

H.M.M.L. 338
c/o G.P.O., London

24th December 1942

My darling Linda

Even though it is Christmas Eve and I suppose I should be full of benevolence and goodwill to my fellow beings I cannot claim that those words would accurately describe my feelings towards you at the moment. In fact I'm damned annoyed with you. Three mails have arrived in the last three days but nary a word from you. Look my sweet there may be some perfectly good reason for the lack of correspondence on your part but whatever it is I want to know it very badly. Have you become tired of me and were those many promises of eternal devotion just so many words or what is the reason? Darling I do appreciate that letters take a long time to get here and that many probably get lost on the way but the fact remains that other letters have arrived and it shouldn't be just yours that go adrift. You know quite well how much I love you and I really have written to you a hell of a lot – still I'm not really angry with you but I'd like to give you a hell of a spanking just the same!

Well it's been a good X'mas Eve so far; wet, cold (I don't wish to see the words "Sunny Mediterranean" anymore!) and I'm duty boat with the knowledge that I am to go out in the early hours of X'mas morning. Actually we've been working extraordinarily hard and everyone is showing some signs of strain – amazing what you can stand up to when necessary.

I've seen John. He is able to get about again and he will be going back home in the near future – must make sure that I catch pneumonia one way or another. He really has had rather a rough time of it but the Doc assures me that his illness has left him with no lasting ill effects – so that's a pretty good thing. When he does get back I hope he'll get in touch with you – I'm sure he'll get in touch with Johnny – or so he assures me, at any rate.

I'm a little concerned about the news from home. Mother apparently is rather ill and with the delay in the arrival of news it makes it a little worrying. However matters aren't quite so bad as when I was at Freetown and received no mail for about four months – I've never seen such a wildly excited mob of matelots as when our mail did arrive and contained about fifty letters apiece; it certainly kept them busy for the next couple of weeks.

Went ashore a few days ago with a friend of mine who has turned up here and who informed me that I exaggerated the potent qualities of the champagne cocktail served at the Paris. Anyway we went there. After one he didn't think much of them; after two he thought that they improved with acquaintance; after three he thought this dump wasn't such a bad place after all; after four he could keep on drinking them all day; after five, I took him back in a taxi – need I add that through experience I had stooged and had only had two.

Incidentally my people are very keen on meeting you, so they inform me and they don't seem at all sure that we are not already married. Linda darling I was a rat and I did make a very big mistake, one which, if I had that time over again I most certainly wouldn't repeat. I do love you so and, assuming you don't get too bored with me in the interim, we'll get married as soon as I get back. Actually there's a pretty good story going the rounds at the moment – on account of (a good 25th expression) the excessive strain! placed on all ships taking part in the initial assault, reliefs will appear sometime in March and we'll then get home. It's a good story!

Darling I must finish as I've got to go and very soon – heaps of love and please do write soon.

All my love
Eternally
Don

P.S. Have you sent the photo yet?

As usual

26th December 1942

Linda darling

Surprised at the postmark (whatever it may be)? As I told you John is going home and he is taking this letter with him – so have no illusions about my return.

Well Christmas, such as it was, is over and you'd scarcely have noticed it in this place. Actually we were in harbour all day yesterday until the evening when we had to go out on one of these boring patrols – I may add that I didn't particularly enjoy it. In true naval fashion we had lunch down on the mess deck with the crew, dressed three of [them] in my uniforms and crawled into [the] matelots rig ourselves. It really was very funny and we certainly had a better time than I would have believed possible here. Dudley and Gibby also stooged down to my mess deck and entered into the spirit of things. Incidentally you remember Bob Harrison who was Secretary of the D. Club Tenby, I gather from Dudley that he has turned up in this place – it's a small world (platitudinous remark!)

At the moment I'm most anxiously awaiting the next mail in which there must be a letter from you. Darling how often are you writing – you've no idea just how much everyone looks forward to receiving mail, probably because it's our only contact with home. Actually I'm a little worried at the moment as its some time since I had any word from home and I gather that mother is rather ill – I wish letters didn't take so long to get here.

How go things in Weymouth – do you ever go into the Crown? If you do give old Batty the best wishes of the flotilla – I think he'll remember us. We used to have some pretty good times there just over a year ago – more arguments than that.

It's fairly quiet out here now, a few air raids but nothing on the scale of those in the first few weeks, need I add that I'm not sorry for that.

Must finish and get some sleep. Darling I do love you so very much and I am missing you most horribly. Are you quite sure that you won't change – two years is a long time to wait especially with the distractions offered at home. God knows I want you to wait for me – I shan't change as you well know.

Do write lots wretch

All my love angel
As ever
Don.

P.S. Where's that photograph?

H.M.M.L. 338,
c/o G.P.O., London.

29th December 1942

L.A.C.W. Russell W.A.A.F.,
R.A.F. ~~Ringstead,~~ Worth Matravers
Near ~~Dorchester,~~ Swanage, Dorsetshire, ENGLAND.

Linda darling

This is a foul world - we received today for the whole ship's company a mail which consisted of three letters, two of them for me - a X'mas card from Mrs Arnaud and a new tiddley calendar my father has printed. I can only hope we are more fortunate next time as it's now about three weeks since I heard from you - the last letter I received from you was dated 16th November, which, you must admit is some little time ago and doesn't exactly make for the alleviation of worry. Please sweet, do write a hell of a lot. I fully realise that a lot of the mail doesn't make the distance but if you write sufficiently frequently some of it is sure to get here - I hope!

Been a bit seedy for the last few days - don't know what it is (ain't booze as we've been too busy) but I imagine these interminable night patrols have something to do with it. The Doc tells me to get as much rest as possible - might as well tell me to arrange my passage home in the present circumstances.

Incidentally you'll be pleased to hear that I lived up to the reputation of "glamour boy" today. We were due for a patrol tonight but it was so bad outside I made representations against it. I was to go out and try it. I did. But not for long. So, here I am tucked away inside until the weather moderates. And no cracks chum - life doesn't amuse me at the moment.

Darling I'm missing you so horribly. I had never before realised that I could be so completely in love with anyone that this enforced absence would drive me nearly crazy. I'm missing you more even than I thought I would when we parted and all I long for is this whole mess to finish so that I can get home again to you. Do you realise that it's only two and a half months since I left you in that taxi in Falmouth - to me it seems an age. But I can't be out here forever and we'll have all the more to celebrate when I do get home again. Not excluding a honeymoon! Incidentally Linda I think an official engagement is a very good idea - please say yes, and I'll make the necessary arrangements.

By the time you receive this letter you should have heard from John Bick - or at any rate received the telegram I asked him to send. I gather from John that Johnnie has got herself engaged. I don't know her address but I should be grateful if you would offer her my most sincere congratulations - though I don't advise you to get up to similar tricks while I'm away.

What's happened to the photograph? I have a horrible suspicion that it's at the bottom of the ocean - if it really was sent some time ago will you send me on a further copy please? Should hate to have to fill the place of honour in the wardroom with that of someone else. Alright chum - you know I wouldn't anyway!

Alan stooged ashore by himself yesterday and turned up just before we left in the most perfect condition I've seen him since that party on 280. He informed me he'd only got back by pushing his fingers down his throat, being very ill and then sobering a little. What it is to be a T.T. (well, what is it anyway?)

Must finish my angel. Do write a hell of a lot as I am rather worried. Please don't change.

All my love sweet and just occasionally remember your lonely, pining
Don.

H.M.M.L. 338
c/o G.P.O.,
London

31st December 1942

Linda my darling

This is a bloody existence. It's blowing hard, the rain is falling in torrents and, although we are lying alongside, we are doing a 40 degree roll – which isn't exactly pleasant. Still shouldn't care to be outside. The sea is hitting the breakwater and the spray is dancing up to forty or fifty feet (Forbes my spare officer has just made the comment "Don't let me hear anyone talk about the Scottish climate after this"!)

But away with the blues! It is New Year's Eve and although we are duty boat I hardly think that we will be sent out in this sea – just glamour boys through and through.

Had some quite amusing French types down on board yesterday – in case you are suspicious I'll tell you the whole story. In the early days here we met a most amusing bloke whom everyone calls The Admiral (apparently he was in the French Navy some years ago). We've tried hard to teach him English but all he has mastered to date is "The German Navy – bottoms up". Anyway he stooged down at gin time and brought with him two girls who are the principal attractions at a concert which is to be held tonight – one is a ballet dancer and the other is a singer. We were all chatting quite happily if a little uncertainly when down the hatch come Gibby and Arnaud – Gibby's as good as a bloodhound where women are concerned. Well that was OK and we all arranged to meet in the Patio at 18.00. At 17.00 I wandered along to pick up Dudley and Gibby and that of course is where the session started. Instead of arriving at the Patio at six it was after seven and the girls had gone and left a message for us to follow them to their flat – no address given. So that was that. We had several aperitifs (I don't drink champagne cocktails anymore!) and decided that the hootch was better on board and in any case leave ends at 20.30 so we went (almost) rejoicing on our way. But instead of the usual happy session something went adrift and it developed into a quarrelling party. Anyway I got a few things off my chest – they'd been in cold storage for some time and then everyone was quite happy again – anyway it's a matelot's privilege to "drip" occasionally.

I haven't seen Gibby yet this morning but Arnaud looks as though walking around in the middle of an unpleasant nightmare. I'm just numb – as you can see from my writing.

Well it's New Years Eve and this haven of rest is hardly the ideal place in which to commence 1943. Next year I hope to be back home once more and then we can make up for the enforced separation. I love you desperately darling and I'm only awaiting the time when every week will be a continuation of the heavenly time we had together at Tenby. I promise that I won't change wretch and there'll be a hell of a lot of trouble if you dare do so. Incidentally where do you want to live after the war? As you know my job will probably be in London (unless they won't have me back and then it will be a question of which Public Assistance Committee will look after me) so it will have to be within a reasonable distance of town. Personally I like living in town (or rather Hampstead or Putney) but I have no objection to being further out. Quite frankly sweet all I want is to be with you again, to make love to you again and forget about wars and all the things that go with them. Without the thought of going back to you I don't think I should honestly care whether I got back or not – but let's keep off depressing subjects.

Incidentally you remember the multitudinous subjects we discussed on one never forgotten walk to Saundersfoot – the views I expressed on that occasion still hold – just in case you thought they didn't! Still I promise to behave myself chum.

Alan is changing place with Gibby's No 1. You may remember that Gibby and his No 1 were always quarrelling at each other and now matters have apparently come to a head and they have had to be separated. How I shall get on with Denton I don't know but I'm hoping for the best.

John the rat is now on his way home and I imagine that by the time you receive this letter he will have been in touch with you – if he hasn't he'd better look out for squalls.

Must finish pet. I do love you so much and I do so want to be with you again.

As ever
Don

P.S. Darling it's so long since I heard from you – please write often.

Chapter Six

JANUARY – MAY 1943

After Operation Torch, the Axis powers built up their troops in Tunisia to fill the vacuum left by the defection of the Vichy forces to the Allied side. The Allies were hampered from increasing their strength into Tunisia, because of uncertainty regarding the status of the French troops, and their advance to Tunis was halted and repelled. Thus during the winter a stalemate ensued, during which both sides took advantage by building up their forces.

In the second half of February, Rommel would rout an inexperienced French/US Corps at the Battle of Kasserine Pass (see **Map C**, on page 43). However, by early March 1943, the British Eighth Army was advancing from the west and the Axis found their troops being trapped between the two armies in a pincer movement. A major offensive in mid-April 1943 would crush the Axis forces in North Africa, leading to their surrender on 13th May 1943 - yielding over 275,000 prisoners of war, although a larger number of Axis troops were evacuated.

In his book, *Flag 4*, Dudley Pope records that by the end of January 1943, Coastal Forces strength in the Mediterranean had grown to over 100 ships, of which some 40 were MLs.

Don's first letter of 1943 is dated **2nd January**. He reports that he had come upon a tearful Dudley writing to Jane to break off their relationship. In Don's opinion, he does not have the moral courage to go through with a divorce and is genuinely attached to his wife, Eda. Anyway, they had a few drinks and wandered on to see Gibby and a party had ensued. As on many recent occasions, Don's letter ends with appeals for letters and the elusive photograph.

On **4th January 1943** Linda at last writes (in a letter headed "night watch"), thanking Don for the perfume (Elizabeth Arden 'Blue Grass'), lipstick and rouge. She mentions a New Year's party at The Picnic, which had finished, in her absence, in her room. She has counted 29 letters and 26 wires from Don. She reveals that she is not doing too badly for wine and that oranges were available at Christmas. She is sorry to hear of John's illness and reports that Louise has not heard from Max. She pledges her love and loyalty and asks whether Don is receiving all her letters. From the tone of Don's correspondence it seems that many of those had gone astray or were still delayed.

In his letter of **6th January 1943**, Don advises that the Coastal Forces Base at Algiers has now been officially established and that he is at liberty to reveal more of the happenings of the last month. Don's tells how his ship was the first in before moving up the coast to Algiers Harbour. The operation was a success and everything was quiet after the landings and he considers the experience to have been good fun and thrilling. They went ashore and were made welcome by the locals. However, after a month, he has become bored and the food and social life ashore leave much to be desired.

On 8th **January 1943**, Don writes probably his longest letter, having received Linda's communications of 5th, 9th and 10th December 1942 (only the first of which survives). When he has received correspondence from her, his letters always strike an upbeat note. Depression seems to set in and gradually increases the longer the gap grows in hearing from her. He regrets that the war has kept them apart and speculates that they will be reunited within 12 months. He reminisces about their first meeting in the County Hotel at Haverfordwest, their drinks in the Castle Hotel and their walks by the river.

1950s Painting of *Castle Hotel* and Square, Haverfordwest by David Lindley
Courtesy *Haverfordwest Town Museum*

He describes the events of the previous evening in lengthy detail when he, Peter and Dudley had gone ashore, initially to the Paris Hotel. There, he relates, all the tables were occupied by "pongoes and yanks". Apparently 'pongoes' was a derogatory term used by the other services to describe army personnel who 'ponged' after roughing it in action. 'Yanks' is still used as a slang term for Americans. Eventually the evening ended with a drinking session, which did not finish until 02:30 the following morning.

The envelopes of Don's letters dated 6th and 8th January are both postmarked by Weymouth Post Office on 30th January, indicating that the mail is taking between three and four weeks to arrive.

In a short letter that he writes on **14th January 1943**, he says that, as he has not heard from her recently, he is consoling himself by reading and rereading Linda's previous three letters until he knows them by heart. He gives an amusing description of the events of an evening spent ashore with Dudley with the express intention of meeting six English nurses who did not match their expectations. That had not prevented Don and Dudley from having a 'skinful' and, on the way back to the quayside, Dudley had fallen down the steps into the dry dock, thankfully without damage. He signs his letter from the "lonely, pining, horribly lovesick Don".

Linda writes on **18th January 1943** saying that she has received a pile of mail from Don. She confirms that she will write to Mrs Arnaud and will visit Don's aunt in Bournemouth. She also describes the confusion arising after Don gave John some letters to post on his return to England whilst on sick leave. Linda was also on leave, staying with her sister, Peggy in Southbourne, when Melba (presumably a WAAF from *RAF Ringstead*) phoned to say that a letter, postmarked Reading, had arrived and she had assumed Don must be in hospital there. One can imagine the ensuing panic as, in the war, loved ones must have been on edge in case of bad news. John must have been moving around as another letter arrived, postmarked London, and a telegram was sent from Gloucester. Linda now regrets having told Johnnie that John (Bick) is back home because Johnnie is now in a new relationship.

Linda tells how, after the panic about Don, she had composed herself and had taken part in her nephew Derek's Christmas Party. (Derek was Peggy's stepson and would have been aged nine.) She describes meeting a naval Sub-Lieutenant at a Wren dance at the Gloucester who knows Don and Dudley Arnaud. Her letter ends with a promise to write frequently and to send her photograph.

On **22nd January 1943**, Don writes a short letter. Dick has "rejoined the fold" and he and Dudley have shown him around Algiers, including the Bristol and the Oasis. The Oasis Hotel is open to this day, but it seems that the Bristol Hotel is no longer trading.

In his letter of **25th January 1943**, Don expresses frustration and disappointment that the mail has arrived but contained nothing from Linda. The last letter from her was dated 10th December 1942, more than six weeks earlier. If she does not write more frequently, he threatens a "whole heap of trouble coming to those blond curls of yours". (I found one such curl in an envelope, enclosed with one of Linda's letters, which Don had saved and which has survived to this day.) He declares that he is a reformed character and not attending all the parties, and he describes life there as boring. He reports that his radio has been repaired and that he heard Billy Ternent playing *South Rampart Street Parade*. Billy Ternent (born in Newcastle upon Tyne in 1899) was a popular orchestra leader, best known for backing Frank Sinatra at the London Palladium.

On **1st December 1942**, the *Beveridge Report* had been published, which would provide the foundations of the Welfare State. In his letter, Don asks Linda to send him a copy of G D H Cole's booklet on the subject, saying that he will not have time to read the whole report.

Before the war, he had been working at the Ministry of Health. If adopted, the Beveridge proposals will have huge implications, not just on the general populace but on Don's job, to which he anticipates he will return.

In fact, it was the Labour Party's promise to adopt the Beveridge recommendations that would lead them to a landslide victory in 1945. The General Election fell on 5th July 1945. Don returned to the UK on the previous day and would, most certainly, have voted Labour. Soon after the war, he was moved to the Ministry of National Insurance, created in 1944 as a product of the *Beveridge Report*, where his role in public relations would resume.

Don's letter of **25th January 1943** finishes in familiar tones reminiscing about halcyon days in Tenby and Falmouth. He chastises himself for being "a beast" in Falmouth and begs forgiveness for wasting and spoiling their last week together. Don blames it on pressure of work. He vows to obtain a special marriage licence upon his return.

A joyous Don writes to Linda on **9th February 1943**, confirming that he has just received her letters of 4th and 18th January, the first mail he has received for two weeks. He jokes that the occasion warrants a celebration equal to an armistice declaration and wonders whether she has received all 21 of his telegrams. He speculates that he might be abroad a further 18 months which, as events unfolded, turned out to be an underestimate yet again. He tells her how much he misses her and wonders how he manages to exist without her. He inscribes his letter 'No. 1' and says he will number future letters so that Linda can monitor how many are getting through to her. There is again a request to hurry the photograph. We cannot be too sure what motivated her after she received this letter, but at some point Linda wrote "answered" and "bad mood!" on the envelope.

Unfortunately, pages 3 and 4 of Don's six-page letter of **16th February 1943** (inscribed 'No. 2') are missing. He has just received Linda's letter of 26th January (also not found). However, he does answer several matters that she has raised. He says that Phyllis (the nickname for Eric Denton, who had swapped places with Alan to become Don's No. 1 – see earlier letter) is not doing too badly and that Gibby is regretting the exchange. He lauds Linda's father's good taste in liking Rosalind Russell, an American actress, who started her career as a fashion model before finding success with MGM. By the mid-1930s she had become a big star. Her most famous film in the 1940s was His Girl Friday with Cary Grant. She won all of the five Golden Globes for which she was nominated and her career continued until the 1970s.

Returning to Don's letter, Linda has transferred to *RAF Worth Matravers* from *RAF Ringstead* and he asks if she is enjoying Swanage. Don declares that an official engagement was an excellent idea, and he proposes to send a remittance so that she can purchase a ring.

A letter dated **21st February 1943** is sent by LACW Russell WAAF, c/o Ingleston, Victoria Road, Swanage, which is presumably the address of Linda's lodgings. In his previous letter, Don had mentioned that she is lucky having two old maids to run around after her. She thanks him for his three cables and is looking forward to nine days of leave at home on the Isle of Wight. She reports that two of her friends have been injured and one killed in an accident but there is no mention of the circumstances. She says that she has not heard from John (Bick) and has not had a cigarette for a month. She confirms that she will forward, as requested, Cole's booklet on the *Beveridge Report* and a photograph of herself. She asks Don to write to Bacon's (a Liverpool photographer who no longer seems to be trading) in order for her to have an enlargement of his photograph. She considers life to be dull in Swanage, but there are occasional dances at the Grosvenor Hotel (which was demolished in 1988) and there are two cinemas in the town. She has seen the films *The Major and the Minor* and *Sherlock Holmes and the Secret Weapon* and wonders whether Don has watched any new films, such as *You Were Never Lovelier*.

On **28th February 1943**, Don writes in rather a depressed mood. He designates this as letter No. 5, delivered by sea. His sea mailings Nos. 3 & 4 are missing, although there is an empty envelope, sent from him and dated 21st February 1943, which would have contained one of these. He has found the five months that they have been apart quite an ordeal and anticipates that it will finish up as two years. It seems an age to him since he saw Linda off in the taxi at Falmouth. He reminisces fondly of their time together, especially their week in Tenby. He wants them to go to Tenby on his return and visit the Lion (probably the Royal Lion Hotel) and see Alice there, to walk to Swallow Tree Woods at Saundersfoot, and so many other things. He then dreams of a visit to Haverfordwest, to the cinema, and even to have some of "that dubious fish" at the Castle Hotel. He reminds her to arrange a visit to his aunt in Bournemouth and to send the long-awaited photograph. He says that she should consider herself officially engaged and that he will send a remittance for a ring.

Don's letter dated **9th March 1943** is the first one addressed from Mess 17, Coastal Forces Base, Malta and he declares triumphantly that he has received two photographs of Linda. There is not much news apart from one party ashore and a celebration with Dudley and Dick. He is enjoying the good weather and, having been sunbathing, he is planning a swim. His air letter of **13th March 1943** (air letter No. 1) is also addressed from Malta and he comments that Coastal Forces are at last getting some recognition but are consequently being worked hard. The second half of his letter is again devoted to reminiscences of better times with Tenby receiving special mention. He attributes his homesickness to playing cards with Richard and talking about Falmouth.

Linda writes from her lodgings in Swanage c/o Mrs Klitz (presumably her landlady) on **15th March 1943**, acknowledging receipt of his letters of 28th February and 9th March (her letter says February – probably an error). Her nine days of leave have been cancelled. She is still officially attached to *RAF Ringstead* and will be returning there shortly. She says that she has not yet visited Don's aunt in Bournemouth and sounds reticent. She expresses joy at being officially engaged, even though rings are a shocking price. Although there have been no parties or dances, she has been to the cinema to see *Smilin' Through* and *Road to Morocco*. She anticipates them celebrating Christmas together and vows that they will have a ginger beer on the way to Saundersfoot. Finally she asks about Richard, Alan and "bad types" Gibby and John.

Don's next letter, of **18th March 1943** and addressed from Algiers, comprises just a few lines written at 06:00 (under the weight of a hangover) saying he will write properly that evening.

However, his next surviving letter is dated **1st April 1943** and is again from Algiers. He blames pressure of work as the reason for not having written. He thanks Linda for her mailing of 5th March (which is missing from this collection). The usual topics surface: the photographs, drinking with Gibby and their week in Tenby, to name but a few. A second brief communication is sent by him on the same day via a new service in an unsealed format that he considers gives insufficient privacy.

In his next air letter, dated **3rd April 1943** (air letter No. 4 – therefore 2 & 3 are missing), he acknowledges receipt of Linda's letter of 15th March. He surmises that his communications of 16th, 21st and 24th February have gone astray. (In fact, only the last of these is missing.) He says that his mother is pleased to hear of their official engagement and looks forward to meeting Linda. He has been to a party ashore at their Engineer Officer's flat, where he relates there were eight blokes and ten French girls. Apparently, Gibby was in good form and Teddy Rose was barman, and Don claims to be one of only two sober at the end of the evening.

Don's letter dated **13th April 1943** but completed the following day, celebrates the receipt of Linda's photograph – at last! He reveals that the address on his letter is a little deceptive, presumably meaning he is not now in Algiers all the time. There had been a farewell party for

Max, a few nights earlier (it also happened to be Alan's wedding anniversary) and Don reported that he had performed *Darktown Strutters' Ball*. This must have been his 'party piece' as he previously mentioned singing this in his letter of 18th November 1942 (see Chapter Five). The next day, he and Dudley had undertaken some physical training, followed by a long walk round the face of the cliff and up and over the mountain. He says the country there is delightful but there is no clue as to his precise whereabouts.

Don's letter of **18th April 1943** (air letter No. 7) starts with a severe reprimand regarding Linda's lack of correspondence. Apart from a couple of hours' walk the previous day with Dudley, he has not been ashore. The drinking session they have just had led to feelings of homesickness and thoughts of Greenbanks (a hotel in Falmouth – see page 126). He reiterates that they should marry as soon as he returns and honeymoon at their haunts – Tenby, Saundersfoot, Falmouth, and even Haverfordwest. He says he will never forget that night when he and John visited the County Hotel in Haverfordwest and he first met Linda and then they went on to the cinema. He finishes saying that he will send powder, as perfume is not available.

In his next letter, **five days later** (air letter No. 8), he has still not heard from Linda since her communication of 15th March 1943. He says that they are being worked pretty hard. He tells of a party with Dudley and Gibby, which resulted in a bad hangover the next day, and the letter ends in the traditional, tender way.

Don writes again **the following day** (sea letter No. 6), in a depressed mood, explaining that he is only allowed one air letter per week. He has been reading Linda's old letters. He particularly enjoys the ones she wrote before he left England, when he was "stooging around the Bristol Channel". Despite his "near escapes of marriage" he now recognises that Linda is his only love. He looks forward to life with her immediately after the war. He says he will avoid work for three months, look up old friends and repeat that heavenly week in Tenby. On his return to Whitehall, he thinks he will find himself out of touch with events. He agrees with Dudley that it will take some adjustment for the men of the 25th ML Flotilla to adapt to civilian life. He returns to the present: the weather is cold, cloudy and wet and Phyllis is back from hospital following his jaundice. Again, looking forward, he favours a flat in Hampstead close to the Heath and he knows some good pubs nearby.

Somehow he manages two letters on **10th May 1943** (air letters Nos. 10 & 11). He has just received Linda's letter of 15th April (unfortunately missing). He comments that it was numbered 11 and her previous letter was No. 3, so either her numbering system has gone haywire or a lot have gone astray. Apparently, Linda had reported that Johnnie had returned to *RAF Ringstead* and that she, herself, had been on leave. Don wishes he could have a break from his ship. He says he had been ashore in Algiers to a party at their Engineer Officer's flat with, amongst others, Teddy Rose and Ronnie Perks from Falmouth and some Wrens (Women's Royal Naval Service). Apparently Dudley has fallen for a French female, but Don assures Linda that he has no interest in other women.

Don starts another letter on **15th May 1943** (air letter No. 12) in a state of depression, probably not helped by the previous evening's all-male party ashore. He has sent off the money for Linda's engagement ring. He completes the letter the next day, having just received hers of 1st May 1943 (also missing), in which she must have related that her visit to Don's aunt in Bournemouth had not gone well. It seems that his aunt had not received either his letter or a letter from his mother explaining the situation, and that his previous engagement and flirtations were aired by his aunt!

Don reveals that he has now finished in North Africa and will be venturing into other theatres. He finishes the letter by congratulating Linda on her promotion to Corporal and says that he is sending a pair of silk stockings size 9½.

Don commences writing his next letter (air letter No. 13) later in the day on **16th May 1943** and completes it the following day. Apparently, Alan has announced that he is being sent home for leave and a shore job in a quiet place as he has been diagnosed with "anxiety neurosis". Don tells of an impromptu party which he blames on Dick, with whom he is sharing a hangover. The party broke up at 04:00 that morning. He suggests that Linda should visit his aunt again to clear matters up. He has heard from home (Liverpool) that his younger brother, Leslie, has got himself all entangled with a ballet dancer. He reports hot weather resulting in sunburn.

Linda writes on **28th May 1943**, having just received Don's air letter No. 12 (see above). She apologises that her letter of 1st May had upset him (her letter and his reply are both missing). Her excuse is that she was feeling depressed, and of course she loves and trusts him completely. Neither the £25 remittance for the ring nor the powder and silk stockings he had sent have yet arrived. She has been on a three-watch system for the past few days, but last week she had 36 hours' leave and stayed with her sister, Peggy, in Bournemouth. She says they had "a bit of a shaking" during a recent air raid and she had been very worried. However, she continues that the picture is not quite as black as it is painted but bad enough.

In fact nearly 200 people, mostly Allied airmen staying at the Metropole Hotel, died in the Luftwaffe raid on Bournemouth on 23rd May 1943. The raid was the deadliest wartime attack on the town - 26 Focke Wolf 190 planes dropped 25 high-explosive bombs on the town, destroying 22 buildings and damaging a further 3,000. Photographs of the Metropole Hotel before and after the raid are shown on the following page.

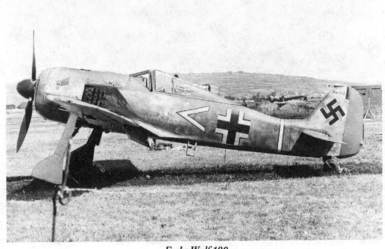

Focke Wulf 190
By *RAF* [public domain], via *Wikimedia Commons*

Metropole Hotel in its heyday around 1910

Metropole Hotel after the raid (from *Bournemouth Times*)
Images on this page provided by *Moordown Local History Society*

In wartime, life has to go on and Linda and her sister had been to the ballet – *Swan Lake* and *Polonica*. She says that, at the time of writing (8 am), she and Johnnie are on watch together. Johnnie has now got over her broken relationship with John. They are going to Weymouth to see the film *The Major and the Minor* (in her letter of 21st February 1943, Linda had already mentioned seeing this film in Swanage).

On **1st June 1943** (air letter No. 14) Don reports continued hot and sunny weather and more sunburn following sunbathing on a beach with Dudley. They are now in white uniforms but laundry is a problem because of a shortage of soap. He has also been to a small fishing village with Gibby where, nearby, there is an Army officers' rest camp and they were invited into the bar. He met an English nurse and stayed with her for the evening but stresses, by way of assurance, that this was not the same as being with Linda.

**Letters:
January – May 1943**

c/o Ingleston,
Victoria Road,
Swanage,
Dorset.

My darling Ron,

Very many thanks for your three cables. I really had you known all of...

H.M.M.L. 338
c/o G.P.O.,
London

2nd January 1943

L.A.C.W Russell W.A.A.F.
R.A.F. Ringstead,
Near Dorchester,
Dorsetshire,
ENGLAND

My darling Linda

I don't know what on earth I have to say as so little has happened since my last effort, except to tell you that I love you rather a lot and even that will hardly fill a complete letter.

As I say very little has happened. After I had completed my letter to you on New Year's Eve I wandered across to see Dudley whom I found almost in tears in the middle of a letter to Jane. Apparently he has decided that it is one of those things which can never really come to anything and he was informing Jane of that fact. The whole trouble is of course that he would never have the moral courage to go through with a divorce and, in any case, I think he is genuinely attached to Eda. We'll see what happens when he does get home and is faced with facts – rather than daydreams. Anyway we had a couple of drinks and then wandered on to see Gibby – and that started the party. It is with much regret that I confess that I did get rather tight for the first time for many weeks – reformed character, that's me! Still it was good fun and I'm told that my rendering of Dark Town Strutters' Ball is not slipping.

Next morning things didn't seem quite so rosy – in fact I doubt whether I have ever felt worse in my life and please don't say it serves you right – I'm fully aware of it. I mooched around during the morning and as soon as I had finished lunch decided that sleep could effect the only cure. In the evening just loafed around and read.

The weather has been pretty foul today and as I'm duty boat I'm praying that I shan't be sent out on patrol today also Denton took over from Alan so I'm anxious to see how things go – there'll probably be fireworks before long.

Darling I do love you a hell of a lot and I'm just eagerly awaiting the next mail – it's about time we had one. Incidentally have you sent the photograph yet or was it so bad that you decided to destroy it? Just curious!

Must finish wretch. I am missing you so much and I needn't tell you that all I want is to be back with you once more.

Don't change pet

All my love and write lots to your miserable pining
Don

R.A.F. Ringstead,
Dorset

04/01/43 (night watch)

Lieut F.D. Bickerton R.N.V.R.,
Mess 45,
Coastal Force Base,
Gibraltar.

My darling Don,

A million thanks for the perfume, lipstick and rouge – absolutely perfect and terribly sweet of you. Elizabeth Arden 'Blue Grass' – oh boy!! a heavenly perfume, which at present is safely locked away in my case as such things have been known to vanish. I wish you could see my rosy lips and cheeks (yes, more conceited than ever!). I must admit that your good taste has shaken me considerably – thank you darling.

I suppose that your New Year celebrations were pretty hectic!! We had a party at the Picnic, which fortunately I had to leave early for night watch – in one of my 'coping' moods! Apparently the party finished in my bedroom about 5.30, as when I came off watch things were somewhat disorganised – more about this later as it was very amusing. Anyway, I eventually rolled into bed only to find it full of empties.

I received your letter card this morning, dated 7/12, which should have arrived by Xmas! I/C mail must be a big job, and I hope, for my sake, that there was at least one letter from me amongst those 157 bags (you might let me know). I was looking through your letters t'other day, yes, you have written a lot since I've known you – 29 to be exact and 26 wires (not with blue ribbon though!).

Darling, must you harp on glorious sunshine, fruit and wine etc: although we're not doing too badly for the latter <u>and</u> we had oranges at Xmas, the former will come later (I hope). You are lucky and how I'd adore to be with you all the time. I wonder why you think I have a nasty mind of course you're behaving (there ain't much choice). Seriously, I do believe you but do have a good time (I bet you will – fool if you didn't). Please ignore cracks but I am reasonable. I'm spending my life thinking and talking about you and always muttering I must write to Don! (no cracks).

I'm sorry to hear that poor old John has been ill and I'm wondering if he'll wangle sick leave (probably a few others but I mustn't put ideas in to your head). So Max is making a nuisance of himself, he is a dog, no Louise hasn't heard from him he dropped her like a ton of bricks.

Darling I'm missing you horribly I only hope that you won't be away too long – well, it's three months now, every day is a day nearer! We'll make up for lost time and do lots of crazy things – you once said 'two years and then a lifetime', I hope and pray you're right – you must know by this time that I love you and will wait no matter how long.

Do take care of yourself and please write as much as possible. I won't change darling.

All my love,
Ever yours
Linda

P.S. Are you receiving my letters?
P.P.S. I love you.

MESS 17,
Coastal Force Base,
ALGIERS,

6th January 1943

L.A.C.W. Russell W.A.A.F.,
R.A.F. ~~Ringstead,~~ Worth Matravers,
~~Near Dorchester,~~ Swanage,
Dorset~~shire,~~
ENGLAND

Linda darling

At last we have been able to organise our base and therefore an address – and I can also give you a rather fuller account of happenings over the past few months.

We were here right in the beginning in fact I think we may claim the doubtful honour of being the first here. Everything was quiet after the landings had taken place and we moved up the coast to enter Algiers harbour. It was good fun and we were all thrilled to death with the success of the operation. Of course we stooged off shore at the first opportunity and were made quite welcome by the great majority of the local inhabitants. The cafes with their chairs and tables on the sidewalk were reminiscent of France but, I regret to report, the quality of the drink was not.

But I'm afraid those first thrills wore off very quickly and now I'm bored to tears with the place – so much so that I rarely bother to go ashore. And I suppose you'd like some information of the female element. Well chum it ain't so good. The only girls who will have anything to do with the British Forces are those of somewhat doubtful reputation and personally I just ain't interested. The food situation is bad and only on two occasions have I eaten ashore. Still I suppose we could be in a worse spot – I can think of many places in which I would prefer to be e.g. Weymouth!

Well sweet the mail is almost inevitably conspicuous by its continued absence but as usual we are still living in hopes of its impending arrival – even to the extent of visiting the mail office about three times daily.

I told you about the photograph we had taken on X'mas day – I saw it today. Well chum it's not so good but I'm getting some copies which I'll send on and you can judge for yourself.

Darling did I ever tell you that I love you? No? Well let me hasten to remedy such an omission! I love you but oh sweet, I do so wish I could be with you and able to tell in words just how much I'm missing you, Do write lots and when this ruddy mail does arrive maybe I'll get a whole bag from you.

All my love pet
As ever
Don

Mess 17,
Coastal Forces Base,
Algiers.

8th January 1943

L.A.C.W Russell W.A.A.F.
R.A.F. Ringstead,
Near Dorchester,
Dorsetshire,
ENGLAND

My darling Linda

Spring is here again – in fact a mail has just arrived containing your letters of the 5th, 9th and 10th December so I hasten to reply to withdraw any past remarks I may have made about your lack of correspondence. Seriously sweet I am most relieved as absence of any word from you was making me rather worried. Darling I really have been writing a hell of a lot but I have had a suspicion that it could not all be reaching you, the gap between my letters of 15th and 26th November for example is not lack of literary effort on my part but merely another of the numerous misfortunes of war. Still it's some consolation to learn that you do receive part of it!

I'm missing you equally as badly and you should know wretch that I won't change. Angel I'd give anything in the world to be with you so that once more we could stooge around together and do all those things that this war prevents us doing. I hope that by this time next year that at present fanciful daydream will be fulfilled. Please don't worry pet I'm awfully good at taking care of myself. And, says he, adopting a sterner attitude, will you please take care of yourself – you know quite well you catch colds very easily. Do take care – please.

I honestly never thought the day would come when I could truthfully say that I should be pleased to be back at P.D. Even with you at Weymouth it would mean that I could see you every three months at least, and that would be absolute paradise, and say once more a la Milnes "It is shocking, it is scandalous to enjoy life as I do" – or, more probably, words to that effect.

I, too, used to enjoy the walks by the river (even in the rain), the beer in the Castle (the fish <u>was</u> pretty foul) and perhaps my happiest moment was the evening I met you in the County. Quite honestly chum I only went over to Haverfordwest because I was curious to see the town – little did I know what was to come out of such curiosity (no believe it or not I'm not regretting – but if I hadn't gone I shouldn't be feeling nearly so homesick as I am at the moment). Yes I think we will go back to all the old places one day.

Must say I'm looking forward tremendously to receiving this much discussed photograph – it's alright pet, I do appreciate the difficulties you must be having with the photographer, but please hurry him up and don't forget to send it by registered air mail. We seem to have so much mail adrift that particularly in this case I wish to take the minimum of chance.

You seem to have enjoyed your kit inspection – I believe I have a "men only" cartoon on the subject; I'll try and dig it out – you've probably seen it!

Incidentally I'm not at all sure that this business of showing my photograph to odd people won't get you into trouble at some time or other. Imagine how you would feel if someone were to exclaim in a dramatic sob "He is the father of my child!" (Knowing your low mind I'd better state immediately that it won't happen!). Why everyone at Warren should appear to know Dick and I, I can't imagine. Never been to the place in my life.

Can't understand why you are not taking part in your X'mas show. Couldn't you put on a one act play on "How I got back to the Greenbank" OK pal – just wondered!

I had a long depressing letter from Dick yesterday. He's fed up both with his base and the people with whom he is working. I was therefore very glad to learn that he will be rejoining us in the near future – I'll certainly be glad to see him again.

Regret to report that I was nearly led astray last night (not what you're thinking). Peter, Dudley and I decided that it might be a good thing if we had dinner ashore but no, repeat no, session. On the way to the Paris we looked in on some army types and managed to hold our own with only one drink for about an hour. So far so good. On to the Paris. Here we are politely informed that there are no vacant tables (full of pongoes and yanks) but if we care to wait just a moment he will be enchanted to accommodate us. To while away the interval we have "mais une touché" (which incidentally appears to have become the flotilla slogan). And then I met some French people I know and they insist that we have one with them. Well I had no desire to appear insulting so we did. And another and so on ad nauseam. Dinner? Well frankly we forgot all about it! I couldn't get Dudley away from the place as he insisted that we should go to one of the low dives in this place. Well we left to go there and very fortunately after tramping half Algiers just couldn't find it. Then we met a French Army doctor who we invited down on board and really started the session – amazing how fluently ones French flows after a mellowing of whisky. On his departure (God knows how he got back) we brought out the records, many of which I'm sure you'll be glad to hear are broken, and started to swing until I regret to say 0230. Then I went back on board and had my dinner. The end of a perfect night. My thoughts ran in different channels this morning.

Must finish now pet as I've promised to go over to Gibby's for "mais une touché" – I may add that it will be.

Please write lots to me. You know I love you terribly – I won't ever change darling. Believe me you are the first and only person I have ever loved in this way – and then almost as soon as I meet you I get dumped in this joint. Incidentally sweet I honestly don't make a practice of asking someone to marry me in every letter just for the mere joy of it. I'm missing you so horribly please write often.

All my love
Ever thine
Don.

Mess 17,
Coastal Forces Base,
Algiers.

14th January 1943

Linda darling

No more mail yet but I've read and reread your last three letters until I nearly know them by heart – anyway there should be lots of stuff when it does arrive.

The other evening was quite amusing. Dudley and I were invited to dinner by an Army Major for the express purpose of meeting six English nurses. Big stuff! Had a bath, tiddlied ourselves up – even put on one of my remaining few stiff collars and started cheerfully on our way to the Hotel Oasis. Arrived fifteen minutes adrift at 1745. No nurses. Meet some blokes we know and start on champagne as there isn't anything else to drink. 1845 I look round, I can't speak but I clutch Dudley's arm and point. His mouth drops. Well chum believe me I can understand why they came abroad but why inflict them on us. Dinner was foul and then I espied the Admiral with the singer and the dancer so we make our apologies and have a touché with them. But we are so polite and therefore rejoin our own party and make small talk until we consider we have a reasonable chance of escaping. Then on to Gibby's boat where we tell our story to his undisguised amusement and numerous low cracks. Anyone would have thought that that would be enough for one night but no! – on our way back Dudley has to fall down the steps into the dry dock fortunately without damage of any kind. In fact not one of our better efforts!

Last night I didn't do anything except have a quiet nightcap with Dudley and reminisce about Falmouth and Tenby. We nearly finished by weeping in each others arms.

Darling you are writing a lot aren't you. I do miss you so terribly and your letters are the only consolation I possess. I love you so very very much and I just want to be back with you again to be able to hold you so tight in my arms. In fact I feel "real sloppy".

Don't change my sweet and write often to your lonely, pining, horribly lovesick

Don.

P.S. How's the photo coming along
P.P.S. Sorry for such a short letter – I'll write again tomorrow.

R.A.F. Ringstead,
Dorset
England

18/01/43 (postmark)

My darling Don,

I've received a whole pile of mail from you which has kept me busy for quite a while, it's grand to hear all the news and to know that you are safe, and well, in spite of machine gunning and dive bombing!! You're right they have absolutely no sense of proportion – mind you shoot him down the next time.

I'll write to Mrs Arnaud, thanks for her address, perhaps I'd better not mention the amusing scene of her husband with a whisky in one hand and a French girl in t'other, somehow I don't think she'd approve! Will call on your Aunt in Bournemouth, it looks rather a nice hotel – glad she is young as I'm usually terrified of chattering old women.

A few days ago I was at my sister's house in Southbourne when Melba phoned me, in a shocking flap, tongue tied, puffing and blowing etc. Anyway she eventually managed to tell me that a letter of yours had arrived from Reading, should she open the letter as she was certain that you were in hospital. Of course I screeched down the line 'for God's sake do' (my sister came tearing out of the kitchen and afterwards told me that I was as white as a sheet – I wish she could see mine, the RAF should try Persil!). Later she phoned to say another letter had arrived from London and a wire from Gloucester. Darling, I can't stand such shocks at my great age! Please thank John, I'd rather like to see him and collect a bit of gen, but suppose it's not possible? I've rather stupidly told Johnnie that he's in England, although I don't suppose for a minute that he'll contact her. My small nephew's Xmas party got me down after my alarming phone call. Anyway I managed to pull myself together and helped organise such games as 'hunt the thimble' and 'blind man's buff'!!! Tea-time was a scream – twelve small boys and four girls eating, talking and drinking pop as hard as they could (I thought I was a pig!) It was a relief to see them go at 6.30, we were completely exhausted and had a quiet evening listening to gramophone records.

We were invited to a Wren dance at the Gloucester Friday, quite good fun but as usual I was bored part of the time and wished that you had been there. I danced with a Sub-Lieut from 123 who vaguely knew you, and Mr Arnaud, until I produced your photo then he was quite certain that he knew you. Unfortunately I didn't think of asking him his name, apparently he knows Falmouth Greenbanks quite well – which was all very depressing and made me feel even more miserable, the bar had sold out by 10 and no chance of drowning my sorrows! I haven't been to The Crown but it's an idea for discussion sometime, I'll remember you all to the old man (trust you're popular!!) If all's well the photo will be on its way next week. My apologies for delay but it was necessary for another sitting, by this time you must have forgotten what I'm like and when you see my photo – what a shock you will have.

Life goes on here much the same which doesn't help letter writing, no doubt it's the same there (what a sentence). Nevertheless you manage to write pages most days. Darling, surely some of my letters have caught you up by this time – I'll try sending via Mess 45 etc. which should be the better way, these letter cards are useful. I've bought two dozen so there should be no excuse for my lack of correspondence! Please write soon and let me know if you're receiving them quicker this way and darling please don't be angry because I haven't written every day. I do love you a hell of a lot and you know perfectly well that I'm sincere and will never change and remember that I'm thinking about you every minute of the day. When I saw the Navy at the Gloucester and remembered that you had danced there so often, it made me feel so sick and miserable that I just couldn't enjoy myself, and as you probably know I'm not much of a dancer (ballroom anyway!) myself so towards the end I completely lost interest.

I hope you've had a letter from your mother and that she's better, it must be very worrying, wish I could do something about it.

Well darling, I'm almost out of paper but will be writing again later. I do love you so very much, take good care of yourself.

All my love,
Ever yours
Linda

P.S. Love to Mr Arnaud, Richard, Gibby and Alan

Mess 17,
Coastal Forces Base,
Algiers.

22nd January 1943

L.A.C.W Russell W.A.A.F.
R.A.F. Ringstead,
Near Dorchester,
Dorsetshire,
ENGLAND

My darling Linda

Still our mail like the Scarlet Pimpernel eludes us but hope springs etc. And frankly I haven't done very much since I wrote to you two days ago - so you may expect this letter to be rather short.

Dick has rejoined the fold (perhaps lair would be more appropriate) and it was made an excuse for general celebration. Dudley and I staggered along to show him the sights of Algiers including the "job". I don't think I've described the job yet so I'll do my best. It's a very small Arab boy who travels along on all fours, right hand holding left foot, in a crabwise fashion and when he gets up to you holds out his left hand for money at the same turning up a face with an expression of trusting pathos. I fear that we must have become a little hard and we remain quite untouched. However the sight of Gibby, Dudley, Peter and I carrying out a faithful imitation on the way back is an inspiring sight.

From there we went on to the Bristol and had some of the "banana things" (actually crème de banana, but I regret to report that our vocabulary grows more stereotyped everyday) and introduced Dick not only to the crowd but our more recently acquired bad habits - by that I mean a [illegible] and "unpartyroute" - to quote Gibby. In fact it was quite a successful morning and I'm certain we were fortunate in returning for our lunch at 1400.

In the evening we decided for the Oasis to show Dick the lovely English nurses who have recently arrived here. Honestly chum you've no idea how disillusioning it can be to sight some honest ugly English faces again. Frankly they were not chosen for their beauty but they are quite good sorts. Thus concluded our day's entertainment. Not quite up to our old standards, I fear!

Darling how is that photograph progressing - you've no idea how I'm longing to receive it. Sweet please believe me when I tell you that I love you more than everything in the world and life is just hell without you. Please write as often as you possibly can and give an occasional thought to your pining Linda missing

Don.

P.S. I managed to get someone to send a cable to you from Gib in case of difficulties about mail. Did you receive it?

Mess 17,
Coastal Forces Base,
Algiers.

25th January 1943

L.A.C.W Russell W.A.A.F.
R.A.F. ~~Ringstead,~~ Worth Matravers,
Near ~~Dorchester,~~ Swanage,
Dorsetshire,
ENGLAND

Linda darling

A mail has at last arrived but wretch no word from you and therefore more than a little disappointing. If you don't write more frequently my pet there'll be a whole heap of trouble coming to those blond curls of yours and believe me I mean it. The last letter I received from you was dated 10th December or over six weeks ago and though I fully appreciate that there are long delays in the mail nevertheless it remains a fact that I have received letters from home in the interim. Sorry sweet this has become more lecture than letter and I promise to be good but please write as frequently as you can and then some of it, including the photograph I hope, is sure to get through.

I haven't much news for you as things have been rather hectic during the past few days. I saw Dudley this morning and he confirmed the story told by a strained face of a couple of rather hectic parties - they sounded so awful and he looked ghastly that I was thankful I wasn't able to be there! And coming from me you may guess how bad they were. Incidentally I forgot to mention that I am now (flourish of trumpets!!) a reformed character - in fact I've felt so foul after some of these parties that I've decided it's becoming too much of a good thing and that it would be a far, far better thing to lay off for the time being - except in moderation of course. And chum I don't want any cracks!

Life here remains as boring as ever. I haven't been ashore, says he righteously, since my last letter although I must admit I haven't had the opportunity. And the weather! At the moment it's blowing, raining, cold and to crown it all I'm not in harbour - which is of course a very good thing.

Our radio has been repaired and we managed to get the forces programme last night. To my delight I heard Billy Ternent playing "South Rampart Street Parade" and playing it quite well in true Bob Crosby style. But you wouldn't appreciate that!

Incidentally would you do me a favour? Please send on a copy of GDH Cole's booklet on the Beveridge Report - as I haven't time to go through the whole report and this appears to be factual and not critical survey.

Sweet I am missing you lots - all that happens when Dick, Dudley and I get together is a discussion of the things we used to do at Tenby and Falmouth. I was a beast during our last week together at Falmouth and I'll never forgive myself for behaving as I did. Angel please say that I am forgiven for wasting and spoiling that only too precious week - I didn't intend it should be spoiled and I can only plead pressure of work which although a hackneyed excuse is none the less true. When I get back we'll go to some place to make up for it - I hope to God that that day is near. You know that I love you so very much and, assuming your agreement, I propose that we get married by special licence as soon as I return. It is no mere rhetorical conglomeration of words when I tell you that without you life would be impossible - never before had I even dreamed that anyone could exercise so much influence upon me. But you see I love you as I, in my sophisticated innocence, never believed to be possible! Darling we will be so happy together and there are so many things that we'll be able to do – almost too many things to cram into one short and crowded lifetime. But oh boy! Won't that cramming be fun!

Must finish my darling as this roll is becoming too bad to continue writing. Do write soon wretch – your letters are the only thing which make life bearable. I do love you Linda; I shan't ever change as long as I live.

Spare a few thoughts for your far-away, pining
Don

P.S. How about the photograph?
P.P.S. I turned out the pockets of my sports jacket yesterday and discovered a bill from the Lion and two automatic weighing machine tickets. Still putting on weight?

Mess 17,
Coastal Force Base,
Algiers.

9th February 1943

L.A.C.W. Russell W.A.A.F.,
R.A.F. ~~Ringstead,~~ Worth Matravers
Near ~~Dorchester,~~ Swanage,
Dorsetshire,
ENGLAND.

Linda darling

A mail has arrived!!! And the celebrations are worthy of an armistice declaration. Anyway multitudinous thanks for your letter of 4th January and the undated one postmarked 18th January – I trust the strain wasn't too great.

It's good to know that you received the perfume etc as I was afraid that it had gone adrift – why my good taste should shake you I can't possibly conceive; to me it is purely of nature. And when you write of becoming "more conceited than ever" it is not unnatural that my credulity refuses to stretch so far!

Your New Year celebrations sound rather hectic and I imagine that it was probably rather a good thing that you had to go on watch – I don't think it's particularly nice of you to lead these people astray and then assume an air of virtuous innocence in your letters, you seem to forget that I have had some experience of you at odd parties. Just as a matter of interest what did you expect to find in your bed apart from the empties?

It's something to know that you did receive my airmail card albeit a week late, and, as you are so interested there wasn't a letter from you in the 157 bags of mail. Honestly sweet the mail situation here is absolutely bloody. This is the first mail we've received for well over two weeks and it contains only two letters from you (only four for me in all) and not a word from my people which is most unusual. Incidentally I didn't realise that I had sent you 21 wires – the total must have increased considerably since that date. I have been sending wires by odd people who have been venturing into a civilized proximity – have you been receiving them?

By far the best news in your letter is that you do miss me a little. Darling I feel so horribly lonely without you and the prospect of a further eighteen months or so abroad doesn't improve my present ill temper. Anyway eighteen is well nigh countless months isn't, I suppose, so great a hardship as it may seem and as soon as we are together once more they should only serve to sharpen my enjoyment at being with you once more. Linda you wretch I do love you so terribly that I feel it doesn't matter how many things may happen in this war I will always come back to you and you will always welcome me back. Please solve one mystery for me – how did I manage to exist before I met you? (if such a time did exist and is not a full hallucination).

And your other letter. It's something to know that you have received a whole file of mail from me – however I should be most grateful if you would quote the dates to give me some idea of the proportion of mail that is getting through – in fact I think it would be a good idea if I numbered the letters starting now.

I'm sorry about the confusion you apparently experienced with letters and telegrams coming in from every corner of the British Isles and frankly I can't understand the one postmarked "Reading" as I know no one who lives there. Still it's something to learn that letters are reaching you.

Darling I must finish but I promise to write in a couple of days. I don't need to tell you how much I love you and how terribly I'm missing you. I promise never to change but I do wish I could tell you in person rather that by inefficient letters.

All my love my angel and don't forget to hurry the photograph.
I do love you so much

As ever
Don.

Mess 17,
Coastal Forces Base,
Algiers.

16th February 1943

Linda my angel

It just can't be true – another letter from you and dated 26th January at that! And you are actually receiving my mail – sorry about the depressing New Year letter but I just felt that way.

You ask how I am coping with Phyllis. On the whole not too badly, he's not exactly my idea of an ideal companion but he annoys me rather less than Alan does on occasions – I fear that Gibby is regretting the change!

So you are attempting to teach your father some of your own evil habits – anyway I congratulate him in his good taste in liking Rosalind Russell.

Are you still enjoying Swanage? You always seem to fall on your feet – this time with two old maids to chase around for you; no doubt they've discovered your true low character by this time. And frightfully overworked indeed! Chum you want to come out here and discover what work really means. (This seems an ideal opening for a moan so I'd better leave it alone). Seriously we have been working very hard and I hate to confess that it is exactly a week since I last wrote to you. Darling I'm truely sorry but things have ....

[pages 3 & 4 of letter missing]

.... had some very good parties together in the Crown. He came out with me today as we expected excitement but, as usual, were disappointed – still the sea experience wouldn't do him any harm.

Do you still go to the Picnic Inn or have you learned your lesson? Incidentally wretch please hurry up the photograph – I really am awaiting it most expectantly (I hope you aren't wearing that awful cap!!!).

About an official engagement. As you know I consider it an excellent idea and I propose that I send a remittance via Naval channels (cheque is impracticable in view of its possible loss en route) and that you get an engagement ring. It really is impossible for me to get anything from this end – I only wish I could be with you to help you choose it (if you remember you once admitted to being shaken by my excellent taste!).

I really must finish as it is 0145 and tomorrow an early start seems indicated. Please write lots Linda sweet and may I say once more that I love you terribly.

All my love darling and don't forget on some occasions to think of a horribly Linda missing

Don.

P.S. Gibby sends his best wishes and he also says, "Beware of the Poles, they're worse than the 25th."

L.A.C.W. Russell W.A.A.F.
c/o Ingleston,
Victoria Road,
Swanage.

21st Feb 1943

Lieut F. D. Bickerton,
R.N.V.R.
Mess 17,
Coastal Force Base,
Algiers.

My darling Don,

Very many thanks for your three cables. I nearly had you thrown out of Greenbanks – zeh, when ze go to the Picnic Inn ze will keep sober, I've seen too many people fall into that stream.

By the way, I am only attached here so please continue sending mail to Ringstead. I slipped over there the other afternoon for some clothes, and the camp looked so miserable and depressing that I dread the thought of leaving here. Thank Heaven my leave is here. 9 days at home – what a blessing.

Darling, I do hope a few of my letters have turned up, especially the one thanking you for the lovely perfume etc. We've had a sad time as two of my friends were injured and another killed in an accident, a horrible business but might have been worse.

I haven't heard from John so I gather that by this time he is thinking of joining you. I hope you are better, do take good care of yourself. It's grand to know that you are not drinking so much – please continue the good work, I haven't had a cigarette since the 19th Jan – and darling no cracks (I don't pretend to be good) about bumping my halo!!! By the way I've ordered you a copy of Jones' Beveridge Report, and will send it on shortly, with the photos. Darling, I've had some taken down here. There are several proofs but I can't think which you'd like the best, anyway I'll send two and if you don't like them please tell me, and will you write to the Bacons of Liverpool saying that its OK for me to have an enlargement of your proof – don't forget darling.

Things are pretty dull here there are just two cinemas and occasional dances at the Grosvenor. I saw two quite good films this week, Ginger Rogers in "Major and Minor" and "Sherlock Holmes' Secret Weapon". I wonder if you have seen any new ones – Fred Astaire in "You were never Lovelier"?

Darling , I have a feeling that you will not be away from me for very long, I'm just longing to see you again. I wonder if Alice is still at the Lion, I'll never forget the morning Johnnie phoned!! Do write soon and let me know if you are better as I am very worried.

I love you darling and believe me I won't change. I just want to be with you forever. You won't forget to drop Bacons a line will you? And tell me if the photos are good enough. I think there is something wrong with the lighting!

Cheerio now darling,

All my love
Yours
Linda

As usual

28th February 1943

My darling Linda

It seems an age since I last heard from you but no doubt many letters and I hope the photograph are on their way. I must admit that I'm feeling thoroughly depressed tonight and only intend to inflict myself upon you for a short time.

My sweet I am missing you so terribly that everything seems pointless and empty. All I want is to get back to you again so that we can pick up the threads where we were forced to drop them. I love you more than everything in the world and you know fully well that I always will do so. You see wretch I just feel that you are an indispensable and integral part of me and that while I am away from you I can never be really happy. I suppose it seems all rather sloppy but it is nevertheless very real. There are so many things we must do and we have had so little time together in which to do them. Two years is a long time but already five months of it has passed – I only hope the next eighteen pass as quickly. In some ways it seems an age since I saw you off in the car at Falmouth but the whole memory of our times together, especially Tenby, is so bright that on occasions it seems as yesterday. Angel we simply must go to Tenby when I get back home – see Alice in the Lion, walk to Saundersfoot and through Swallow Tree Woods and so many other things. Then I think a visit to Haverfordwest (not forgetting the cinema!) is indicated, we might even have some of that dubious fish at the Castle. In point of fact what I'm really trying to say is that I love you and just want to be with you.

How go things with you? Have you yet managed to get to Bournemouth and looked up my aunt – incidentally don't believe any of the stories which she may care to tell out of school and you might tell her from me that I always behave myself.

What has happened to the photograph; every letter I receive informs me that it will be posted the following week. The days appear to be drawing out.

Darling consider yourself officially engaged – I believe I have already told you that it would be quite impossible to get a ring out here and that I would be sending a remittance home to you. Wish I could help you choose it but that unfortunately is quite impossible – still you'll be able to tell me all about it.

Must finish my precious. All my love and do write as often as you can.

Ever yours
Don.

Mess 17
Coastal Force Base
Malta

9th March 1943

L.A.C.W. Russell W.A.A.F.,
R.A.F. Ringstead,
Near Dorchester,
Dorsetshire,
England.

My darling Linda

I've just received the two photographs and I think they are absolutely terrific – sweet you look more perfect than ever and I am missing you so very badly – I'm only living for the day when we can be together again. Again thank you very much for the photos – the place of honour is now rectified! Incidentally was there a letter in the envelope? The reason I ask is that both letters were, according to a note inside, received open. The photo I like best is the one in which you are looking into the camera – you see you're smiling at me even as I write this letter.

I haven't very much news for you. Have had one party ashore and found it quite amusing but apart from that life has been very dull. Caught up with Dudley and Dick again yesterday and celebrated rather hastily last night – in fact Dudley is as great a menace as ever!

The weather is absolutely terrific in fact I've been sun bathing on deck all afternoon and, methinks, I'm going for a swim as soon as I have written some letters. But angel I am missing you a hell of a lot and I'd be quite happy back in England in cold or rain. Just by the way, did I ever happen to tell you that I love you rather a lot. I did? I rather thought I must have mentioned it on some odd occasion. Seriously wretch I do love you so very much and I'm longing to get home to you so that we can get married with the minimum of delay – believe me I made one mistake and I'm going to make quite sure there's no slip up next time.

How go things at home – the only reminder I have of civilisation is an occasional bottle of Simmonds beer and it tastes pretty good to me.

Darling please write more often as your letters are the only event I have to look forward to.

All my love sweetest
I'll always be ever yours
Don

P.S. All the gang send their love. Gibby may even write one day!
P.P.S. Mother's dying to meet you – she asks about you in every letter.

Mess 17
Coastal Force Base
Malta

13th March 1943

L.A.C.W. Russell W.A.A.F.,
R.A.F. Ringstead,
Near Dorchester,
Dorsetshire,
England.

No 1

My darling Linda

An airmail service has been inaugurated so I hasten to take advantage of it in case you should think that I have forgotten about you. I know that its five days since I last wrote to you but honestly sweet you'd be annoyed at the amount of sea time I'm doing these days. Incidentally we are only allowed one of these peculiar forms per week (at the time of writing anyway) and I think I'll start numbering the letters once more.

It must now be about a month since I last heard from you and it already seems years. I've heard that a Rear Admiral has been appointed i/c mail at the Admiralty but to date my clouded perception is unable to distinguish little change.

As you know I'm away from Algiers at the moment and someone at last appears to have recognised that Coastal Force craft are capable of doing a goodish job of work – unfortunately this has dawned all of a heap and we're working harder than that. However it does keep us out of trouble!

Wretch I'm still missing you so horribly. Do you realise that it's almost exactly five months since I left England and it already seems nearer five years. Tenby (quite the happiest week of my life) seems far away and all that remains are hopeful dreams of our next visit there. My angel I could fill pages telling you how much I adore you but how much more satisfactory it would be to be able to tell you by spoken rather than written words. Linda pet you must know full well that I shan't ever change and that I'll love you always. Wretch promise me that you'll never change – you know that I shan't. My only desire is that I should get home and that we may be married as soon as possible. There are so many things we must do together that life seems more precious, more vitally necessary than ever before. However even foreign service doesn't last forever and I think that we will have ample time to make up for the time we have been forced to spend apart.

Sweetest I know that this is a horribly sloppy letter and I do love you so terribly and a letter is the only outlet for pent up feelings.

Been over with Richard tonight playing cards and talking about Falmouth – hence the modicum of sentiment!

Darling do write lots and do hurry that photograph – you've no idea how anxiously I'm awaiting it.

The limits of the card force me to close – I'll write again soon.

You know I love you terribly and that I won't ever change.

Eternally yours
Don

L.A.C.W. Russell W.A.A.F.
c/o Mrs Klitz, Ingleston,
Victoria Road, Swanage.

15th March 1943

Lieut F. D. Bickerton, R.N.V.R.
Mess 17, Coastal Force Base,
Algiers.

My darling Don,

Very many thanks for your letter dated 28 Feb (5), the last I received was dated 9 Feb (1), so I'm hoping that the others haven't altogether gone astray – no doubt Ringstead is to blame for the delay.

As you will see I am still attached here but expecting to return to camp quite soon, unfortunately my leave, which was to have commenced Saturday, has had to be cancelled, temporarily. I'll be more than pleased to get home for 9 days rest after 5 months hard work (no cracks!).

No darling, I'm afraid I haven't had an opportunity to look up your aunt but I will do so during my leave, or beforehand if possible – and I'm looking forward to hearing all about your gay past, 'bags of gen'!!! Frankly I'm rather terrified to meet her, does she know about me? I wish you would mention me in your next letter to her.

Darling, how marvellous being officially engaged, although rings are a shocking price these days, but I agree it will be nicer and will make me feel even closer to you. I do miss you so much but somehow I feel sure that it won't be many months before you are home, won't it be grand and how exciting our first meeting will be. (even if I'm still in my tailor made uniform! And W.A.A.F. cap which you like so much!)

I've done very little since my last letter, apart from duty, eating and sleeping. Monday I broke out and went to the cinema and saw 'Smiling Through' Jeanette MacDonald version, very good but frightfully sad. (I wept buckets) also 'Road to Morocco' once again. Naturally the camels amused me most of all!!! No parties, dances etc. For weeks but we are due for a celebration when we return to R. – SO's birthday, when I'm hoping to be on leave. Incidentally, I'm behaving myself too, in point of fact, leading a painfully dull life without you. I'm still very proud of the fact that I haven't had a cigarette since Jan 19th!! Not bad going, considering Melba smokes like a chimney!

Darling when you come home do you think you'll be able to get plenty of leave only I'll soon have to start saving time. I suggest we celebrate Christmas together!!! By the way we mustn't forget to have a ginger beer on the way to Saundersfoot, damn good stuff, although if I remember rightly you suggested that a double gin would be an improvement!! I hope you are taking good care of yourself and not too many celebrations – one of my biggest worries you know. You haven't mentioned Richard, Alan, or bad types Gibby and John recently, do let me know how they are.

No more now, always all my love and please be careful.

Ever yours,
Linda

P.S. Have you received the photo?
P.P.S. Please write soon xx

Mess 17,
Coastal Forces Base,
Algiers.

18th March 1943

My darling Linda

Just a very short note to tell you that I'm still in the land of the living and that I love you as much as ever.

I've just received your letter of 21st February but as the air mail service now appears to be in operation this is only a trailer of the reply which I intend to write tonight – believe it or not the time is 0600! But someone has promised to deliver this letter for me and the opportunity seems too good to waste.

Life is very quiet these days or perhaps I should say has been very quiet apart from the parties of the last couple of nights. You may have guessed that I am suffering a hangover at the moment and life doesn't taste too sweet.

Angel I am missing you so terribly and I'm only longing for the day when I can be with you once more. Please hurry up the photo and <u>please</u> write rather more frequently than you have done in the past.

All my love darling
Your devoted
Don.

P.S. All I really want to say is "I love you"

Mess 17
Coastal Force Base
Algiers

1st April 1943

L.A.C.W. Russell W.A.A.F.,
R.A.F. Ringstead,
Near Dorchester,
Dorsetshire, England.

My darling Linda

This service has just started so I hasten to take advantage of it. I have today written to you by air mail but as it is over a week since I last wrote I thought maybe I'd better let you know that things still run smoothly out here.

Please write as soon as you can and please hasten those photographs. I love you very terribly but these things strike me as being a little too public for comfort.

All my love angel
Ever yours
Don

Mess 17,
Coastal Forces Base,
Algiers.

1st April 1943

L.A.C.W Russell W.A.A.F.
R.A.F. Ringstead,
Near Dorchester,
Dorsetshire,
ENGLAND

My darling Linda

I'm most frightfully sorry to have been so long in writing to you but life hasn't been all beer and skittles recently and I've been kept rather busy. Please – am I forgiven! And many thanks for your letter of 5th March which appears to have chased me around for some time – it was the first letter I had received from you for ages, please write more frequently.

Sweet you've got me all wrong. I didn't intend taking your letter in the wrong way – my remarks were merely intended to be humorous but apparently I missed the boat. Sorry! And you know quite well that I trust you.

Instead of writing to Bacon's I have written home and asked them to call in and tell them it is O.K. but as airgraphs are now available I will send one to Bacons in addition.

There's not very much news I can tell you about except that we have been working exceptionally hard recently – in fact more sea time than that. I went ashore with Gibby last night for a quiet drink and fortunately it stayed at that – until we got back aboard anyway! Gibby really is a menace these days and I must say we all take full advantage of any time we have in harbour.

Angel I miss you so frightfully – all I want is that this awful mess should be cleared up and then I can come home to you again. I had hoped that after six months I might have become resigned to it but instead it becomes worse than ever. I do love you so terribly Linda darling. I want to be with you and hold you so very tight in my arms again – in other words wretch I want life to be a permanency of that week in Tenby. I promise you that I shall never change and that I'll always love you just as much – it can't be more as that just isn't possible. I know you'll wait for me.

Incidentally Mother says that she is looking forward to meeting you – I'm sure you'll like her pet.

Haven't received the photographs yet but I'm still hoping – please hurry them up.

Write soon and do write as often as you can.

All my love sweet
Always your
Don.

P.S. Gibby sends his love and says he'll write sometime but as he hasn't written one letter for 4 months I shouldn't bank on it.
P.P.S. Give Johnnie my love when you write.

Mess 17,
Coastal Forces Base,
Algiers.

3rd April 1943
Air letter No 4

L.A.C.W Russell W.A.A.F.
R.A.F. Ringstead,
Near Dorchester,
Dorsetshire,
ENGLAND

My darling Linda

Feeling right on top of the world as I've just received your letter of 15th March (No 3). My letters do seem to be going adrift - the missing ones are 16th, 21st, 24th February, I hope they have caught you up by now.

I, too, feel the same way about being officially engaged and Mother in a letter I have received today tells me that she is very pleased I have decided to go all serious and that she is very much looking forward to meeting you – and for that matter who wouldn't. But the day of all days will be that on which we next meet – I dread to think how ill I'll feel next morning after all the celebrations but I think I'll chance it! Angel I do miss you so much that I only hope I'll be home with you again very soon – rather a vain hope I fear.

I must say you sound very righteous at the moment – so you haven't smoked since 19th Jan – I'm almost tempted to ask so what – it sounds as though the halo is getting a little tight. I regret to report that I still indulge in all my old vices and what's more enjoy them! No wretch I am behaving and I'm not drinking too much.

We had quite a party ashore last night at our Engineer Officer's flat – about eight blokes and about ten French girls. Plenty to eat and drink – took my records but no one could jitterbug so what the hell. Gibby was in good form and so was Teddy Rose as barman in a red fez and a not so clean apron – in case your simply 'orrid mind has other thoughts I did behave and was one of the only two sober at the end of the evening!

I think spending X'mas together is a grand idea, I only hope that it can come true. Yes I should get plenty of leave when I eventually get home and then as you say we can enjoy life – incidentally the first thing to do is get married by the quickest possible means. I am so much in love with my darling that all these days apart seem a futile waste of time.

Do write soon and please take very good care of yourself.

All my love sweetest
Don.

P.S. No I haven't received the photo.
P.P.S. Gibby sends his love.

Mess 17,
Coastal Forces Base,
Algiers.

13th April 1943

L.A.C.W Russell W.A.A.F.
R.A.F. Ringstead,
Near Dorchester,
Dorsetshire,
ENGLAND

My own darling Linda

You've no idea how marvellous it is to have you smiling at me all the time but how I wish I really were with you and then perhaps I'd have something to smile about. As the above address is perhaps a little deceptive mail does not come through as regularly as it might and it seems an age since I last received a letter from you – please write lots sweet as they all catch up in time.

Had a farewell party for Max the other night (no! He's not going home) and as it also happened to be Alan's wedding anniversary as well we made quite a night of it. In case it might interest you I stayed perfectly sober and only rendered "Dark Town Strutters Ball" after much persuasion – it's usually the other way round.

14/4/43
I fear that's as far as I got yesterday as Dudley came down bursting with energy, refused a beer and then wheeled me away to do P.T.! I felt alright after it but I don't think Dudley was so good – but he managed to consume the beer without difficulty. In the late afternoon we went for a long walk right round the face of the cliff, up and over the mountain and then back. The country here really is delightful and I must say I feel pretty fit – all things considered. You would love it out here – maybe we'll come here after the war.

In the evening I had supper with Dudley and then an alleged night cap which finished at midnight on my own boat. As usual we became rather sentimental and I had to turn your photo to the wall as you were looking so reproachfully at me. Now this morning it is a smile of forgiveness once more.

Darling I am missing you so frightfully and I only want this b- war to end so that I can get home to you again. Sweetest I do love you so very much and need I add that I always will. I had always considered myself immune to anything except flirtation but this time I apparently used the wrong serum for the inoculation. Please write as often as you can my angel – I'm always thinking of and talking about you.

All my love wretch
Ever yours
Don.

P.S. Dudley sends his love.
P.P.S. I'm sending on some powder and stuff but I fear it must go by sea.

Mess 17,
Coastal Forces Base,
Algiers.

18th April 1943
Air Letter No. 7

L.A.C.W Russell W.A.A.F.
R.A.F. Ringstead,
Near Dorchester,
Dorsetshire,
ENGLAND

My darling Linda

And even that mode of address doesn't prevent me feeling rather annoyed with you. It's ages since I last had a letter from you – in point of fact the one dated 15th March and letters out here are the only things which help me to retain my sanity. For the n th time please write more frequently. Now consider yourself thoroughly told off! You are looking down at me so reproachfully that I promise not to be nasty any more.

'Fraid I haven't very much by way of news for you as I just haven't been ashore – there ain't no place to go no how. Went for a walk for a couple of hours with Dudley yesterday and played our usual game of make believe by carrying on our conversation as though we were at home and making odd arrangements for parties and things. Dudley however rather finished things when he said "And to think we used to say those sorts of things once and mean them." Down to the depths of despondency once more!

In the evening we decided on a quiet game of cards and then a nightcap at ten o'clock. Well we had a nightcap at ten and then Dudley came over to have a nightcap with me. By eleven we were just about weeping on each other's shoulders – we wondered what would happen if we were all suddenly planted back in the Greenbanks. Something tells me it would be a pretty hectic party.

Sweetest I am missing you so badly and I'm only living for the day when I can be with you once more – I don't have to tell you how very much I love you. Darling please can we be married as soon as I get back home? Maybe it won't seem too long as six months of it has passed already. And I think for a honeymoon we should do a grand tour of all those places we've visited together Tenby, Saundersfoot, Falmouth and even Haverfordwest – I'll never forget that night in the County Hotel or the visit to the cinema afterwards – it was fun wasn't it. And I'm more than grateful to John for taking me over with him on that occasion – I certainly didn't know what I was letting myself in for.

Angel the photographs are terrific. I say goodnight and good morning to you every day – and not even Alice to disturb us!

Do write soon and please write lots – I miss you so much.

All my love my sweet
Ever yours
Don.

P.S. Have you visited my aunt yet – I'm writing to her tonight.
P.P.S. Will be sending off some powder – can't get any perfume.

Mess 17,
Coastal Forces Base,
Algiers.

23rd April 1943
Air Letter No. 8

L.A.C.W Russell W.A.A.F.
R.A.F. Ringstead,
Near Dorchester,
Dorsetshire,
ENGLAND

My darling Linda

Mail seems to be horribly scarce these days, in fact it's quite an age since I last heard from you. However I'm still charitable enough to think that there must be a hold up which is no fault of yours - it better not be anyway my sweet.

This can only be a very short note as (1) there isn't much to tell you and (2) I'm horribly tired and simply must get some sleep - you see some unfeeling people believe in working us pretty hard these days. Actually things go on in much the same old way. Dudley, Gibby and I had quite a party the other night and spent the next day rather regretting it. As a matter of fact it was the only really bad one we've had for months and need I add that Gibby started it. The following day Dudley and I tried to walk off the inevitable hangover and barely had sufficient energy to return to the ship.

Have you been able to get your leave yet? I only wish I could be at home so that we might spend it together. I suggest that a week in Tenby would be a week well spent - what say you? Darling I do miss you so frightfully and it really is appalling that my sole subject of thought and conversation is you - and, of course, how I can manage to get back to you. I rather fear that I shan't get home until I have done my two years out here. Still wretch when this rotten business is over we will have a whole lifetime before us and then we can more than make up for this imposed separation. Angel I do love you so very much that I am only living for the day when I can be with you once more. Personally I find lovemaking on paper most unsatisfactory especially as the thing I want most in the world is to hold you in my arms again. Sorry but I must be in a sentimental mood tonight.

Sweetest, do write lots and don't forget to look up my aunt in Bournemouth.

All my love Linda darling
Ever yours
Don.

Mess 17,
Coastal Force Base,
Algiers

24th April 1943
Sea Letter No 6

L.A.C.W. Russell W.A.A.F.,
R.A.F. Ringstead,
Near Dorchester,
Dorsetshire,
England.

My darling Linda

I've been feeling so horribly depressed this morning that in order to cheer myself up I've reread all your old letters and I'm not at all sure whether it has helped or not – but maybe I'll be able to judge before I've finished this letter. Incidentally I'm sorry it has to go seamail but as you know we are allowed only one air letter per week and I used my last writing to you last night.

It's good fun reading the letters you wrote before I left England, more particularly while we were stooging around the Bristol Channel thoroughly enjoying ourselves. Then of course there is the nasty letter in which you quote Louise on my near escapes of marriage (I still think Max is a rat – I wouldn't have objected quite so much if he had told the truth). Anyway my angel you should be quite convinced by this time that I love and always will love only you. I may be a horribly selfish sort of person but when I do get back I intend to marry you then rush you off somewhere and completely monopolise you for the rest of my life. Maybe as a concession I'll let someone see you, say every five years!

I guess that it will be a peculiar life immediately after the war. In our case there will be so many things to do, so many places to visit and so many old friends to look up. Anyway I've no intention of doing any work if I can avoid for at least three months from the time I leave the Navy and I think that it should be just one glorious holiday – say a renaissance of that heavenly week in Tenby.

And work at the Ministry when I do return to the solemnity of Whitehall should be rather amusing. For one thing I will be so completely out of touch with the various problems which must inevitably confront M of H that it will take me months to acquire any standard of knowledge of current affairs at all. Still that's a difficulty which need not be faced for some little time I fear.

Dudley has got something when he questions our general reception when we get home. You see we still do crazy things, to some people they might in fact appear childish, and we have developed a new slang dictionary which will make many people wonder if the Mediterranean sun has had its worst effect. His solution is that the 25th take a large house miles from anywhere and all live together thus no one will be able to question anyone else's sanity! No sweet I don't think we're quite that bad as yet but it is quite an idea for all that.

Today the weather is most depressing, rain with too much low cloud, no sun, pretty cold – in fact the only consolation is that the sea is pretty calm. And to help things Phyllis has recovered from his jaundice and is now back from hospital – together with those awful photographs which I notice are once more lettering the cabinet. However, as you are still smiling so sweetly I assume everything is under control!

Darling where are we going to live after the war? I'm all in favour of a flat in Hampstead very close to the Heath as I know one or two good pubs close by – well one must consider the amenities of the place! Seriously wretch where would you like to be? – I just don't mind at all provided that we are together.

Incidentally have I ever in these odd rambling letters of mine told you that I love you rather a lot? I have – I'm rather pleased as it would have been unfortunate to have omitted so serious a statement. Linda darling you're more precious to me than anything in the world and you must know by this time that I am quite serious and that my feelings will never change.

Well wretch this is rather a rambling rhetorical conglomeration and I'll spare you further eye strain.

Please write lots pet as it is ages since I last heard from you.

I'll always love you my sweet, take care of yourself.

Ever yours Don.

P.S. I do feel more cheerful now.
P.P.S. Did you get the photograph from Bacons.
P.P.S. I'm just about to write to my Aunt in Bournemouth.

Mess 17,
Coastal Forces Base,
Algiers.

10th May 1943
Air Letter No. 10

L.A.C.W Russell W.A.A.F.
R.A.F. Ringstead,
Near Dorchester,
Dorsetshire,
ENGLAND

My darling Linda

Have just received your letter of 15th April numbered 11! Well my sweet either your numbering has gone haywire or a hell of a lot of mail is adrift as the last one I received was No 3. Anyway it's good to hear from you as the long silence was beginning to worry me – do write lots wretch as it's the only thing that keeps me going in this God forsaken dump.

So glad that you enjoyed your leave, I only wish we could have spent it together – maybe we'll have better luck in 1953. You are lucky to get away from things from time to time and I must say that I feel that if I don't get away from the ship soon I shall go bats. Actually it's not nearly that bad but a break would be more than welcome (sorry to be in such a depressed mood – I'll try to be more cheerful!)

So Johnnie has managed to get to Ringstead – I'm very pleased to hear it as I know you are very fond of her. Please give her my love and tell her to try and keep out of trouble in future – if you like I'll give her a few lessons on the lines which people shoot next time I'm home! (And no cracks from you young Linda).

Have you yet seen my aunt? I wrote to her to tell her that you would be coming and Mother in a letter I received today tells me that she has also written to pass on the glad tidings – in fact you should get quite a reception, although I'm not sure if you really deserve it.

Things have been rather quiet at this end but I intend writing a further letter tonight in which I'll confess all my sins – it should look like a blank report. Incidentally as I've recently met a number of people I know, including Teddy Rose from Falmouth, there is something to tell.

Need I add that I love you more than I can tell you and that I promise never to change. I'm still crazy about your photographs and at the moment your sneer has almost changed to a smile of approval. Do write as often as you can sweet – I believe there's an air mail in today so I'm all hopeful at the moment.

All my love my angel I'll write again tonight – but Heaven help you if I don't get a letter.
    *Be good sweet

Ever yours
Don.

P.S. *Sorry I forgot you don't like the expression.

Mess 17
Coastal Force Base
Algiers

10th May 1943
Air Letter No 11

Cpl. L. Russell W.A.A.F.,
R.A.F. Ringstead,
Near Dorchester,
Dorsetshire,
England.

My darling Linda

Supper, such as it was, is over and so I settle down to write the further letters I promised. I make no promise as to the amount of news it will contain but then with so little activity there is little about which I can write.

As I told you I met some of the Falmouth types viz Teddy Rose whom you met and Ronnie Perks who arrived just before you left. To cut a long story short Dick and I decided that we really should celebrate the reunion so, together with our engineer officer who is indispensible because of his flat, we arranged to hold a dance. We got hootch, I provided records and invited the Wrens along (unfortunately there are no WAAFs here!) The whole evening went down fairly well, Teddy gave his now famous Arab impersonation which must be seen to be believed and in case you have other ideas I behaved myself and what's more stayed quite sober. It's such an age since I last danced that I must have lost stones in weight (yes pal, I know I can't afford to). Anyway it was the best evening I've had in Algiers.

Dudley has done it again. This time it's a French female with whom he has "fallen head over heels in love – it's so different this time" (I merely quote). In point of fact I haven't seen the female in question. I gather she's a frightful old bag and I have no doubt that the whole affair will last almost two days. Dudley is an amusing cove but at times he amazes even me.

Sweetest I miss you more than ever – I'm afraid I just can't interest myself in anyone else in the slightest. Normally I suppose at the party the other night I would have relaxed and let myself go but meeting English girls now only has the effect of reminding me of you and all the things we might be doing were we together. My angel I do love you so very much that life without you seems so much a waste of time. You know that my feelings will never alter and that my one ambition is to marry you as soon as possible – I suppose life really is only just beginning but I grudge every moment I am away from you. Please write lots sweet and keep telling me that you love me as much as ever.

Must finish wretch
Good night and God bless
All my love
Eternally yours
Don

P.S. Love to Johnnie & what's all this about Cardiff? Another line someone has been shooting?

Mess 17, Coastal Forces Base,
Algiers.

15th May 1943
Air Letter No. 12

Cpl. L. Russell W.A.A.F.,
R.A.F. Ringstead, Near Dorchester,
Dorsetshire, ENGLAND

My darling Linda

I don't intend to finish this letter this morning as a mail is due sometime today but I'm feeling so horribly depressed that I must write to you – if the letter is too miserable just tear it up and forget it. I have sent off the money for the ring but as it goes as a remittance I'm not sure how long it takes so perhaps you'll let me know when you receive it and also what the ring is like.

I had rather a hectic party (all male!) ashore last night and I'm not feeling too good this morning – well I suppose it might happen to anyone. Yes I promise to behave in future.

16/5/43

Your letter of 1st May has just arrived and I'm not feeling too happy about things. Apparently your visit to my aunt could scarcely be described as successful! Let me say here and now that if you don't feel sure of me by this time that it is quite clear that you never will and that matters can hardly be expected to run smoothly while you are in that state of mind. I hate reiteration but for your benefit let me state categorically (? spelling) that I love you more than everything in the world and that my only desire is to marry you as soon as possible. Surely Linda darling you do trust me. Space is admittedly cramped in air letter cards but I intend to continue if I can't get in all I intend to say on this one. Furthermore I intend to credit you with a mathematical mind and set out the facts in chronological order.

I have written to my aunt but as I believe I have already told you I am limited to one air letter a week, the letter had to go by sea and obviously has not yet arrived.

I told my Mother of your proposed visit and she informed me that she too would write and acquaint my aunt of the said fact.

I have already told you my past history – that I was engaged when I met you and that I have played around a little in the past. Do you or don't you believe that I am serious and that my one aim is to get home to marry you?

Darling this is a stinking sort of letter but I do love you so very much that the idea of you feeling miserable because you think that I might not be serious hurts considerably. Please believe me when I say that I have learned something by experience and never before have I felt as I do about you. My one fear has been that you might change and I just don't dare contemplate that.

Now that we have finished in N. Africa I suppose we will be venturing into other theatres but I have no idea where or when. Do write soon sweet – your letters are the only things that matter.

Write soon
All my love my wretch
Eternally yours
Don.

P.S. Got a pair of silk stockings size 9½ which I'm sending off tomorrow – is the size O.K.? P.P.S. Congratulations on promotion to Corporal and love to Johnnie.

Mess 17,
Coastal Forces Base,
Algiers.

16th May 1943
Air Letter No. 13

Cpl. L. Russell W.A.A.F.,
R.A.F. Ringstead,
Near Dorchester,
Dorsetshire,
ENGLAND

My darling Linda

Having got so much off my chest in the letter I have just finished I now propose to be pleasant (ironical cheers have no effect!)

17/5/43

And that was as far as I got as Alan came down with the glad tidings that he was going home – and he brought three Army types with him to celebrate the occasion. Apparently he is suffering from "anxiety neurosis" (what a beautifully ambiguous ailment) and is to be sent home for leave and a shore job in a quiet place. Well, he made up his mind that he was going to get home and he has certainly achieved it.

Richard really is a bad type these days and is continually organising parties. I hadn't seen him for some little time and we decided to have a quiet dinner ashore. I ran into a pongo whom I knew in peacetime and then other odd people turned up until the two had increased to ten – equally, the whole idea of a quiet dinner was banished from our minds. We didn't quite wreck the place but I did notice what appeared to be looks of relief on our departure. I regret to say the party was only just beginning – we collected more RAF types and returned aboard. Just what happened I don't know (and I couldn't care less!) but the party eventually broke up at 0400. Next day Dick and I became confirmed teatotallers – which just goes to show.

Darling I'm sorry if I was nasty in my last letter but I did think that by this time you should have felt quite sure about me. Believe me sweet when I tell you I spend all my time thinking of you, talking about you and just longing for the time I can go home to you. I love you more than everything in the world – please don't mistrust me again.

And pet do visit my aunt again and please tell her from me that I consider her an out and out wretch and furthermore it would be a good thing to inform her that we are engaged. Maybe she has received my letter by this time.

I've just had a letter from home and they tell me that my young brother has got himself all entangled with a ballet dancer – must run in the family!

The weather here is terribly hot and at the moment my back and legs feel far from comfortable, in fact I'm a delightful shade of purply red.

Darling please write rather more than you do – your letters mean more than anything else.

I do love you so much

Ever yours
Don.

P.S. Having difficulty getting photos developed. Will send 'em when I can.

Cpl. L. Russell W.A.A.F.
R.A.F. Ringstead,
Nr. Dorchester,
Dorset.

28th May 1943

Lieut F. D. Bickerton. R.N.V.R.
Mess 17,
Coastal Force Base,
Algiers.

8 am.

My darling Don,

I've just received your air letter 12, and I'm sorry that my letter of 1st May made you unhappy. Am I forgiven - as I was feeling horribly miserable - please darling. Of course I love and trust you completely and when you come back we must not part for the rest of our lives. The remittance for the ring has not arrived yet but I'll let you know as soon as it does and what I am able to get. Many thanks for sending powder and silk stockings, they should be here soon, it really is very sweet of you but you shouldn't spend your money on me in these hard times, anyway, thanks a million.

I'm afraid there is not much in the way of news as we have been on a three watch system for the past few days - all we seem to do is eat, sleep and duty. Last week I had a 36 and stopped with my sister - where your aunt lives - as they had a bit of a shaking and I was very worried as one hears many rumours, anyway, the picture wasn't quite as black as it was painted, but bad enough. We saw a very good ballet, which I'm pretty certain doesn't appeal to you but just in case it does, a part of the Swan Lake (which I adore) and Polonica.

Johnnie and I are on watch together this morning, she sends her love and says that she hopes you are getting more hot water than you had at the Cambrian! She is in very good form these days - very full of beans, her old self. I'm thankful that she has forgotten John.

We are going into Weymouth this afternoon to see "Major and Minor", an old film which you have probably seen: Ginger Rogers plays the part of a girl of thirteen as she wishes to travel half fare. Ray Milland is the Major - a most amusing film. I've had several bathes but the water is still pretty chilly, and I'm getting brownish - you must be like a nigger in all that glorious sunshine. By the way, what is Algerian wine like? They are importing small quantities here at 6/= a bottle I believe. Also lemons, I can't imagine what they are like.

Darling I love you terribly, won't it be wonderful when this business is over and we are together again? The thought of our first meeting and stooging around keeps me going. I'll have to close now as someone is calling me, writing again later.

All my love darling and do take great care of yourself.

Ever yours
Linda xx

P.S. Give my love to Richard, Gibby etc.

Chapter Seven

JUNE – AUGUST 1943

During the first week of June 1943, Don sailed his ship from its base in Algiers to Malta. He had been based in Algiers since early November 1942 when *ML 338* took part in Operation Torch. There was a brief period in March 1943 when his letters were addressed from Malta and his ship was possibly undergoing a refit. He also mentioned in his letter of 13th April 1943 that, at that time, the Algiers address was misleading – implying that he had been elsewhere. Unfortunately, owing to censorship, he was not at liberty to divulge such information, so we cannot be completely sure of his movements.

Although there is no conclusive evidence, it seems that early June was the point at which Don's *ML 338* detached from the 25th ML Flotilla and transferred to the 3rd. In his book, *A Leaf Upon the Sea*, Gordon Stead mentions that four boats were added to the 3rd ML Flotilla at this time, to make a total of ten. He comments that: "The new officers were good sorts and soon fitted in and several did good work, although some of them were reminiscent of the yachting navy we had left behind in England."

In his first letter from Malta, dated 8th **June 1943** (air letter No. 15), Don reveals that he has just arrived there and has not yet been ashore. The trip from Algiers was uneventful – although he notes that the island of Pantelleria was receiving a bombardment as they passed by.

In fact, the invasion of Pantelleria and the three Pelagie Islands (see **Map D**, on page 120) commenced on that very same day. Pantelleria's capture was to be completed on 11th June followed by the Pelagie Islands two days later. In his paper dated 7th May 1951, H C Atkinson recalls that MLs of the 3rd, acting as minesweepers, took part in these operations.

Don observes that Malta itself has taken a pounding but that the people look extremely cheerful. He anticipates a number of his old mates are in Malta, including Teddy Rose and Smithy, so he is looking forward to a fairly hectic time. He has heard that the beer is an exorbitant price, which will come as a blow after Algiers.

On **12th June 1945** (air letter No. 16), he is gratified to hear of the fall of Pantelleria on the previous day and speculates that he might be home earlier than he had previously thought. He is also feeling sad at leaving friends, particularly Richard, Dudley and Gibby in Algiers. He has now been ashore in Malta and finds whisky to be 2s 3d (11.25p). He is pleased that there are many people he knows in Malta because he is bored to death with Phyllis' company. He again urges Linda to write, not just to him but also his mother.

MAP D

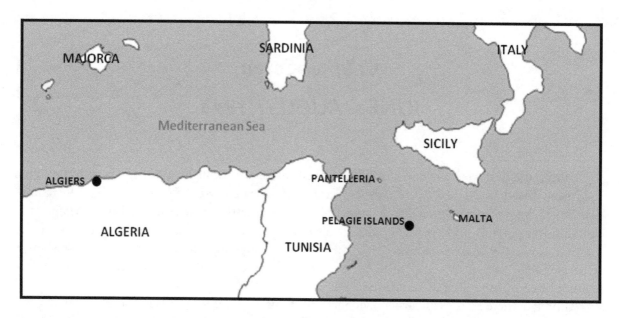

Don writes air letter No. 17 **the following day,** saying that he has had his first shower for three weeks. He says he has met a South African by the name of Gutteridge who was CO (Commanding Officer) at *RAF Hayscastle* between October and December 1941 and who thinks he recognises Linda from her photograph. On the previous evening, Don says he was at a dance in the Reunion Club where he met "an unpleasant little specimen" who was at school with his brother, Leslie.

Don writes another letter on **14th June 1943** (air letter No. 18), although he has nothing much new to say.

On **21st June 1943** (air letter No. 18), Don is still awaiting mail redirected from Algiers and has not heard from Linda since 1st May. He is enjoying living ashore, although it is costing him £5 per day and he has to visit his ship daily. He confirms that he is with a new flotilla (the 3rd) and has enjoyed one or two parties with his new colleagues, with Ronnie Perks and Teddy Rose again getting a mention. He has also walked with Ronnie to Sliema, getting more exercise than for some time. He reports that his crew are excited at the prospect of going to a rest camp, as they have not spent a night off the ship in nine months. He remarks that time is flying and it will be 18 months at the most before he will be back with Linda. (Unfortunately that was to be a seven-month underestimate.) Although he is to be 26 the next day and has been in the Royal Naval Volunteer Reserve (RNVR) since the age of 22, he says there are no signs of grey hairs yet!

His next surviving letter is dated **26th June 1943** (air letter No. 20) and he has just received Linda's of 28th May (missing). He says that he has written eight letters in the last month to her and begs her to correspond more frequently. He has spent his birthday at sea but celebrates in the evening and finishes up sleeping on one of the other ships.

He writes again on the following day, **27ᵗʰ June 1943** (air letter No. 21), on a new format air letter which affords less space. He has been into town with his No. 1, Phyllis, and they had cocktails with Teddy Rose and Ronnie Perks. He says he is becoming sick of Malta – that he is missing the company of Dick, Dudley and Gibby and looking forward to moving on.

On **30ᵗʰ June 1943**, Linda writes from *RAF Ringstead* thanking Don for his cable and air letter. She says that she had dreaded him going to Malta but is thankful that things have quietened down there. She says that this is her first letter since 20ᵗʰ June (missing from the collection) as she has been on a week's course. She tells Don that she has heard from his mother. She complains that, owing to the war, engagement rings are not being made and the ones in stock are subject to 100% purchase tax. She has looked around Bournemouth with her sister but to no avail.

Purchase tax was a tax on 'luxury' goods introduced on 21st October 1940, at an initial rate of 33⅓% in order to reduce the deemed wastage of raw materials. This tax increased to 66⅔% in 1942, and by 1943 it had shot up to 100%, doubling the cost of goods. As so often happens, it was not withdrawn after the war but continued to be levied until 2ⁿᵈ April 1973 when it was abolished and replaced by VAT at an initial rate of 10%, in preparation for the UK's admission to the EEC (now the EU).

In the same letter, Linda announces that she is to go on another course on the east coast, so maybe she will be able to have a look around there. Apparently, Johnnie has been posted back to Pembrokeshire. Linda admits that she is suffering from sunburn following a picnic on the beach the previous evening.

Don writes on **1ˢᵗ July 1943** (air letter No. 22) advising that his crew has returned from their week in the rest camp. The weather is very hot and exhausting. He reminds Linda that it is a year since they first met.

On the following day, Don receives a briefing letter from Admiral Andrew Cunningham, announcing that his ship will be taking part in Operation Husky, the invasion of Sicily. It is headed <u>MOST SECRET BIGOT</u> which was the highest security classification – above <u>TOP SECRET</u>. BIGOT was an acronym for 'British Invasion of German Occupied Territory'.

MOST SECRET BIGOT

Office of the Commander-in-Chief,
Mediterranean,
ALGIERS.

2nd July, 1943.

No. MED(W)/00200/8.

MEMORANDUM.

COMMANDER-IN-CHIEF's MESSAGE.

We are about to embark on the most momentous enterprise of
the war - striking for the first time at the enemy in his own land.

2.   Success means the opening of the "Second Front" with all
that implies, and the first move towards the rapid and decisive defeat
of our enemies.

3.   Our object is clear and our primary duty is to place this vast
expedition ashore in the minimum time and subsequently to maintain our
military and air forces as they drive relentlessly forward into enemy
territory.

4.   In the light of this duty great risks must be and are to be
accepted.   The safety of our own ships and all distracting considerations
are to be relegated to second place, or disregarded as the accomplishment
of our primary duty may require.

5.   On every Commanding Officer, officer and rating rests the
individual and personal duty of ensuring that no flinching in determination
or failure of effort on his own part will hamper this great enterprise.

6.   I rest confident in the resolution, skill and endurance of you
all to whom this momentous enterprise is entrusted.

Andrew Cunningham

ADMIRAL OF THE FLEET.

Distribution:

All ships and authorities
taking part in Operation
HUSKY.

Letter from the Admiral dated 2nd July 1943

Before departing Malta, Don writes on **5th July 1943** (air letter No. 23) giving no hint of the
action in which he will be involved in a few days time. He reports that he has seen the films:
This Above All and *Hi Gang*. He proclaims that life in Malta is as boring as ever and he is
missing the company of Dick, Dudley, Gibby and Peter.

Operation Husky was the codename for the Allied invasion of Sicily. The enemy was not fully prepared because deceptions by the Allies led the Axis powers to believe that the next invasion would be in Greece and the Balkans. In one such deception, the British allowed a corpse dressed as a Royal Marines Officer to be washed up on a Spanish beach. Fake documents on the corpse, declaring that Operation Husky was a planned invasion of Greece, fooled German intelligence. The Allied operation commenced on the night of 9th/10th July 1943, and the bad weather was another factor in the enemy being caught off guard. The operation was successfully completed by 17th August 1943. The Allies' casualties were 5,000 men killed, 15,000 wounded and 3,000 captured. German losses were over 20,000 killed, wounded or captured. Italian losses were over 147,000 killed, wounded or captured.

In his book, *A Leaf Upon the Sea*, Gordon Stead reveals that, late on the day before they were to sail to take part in the invasion, an inch-thick binder was delivered to each participating ship containing the orders for the Sicily landings. It would have taken Don a few hours to wade through all the information. The armada of around 3,000 ships was to sail from ports in the US, the UK, the Middle East and North Africa. The MLs were assigned as escorts to forces destined for the various areas. Beaches would have already been checked by air reconnaissance and surreptitious probes from submarines, and no minesweeping was required ahead of the initial assault.

The MLs set off in groups. Gordon Stead's *ML 126* being joined by MLs *121*, *480* and *565*, and they departed from Malta at 08:00 on 9th July. No conclusive evidence has been unearthed regarding which MLs sailed with Don's *ML 338* or the identity of their group commander. Stead describes a second group of four MLs, commanded by John Peal, being with a convoy of cargo vessels and big LSTs (landing ship, tank). *ML 338* was probably one of these as the final two were detached on other tasks.

As recalled by H C Atkinson in his paper *3rd ML Flotilla*, in the opening phase each ML acted as navigational leader to a group of LSTs sweeping them in to the beaches north of Cape Pessaro.

MAP E

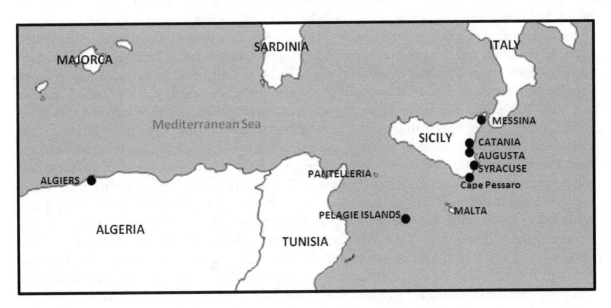

Atkinson says ubiquitous duties were then undertaken by the flotilla, comprising minesweeping, anti-submarine and anti-aircraft patrols. Stead describes his group's activities, including the downing of an Italian aircraft. He reports that the other MLs, which would have included *ML 338*, carried out similar duties including herding landing craft, rescuing survivors from a deliberately bombed hospital ship and escorting convoys. *ML 168* shared honours in the shooting down of a German fighter-bomber and *ML 134* was to shoot up a pillbox and drive out snipers who were harassing British troops. None of the other MLs, he reports, got involved in skirmishes. Two of the boats from the 3rd ML Flotilla had to return to Malta early because of engine defects; another barely managed to keep operating; and the fourth had two-thirds of its crew laid low by seasickness. Otherwise there were no casualties, although two boats suffered minor damage from near-misses. H C Atkinson records that *ML 168* had the honour of flying the flag of Rear-Admiral Troubridge off the beaches and was the first British warship to enter an occupied port in Europe when she made her way into Syracuse on the heels of the retreating German Army. The flotilla continued to keep in the forefront and was mainly engaged in minesweeping operations as ports were occupied, namely Augusta, Catania and Messina (see **Map E**, on the previous page).

A paper entitled *Some Impressions of the Invasion of Sicily* by Eric Thomson, a crew member of the 3rd ML Flotilla and possibly of *ML 338*, was found among Don's belongings. Thomson says that for some days there had been the feeling that some event was imminent, as there was increased activity everywhere and more and more vessels arrived in Malta. Officers were attending conferences ashore and checking details on their ships. Troop ships full of soldiers were also arriving. On the evening of Thursday 8th July 1943 they left harbour and, once anchored, their CO (possibly Don) briefed them on their role for the invasion of Sicily. During the afternoon of the following day, their flotilla and other warships left Malta behind. The wind gradually increased and, by evening, the sea became quite rough. Eventually they reached their rendezvous with the big ships and they were astonished at the size of the armada and wondered how they could fail to be spotted by the enemy. Squadrons of friendly planes flew overhead to blitz enemy positions, mainly in Syracuse. As dawn neared, and it was time for the assault craft to approach the shore, their ML (possibly *ML 338*) was given the signal to escort them from the big ships to the planned places on the assault beaches. All remained quiet until the first troops from the Eighth Army engaged the enemy. Then the ML crew spotted the remains of an Allied glider in the water and the survivors were picked up by another ship. Their ML also picked up survivors from crashed gliders, of which there were 27 in all. Owing to strong winds of up to 45mph, only twelve of the 147 British gliders used reached their targets and 69 crashed into the sea, with 200 airmen drowning. Once the survivors were aboard and they turned seawards, a shore battery opened up on them with shells falling all around, the spray from which soaked everyone. Having disclosed their position, the enemy shore batteries were subjected to a barrage from the Allied big ships and were no more. Later, enemy dive bombers repeatedly appeared and the big guns resumed scoring a number of hits before a merchant ship went up in flames. After dark, air attacks resumed and continued on and off all night. The MLs were ferrying the wounded to one hospital ship and another was deliberately sunk. They also took wounded off a destroyer that had been hit. Fortunately the sea became calm again and, over the course of the next few days, the British Spitfires took control of the skies. Air raids thus became less frequent although another merchant ship, carrying oil, was hit. The MLs were kept busy ferrying supplies and personnel, and then landed supplies in Syracuse Harbour (situated at the headland south of

Augusta). Members of the crew were allowed to explore the town, which had been bombed by the Allies, and were thankful to be on terra firma after being so long at sea. Thomson recalls giving biscuits to small, ill-clad and under-nourished Sicilian children. Some of the older children had postcards, looted from wrecked shops, which they traded with servicemen for biscuits and cigarettes. Don had a number of contemporary Italian postcards in his collection, which he may have acquired by trading in this way. The locals were content to receive the British occupiers; before retreating, the Germans had taken everything of value they could get their hands on. Food, clothing and even furniture had all disappeared. The ML crews were stationed in Syracuse for a while, before returning to Malta.

In *Flag 4*, Dudley Pope records that a total of 30 MLs from Malta took part in Operation Husky, comprising the 3rd, 22nd and 31st ML Flotillas. After the taking of Sicily, many of the Coastal Forces craft returned to Malta and, between 20th August and 3rd September, some 50 ships were overhauled, including 23 of the MLs.

Sub-Lieutenant L H Nixon was No. 1 on *ML 554* and attached to the 31st ML Flotilla. In his memoirs, he recalls sailing from Sousse, Tunisia to take part in the Operation and escorting a fleet of LSTs ashore at Portopalo Bay to the west of Cape Passero. For protection of the fleet, MLs were required to make smoke by towing lit floats. *ML 554* had the privilege of transporting General Montgomery ashore. Shortly after the main operation, the 31st ML Flotilla returned to Malta with 12 LSTs in tow, before returning to Cape Passero to undertake anti-submarine patrols and protect convoys transporting supplies to Syracuse and Augusta. During air raids they would again make smoke to protect the fleet.

Don writes a few lines in the form of an air mail letter (unnumbered) on **19th July 1943**, acknowledging Linda's of 30th June (see above). It is ten days into the invasion, and he admits that things have been hectic and that he is very tired. He has had an exciting time but cannot pass on any information. He says that one of his crew has had the bright idea that he should go home now that he has been involved in two invasions.

In his next letter, dated **24th July 1943** (air letter No. 25), he first answers the points Linda raised in hers of 30th June. He assures her that he is not drinking excessively. He announces that Gutteridge (see his air letter No. 17) is engaged to a Maltese girl and has been promoted to Wing Commander. He was pleased to hear from his mother that Linda had replied to her letter. He, too, has suffered bad sunburn. He says that his part in the invasion went smoothly and there was a fair amount of tension in the ensuing days. However, he has come out safely even though his nerves are not what they used to be.

On **30th July 1943** (air letter No. 26) he has returned to Malta and is disappointed that there is no post from Linda awaiting him. Their stove had broken down and they had to live on corned beef sandwiches and cold water for a couple of days. He has met a friend who is a Sub-Lieutenant on a destroyer and spent an evening out with him. He urges Linda to accept his mother's invitation to visit Liverpool. He is now hoping that the end of the war in the Mediterranean is closer, maybe no more than a year away.

Coincidently, Linda writes **on the same day** from her parents' home at Amos House, Totland Bay, on the Isle of Wight, where she is spending her leave. The last air letter she had received from Don was dated 26th June 1943, and she says she is worried, particularly as Malta had air raids during the previous week. Surprisingly, she does not seem to have guessed that he had been involved in the Sicily invasion. She has collected her small nephew (Derek, who would have been aged ten years old) from his boarding school in Weybridge (St George's RC School). He is to spend a few weeks at Amos House as her sister, Peggy, is in a nursing home (Tuckton, Christchurch) expecting a child (Anthony, born 4th August 1943). She says she has received a second letter from Don's mother, but she is unable to purchase a suitable ring with the £25, so her brother-in-law (Herbert) has banked it for safety. He is a dentist and has been called to the Admiralty for interview.

In his communication dated **6th August 1943** (air letter No. 27), Don moans that in the two months since he has arrived in Malta he has written at least a dozen letters but received only two in return from Linda. He points out that the long silences are not only a worry but give him concern that her feelings for him have changed. In a letter he has received from his mother, he has been informed that his parents have been staying in a pub in North Wales. He comments that, in the past, they had been reluctant to have even one drink in a pub. He has also heard from Richard, who was with Don's former 25th ML Flotilla in Algiers. Dudley is still living with "that awful French girl" and Gibby is abstaining from alcohol. Don wishes that he had remained with them.

On **12th August 1943** (air letter No. 28), Don thanks Linda for hers of 30th July and lists the letters that he has recently sent. He says that he also wired a couple of cables on his return from Sicily to let her know that he is safe. He replies that he does not mind about her not yet finding a ring.

On **16th August 1943** (air letter No. 29), Don has just returned on board from seeing *Babes on Broadway*, although he thinks *Babes in Arms* had been better. He writes that he is still not enjoying the company of his No. 1, Phyllis, and has not settled well with his new comrades in the 3rd ML Flotilla. He has met MacInnes, whom he knows from his Falmouth days, whose No. 1 is Sheppard. He and MacInnes had talked of old times and reminisced about English beer, wishing that the Greenbank Hotel was not so far away.

Image provided by *Greenbank Hotel*

The Greenbank at Falmouth is mentioned several times in the correspondence and was obviously a regular haunt for Coastal Forces personnel and their wives and girlfriends when visiting. Apparently, later in the war, the US Navy used this hotel as an HQ prior to and during the D-Day landings.

In the first paragraph of his letter of 20th August 1943 (air letter No. 30), Don spells out, in no uncertain terms, his continuing frustration at Linda's lack of correspondence and he sounds quite despondent. He misses his former colleagues of the 25th and is desisting from drinking. He has seen a film entitled *The Woman in Room 13*. He continues his letter, reporting that he has been painting his wardroom and has read an edition of the *New Statesman* (a left-leaning political magazine) and thoroughly disagrees with its content.

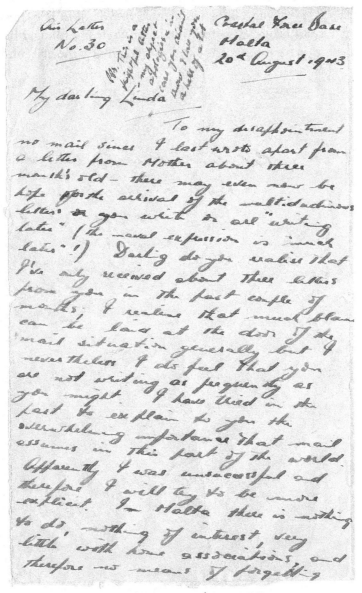

Page 1 of Don's letter 20th August 1943

His next surviving letter is dated **29th August 1943** (air letter No. 32). He has not been well, blaming dysentery. However, he has been ashore and run across someone who was at *HMS King Alfred*, where he received his officer training and, at a dance at the Reunion Club, he met Jack Swift and some RAF personnel whom he knows from Algiers. He has seen Max that evening and he, too, misses their friends from the 25th. Don's mother has written and explained how expensive engagement rings are. He promises that he will send a further remittance. He ends his letter by reminiscing about their farewell party, waiting ages at Neyland for the boat to turn up, the drive to Tenby and then "knocking them up" at the Lion Hotel.

Don is not full of apologies on **31st August 1943** (air letter No. 33) even though he has received Linda's letter of 16th August (another one that is missing). However, he accepts her promise to write more frequently. He hopes she will be able to get up to Liverpool to visit his parents. He has been ashore with Matt, whom he describes as one of the old crowd, and is hopeful of seeing Dick, Dudley and Gibby in the next few days. In her latest letter, his mother has said that she is fed up as his father is fire watching, while his younger brother, Les is in the Home Guard. Don says that his mother has also lectured him on the evils of drink.

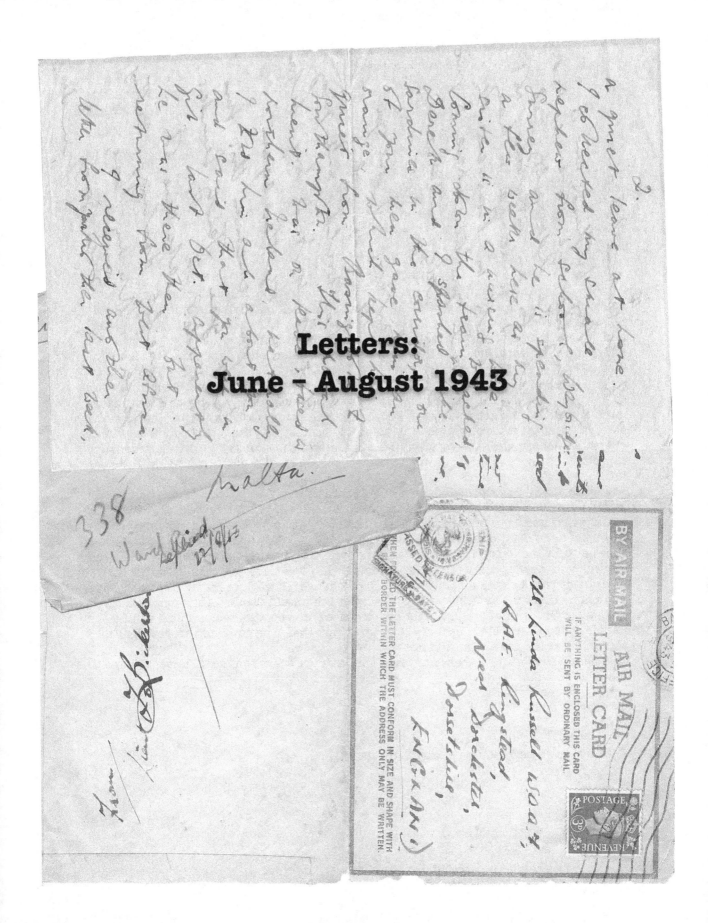

Letters:
June – August 1943

Mess 17
Coastal Force Base
Algiers

1st June 1943
Air Letter No 14

Cpl. L. Russell W.A.A.F.,
R.A.F. Ringstead,
Near Dorchester,
Dorsetshire,
England.

My darling Linda

Sorry that there was such a gap in my air letters to you but there were none available last week and I had to make up for it with sea mail which you have probably not yet received. It is an age since I last heard from you (last letter was that of 1st May) and I'm just longing for some mail to arrive – in fact I want to be told that you still love me as much as ever! Incidentally if it is some little time before you next hear from me please don't worry as I expect to be moving about a bit.

The weather is simply terrific – in fact much too hot for comfort so far as I'm concerned. Last Sunday Dudley and I stooged away to one of the beaches and had a most enjoyable afternoon batheing and lying in the sun - so now my back's sore and skinning and I just daren't touch my arms. It is something that we are now in whites but when ashore we have to wear full whites and the laundry is rather a problem especially as there is no soap in the place – be a question of full blacks in the near future.

Went with Gibby to a small fishing village the other day and to our amazement found a dance in full swing. It turned out that there was an Army officers' rest camp close by and they invited us to refresh ourselves at the bar. Although they had only arrived the day before they had organised all the local talent which I thought to be pretty good – especially for the Army. I danced a few times and then ran across an English nurse and stayed with her for the rest of the evening. She was nice and you've no idea how pleasant it is to be with an English girl for a change. However I regret to say that it's not nearly the same as being with you – sweet I'm missing you so very much that you are never out of my thoughts. The day when we are together once more will be the happiest day of my life – in fact I'll be so happy that I promise not to get tight as I couldn't bear to miss a minute of it.

Please write lots my angel – I do love [you] and you know that I won't ever change.

All my love Linda darling
Ever yours
Don.

P.S. Love to Johnnie & please call on my aunt again.

Coastal Force Base,
Malta

8th June 1943
Air Letter No. 15

Cpl. L. Russell W.A.A.F.,
R.A.F. Ringstead,
Near Dorchester,
Dorsetshire,
ENGLAND

My darling Linda

Sorry about the delay in writing to you but as you see from the new address we do get around a little – and I can't say that I'm sorry to leave Algiers, only sorry to leave so many friends behind. The trip here was completely uneventful and thoroughly enjoyable in most delightful weather – as we passed Pantellaria I was more than gratified to note that it was receiving a hell of hammering as also was Sicilly.

Malta certainly has taken a lot of punishment but the people here look extremely cheerful and go about their work as though nothing had happened – I suppose in much the same way as London, Plymouth etc did at the time of the blitz at home. To improve matters there are an awful lot of bad types here whom I know of old, including Teddy Rose and Smithy, so I think I may look forward to having a fairly hectic time. We have, of course, only just arrived and, as I have not yet been ashore, I don't know what the position really is. I understand however that beer is an exorbitant price – I thought <u>that</u> would please you – and I can't imagine there is very much on which to waste money.

It is ages since I last heard from you but I suppose that with so much moving about it just can't be helped – as long as you write frequently they should all catch me up in time. I do love you so very much my angel and if it's at all possible I promise a long letter tonight. Incidentally Mother writes to say that she very much hopes you will write to her – please do sweet, she's terribly keen on meeting you. Need I add that she can scarcely be as keen as I am to be back with you once more – maybe it won't be as long to wait as I feared.

Must finish wretch – all my love sweetest, take good care of yourself and please don't worry about me.

Ever your
Don.

P.S. The address is:- 93, Thomas Lane, Broadgreen, Lpool 14.
P.P.S. What sort of ring did you get? – that is if the money has turned up yet.

Coastal Force Base,
Malta

12th June 1943
Air Letter No. 16

Cpl. L. Russell W.A.A.F.,
R.A.F. Ringstead,
Near Dorchester,
Dorsetshire,
ENGLAND

My darling Linda

It is alleged that these letter cards are over quicker than ordinary air mail so you may be surprised at my new address – we do get around. It was terrific news to hear yesterday that Pantelleria had surrendered, she was certainly being knocked about aplenty when we passed. Maybe I'll be home in under the two years yet – and then I think that we might celebrate in a mild sort of way of course.

I felt rather sad at leaving so many good friends behind at Algiers, Richard, Dudley and Gibby particularly, but we had quite a party and became quite depressingly sentimental – however it was good fun while it lasted!

Last night I went ashore and was a little shaken by the price of things, particularly hootch after Algiers, - whisky 2/3 for a small tot, it makes you think don't it chum, I see a sober existence ahead! (Need your cheers be quite so loud?)

Fortunately there are many people here I know (Teddy Rose you met at Falmouth) otherwise I would be a little more than bored to death with Phyllis's company, fatuous remarks and (g)nattering. He seems to consider himself the life and soul of the party these days, need I add that it is an opinion held only by himself!

In her last letter Mother asked if you would write to her as she is extremely keen on knowing you – not unnaturally I suppose! – and in reply I gave her your address and asked her to write to you (incidentally I should also be grateful for the receipt of an occasional letter from you!).

I fear that it will still be impossible to have any photographs developed – so I just can't send any on.

Darling I do miss you so very much and I find my only consolation in the receipt of your letters and of course your photograph smiling at me from its place of honour. I love you a hell of a lot wretch and I'm just living for the day when we can be together again. Maybe I'm still a super optimist but I feel that the day may be not too far away – in fact I think I'll take the boat back via the canals and waterways of Europe!

Do write soon my angel – your letters mean so much to me.

All my love sweet
I'll always be ever your
Don.

P.S. Love to Johnnie – keep her out of mischief.

Coastal Force Base,
Malta

13ᵗʰ June 1943
Air Letter No. 17

Cpl. L. Russell W.A.A.F.,
R.A.F. Ringstead,
Near Dorchester,
Dorsetshire,
ENGLAND

My darling Linda

I only really intend to commence this letter today as very little has happened since I wrote to you yesterday – just a slight party ashore and rather more than a slight morning after feeling today.

Yesterday afternoon was terrific – actually managed to get a shower, the first for about three weeks <u>and</u> I don't want any cracks about not looking quite so sunburnt as I was – it unfortunately happens to be quite true! Also met a RAF type by the name of Gutteridge, a South African, who informed me that he was C.O. of Hayscastle in Oct-Dec 1941 – he thought he recognised you from your photograph but he wasn't sure, anyway he seems quite a good type.

In the evening I crawled into long off whites and with other odd folk pushed off into town. I discovered that there was a dance in the Reunion Club and allowed myself to be rooked of a membership fee, then a dance ticket before I was allowed in. Met quite a bunch of people I knew there including an unpleasant little specimen who was at school with my brother. None of us did any dancing but a fair amount of drinking would be cocktails that had as little effect as water – eventually we got rather bored and, by this time quite a collection of us, finished off in a dump called the Monica. Here the drinks were better but we only arrived ten minutes before it closed so there really wasn't much future in that – so back to the dance and the cocktails. Back there I ran into Teddy Rose and some blokes I knew so it appeared to call for a celebration – still unfortunately on the wretched cocktails. Fortunately however we don't drink merely to get tight but rather because we like drinking – just in case you didn't know! We didn't stay very long and arrived back in time to have one decent night cap before turning in. On the whole I must admit that I'm still enjoying Malta but for how long I don't know – every place away from home tends to become boring fairly quickly.

Darling, did I ever tell you that I love you rather a lot – in fact I might even add that I'm quite keen to get home and see you again! Seriously wretch I do miss you badly and I'm just longing to be with you again even in Hotel Itch at Saundersfoot – there will be so many things to make up for when we are together again and I think we may be able to compete.

Please write lots angel
All my love and try and be good occasionally
Ever your
Don.

P.S. I'd forgotten that the RAF type would hardly recognise you without that appalling cap!
P.P.S. I fear I have finished the letter so I'll probably write again tomorrow.

Coastal Force Base
Malta

14th June 1943
Air Letter No 18

Cpl. Linda Russell W.A.A.F.,
R.A.F. Ringstead,
Near Dorchester,
Dorsetshire,
England.

My darling Linda

It's just about midnight but I decided before I went ashore that I would write to you on my return – this is the result. After such a strenuous day it seemed quite necessary to go ashore and relax and I must say that it was about as miserable an evening as I remember. The two blokes who were with me persisted in talking shop the whole time in spite of [illegible] hints and then rudeness on my part – but it was just so much water on the proverbial duck's back. I suppose my fault for the company I chose.

The mail is just starting to catch us up from Algiers and this morning I actually received an airgraph, but to date nothing has arrived from either you or Mother – however I still keep hoping. Incidentally I assume you know that if you should decide to get in touch with me in a hurry there is a cable service available – just a hint!

It really is delightful at sea these days and to date I've grown and discarded about ten skins more or less painlessly! Still if I stay out here long enough I have hopes that I may go some colour near enough to be mistaken for brown.

What about you sending on some snaps of yourself? I promise that I will as soon as it is possible to get them developed although I'm not sure how many of them are censorable.

Did I tell you that I ran into that bad BBC type whom I carted around for some little time a few months ago? So far as I can gather he did have broadcasts on the ship and he must have shot a hell of a line as people have been writing to ask when we are receiving our decorations! The only trouble is he won't tell me what he said which makes it rather difficult for me to tell a convincing story.

Well sweetest it's getting very late and I must get some sleep and I hope, dream my darling love o'thee. I do love you so very much please take care of yourself.

Good night and God bless

Ever yours
Don.

Coastal Force Base
Malta

21st June 1943
Air Letter No 19

Cpl. Linda Russell W.A.A.F.,
R.A.F. Ringstead,
Near Dorchester,
Dorsetshire,
ENGLAND

My darling Linda

I'm still waiting for my mail to catch up with me and it seems to be taking a hell of a time, in fact the last letter I had from you was that dated 1st May – but for once I won't blame you.

At the moment I'm living ashore and quite enjoying it as a novel experience – it's not quite so good as leave as I have to come down to the boat every day but it does make a break. I have been spending most evenings ashore but it really is far too expensive to last (it costs £5 a night!) and we have had one or two parties. On Saturday I went ashore with my new flotilla to a dance, actually we did no dancing at all but as Ronnie Perks and Teddy Rose were also there it developed into quite a session, with the result that yesterday I had the worst head ever – I know I deserved it, don't make cracks pal!

Yesterday was a quiet day and in the evening Ronnie & I wandered into Sliema, had a couple of drinks and walked back – more exercise than I've had for ages.

My crew were all thrilled to death at the prospect of going off to a rest camp for a few days although when they get there and find that there is nothing to do there except rest I'm not sure that their reactions will be quite so favourable – it should do them good as they haven't spent a night off the ship for nine months. It's incredible the way time does fly; do you realise that in about eighteen months at the outside I should be back again with you – Darling I'm just living for that day. I don't need to tell you that I'm missing you more than ever and that I'll always love you as I do now – and a lifetime is quite a long time in which to hold many parties.

Sometimes I feel I'm getting old – 26 tomorrow and only 22 when I joined this racket, although I can find no sign of grey hairs as yet!

Do write lots my sweet – I do love you so.

Ever yours
Don xxx

P.S. Please forgive this awful writing – 'tain't my pen.
P.P.S. Love to Johnnie

Coastal Force Base
Malta

26th June 1943
Air Letter No 20

Cpl. Linda Russell W.A.A.F.,
R.A.F. Ringstead,
Near Dorchester,
Dorsetshire,
ENGLAND

My darling Linda

Many thanks for your letter dated 28th May which I have just received – it's the first since that of 1st May but I trust that the ones in between will catch up, assuming that is, that you have written. I can't understand why I have not yet received from you a letter addressed direct to Malta as it is two weeks since I cabled you. In other words my pet try and write a little more frequently than you have in the past; I have managed to write to you eight letters in the past month so I see no reason why you should only write two – do you? Incidentally I had a letter from Mother at the same time in which she said she was writing to you – have you received it yet?

What makes you think I look like a nigger? – the only affect the sun has is to make me very red and very sore but I have hopes of managing something approaching a tan in the next two years. I can assure you it's not for want of trying. The Algerian wine you talk about is b- awful and the price is normally about 1/- per bottle – anyway I advise you to stick to beer (only wish I could!).

I celebrated my birthday by spending the day at sea but more than made up for it in the evening – it was suggested that a truly novel celebration would be a dry evening, a suggestion that met with little approval! Anyway we went ashore and acted the fool generally – finished up with me sleeping on one of the other boats – in other words a good time was had by all. I got the shock of my life when, next morning, a very old friend whom I'd heard had been lost came down – minus his beard – seemed to call for another party bearing the previous evening in mind, I decided it could well wait – and it did!

It's Saturday evening but for once I'm not going ashore and I'm going to lay and catch up on my back correspondence.

Angel the only thing that really keeps me going is the thought that you still love me and that you will wait until I get home a day that can't come too quickly for me – but even so I begrudge very literally every moment that I have to spend away from you. However I think we will be able to make up for them and really enjoy life again. Darling I love you so terribly that I just couldn't and wouldn't bother to go on without you. All of which sounds very depressing – sorry I'll be more cheerful.

Please write lots pet
All my love
Ever yours
Don xxx

P.S. Love to Johnnie – the lack of hot water at the Cambrian didn't disturb me nearly as much as she did.
P.P.S. Don't forget to number your letters.

Coastal Force Base,
Malta

27ᵗʰ June 1943
Air Letter No 21

Cpl. Linda Russell W.A.A.F.,
R.A.F. Ringstead,
Near Dorchester,
Dorsetshire,
ENGLAND

My darling Linda

This is the new type air letter and I'm afraid that only two sides are of any use so I'll have to cramp as much on them as I can. Not that I have much to write about since last night.

Today has been as uneventful as usual. My idea of a happy awakening is not the Wardroom as viewed through a mosquito net, in fact heads under the sheets at Tenby seems a much better idea! Before lunch my sole companion was Phyllis and together we went to the town for a touché in an attempt to kill the inevitable boredom, as much of each other's company as anything else. There, fortunately, I met Teddy Rose and Ronnie Perks so that the party experienced temporary uplift, mental not moral!, and John Collins helped to complete the gathering. To my amusement I discovered that they had waited for ages for me last night to get into the dance at the Union Club (I happen to be the only one who has paid the sub!) and eventually used a fictitious member for entrance.

This afternoon I slept until nearly 1900 (no I didn't say slept it off - the prices in this place make it quite impossible!) and supper, as usual, came out of a tin - what my cook would do without tins I just can't imagine. Tonight I've been ashore only for an hour or so and I think it's quite the most boring evening I've spent. As I write Phyllis scribbles furiously to his dear wife but about what God alone knows.

Darling do I sound so frightfully browned off - you've no idea how right you are, I'm sick of Malta and I can only hope that we move somewhere else in the near future. I suppose, also, that I miss the company of Dick Dudley & Gibby - what wouldn't I give for a party with the bunch of them now, maybe it would teach the crowd here what parties really are!

Sweetest I love you so very much as I'm missing you like hell - please write as often as you can as you've no idea what your letters mean to me.

I'll always be
Ever yours
Don.

Sender: Cpl. L. Russell W.A.A.F.
R.A.F. Ringstead
Nr Dorchester
Dorset

30th June 1943

Lieut F. D. Bickerton, R.N.V.R.
H.M.M.L. 338
c/o G.P.O. London

My darling Don,

Very many thanks for your cable and air letter, you certainly get around! Perhaps you'll remember that my one hope, last September, was that you would not go to Malta. Thank goodness that it has quietened down there. By the sound of things you are in for a hectic time, bags of parties! Have a good time darling but <u>please</u> don't drink too much.

It must be grand meeting all the old crowd, fancy coming across my old C.O. I remember him quite well, you might tell him that Miss Watts sends her love, she has been down since last September – small world ain't it?

I was on a course last week so I'm afraid this is my first letter since June 20th. When I returned there was a very sweet letter from your Mother, she does sound nice. I'm longing to meet her. Of course, she told me of your wicked past and other little secrets!! She is kindly asking Bacons to send me a photo which I hope will soon arrive (which reminds me of the crack why Gutteridge didn't recognise me without my cap! – cheek).

Darling, I've tried a number of places for a ring but haven't seen anything I like, apparently they are not making any more and the ones in stock are frightfully expensive – plus 100% purchase tax. My sister and I looked round B'mouth a day or two ago and as we could see nothing worth having, I paid the cheque into my brother-in-law's bank in Southbourne. I'm due for a week's course on the east coast, maybe I'll be able to sneak a couple of days in town, where perhaps I'll have better luck, will let you know later.

Poor old Johnnie was posted back to the west coast last week, she was in a frightful state at the thought of Pembrokeshire, but I must admit that she rather asked for trouble. I'm afraid she has no tact, just blunders into things, usually about which she knows nothing.

We had a picnic on the beach yesterday and today my arms, back and legs are so sore that I can hardly bear my clothes. In the evening we had a lobster supper on the lawn at the Picnic, it was jolly good. I made an awful pig of myself – as usual I noticed that a few of your people were doing the same.

Darling, I'm missing you so much, memories of Tenby and Falmouth and the thought of being with you again are keeping me going. I do love you terribly. Writing again later.

Ever yours,
Linda xx

P.S. Don't be angry because my letters haven't caught you up.
P.P.S. If I can't get a ring in London what had I better do? Perhaps it would be easier in the north. I'm wondering if your people have a friend in the trade.

Coastal Force Base,
Malta.

1st July 1943
Air Letter No. 22

Cpl. L. Russell W.A.A.F.,
R.A.F. Ringstead,
Near Dorchester,
Dorsetshire,
ENGLAND

My darling Linda

I was very disappointed that my first batch of mail addressed directly to Malta didn't include a letter from you and I'm wondering whether my cable went astray or if it is just laxity on your part – as I'm in a generous mood I'll give you the benefit of the doubt! But please wretch do write as frequently as you can – it really is important to me.

Mother tells me that she has written to you although she didn't know whether or not to congratulate or merely sympathise with you – a crack on which I went not one iota. Actually I'd rather like you to meet them even before I get home but as you are stationed so far away I suppose it's possibilities are doubtful – anyway should you ever be posted in that general direction they will be more than delighted to see you.

My crew have just returned from a week in a rest camp and in their letters they rhapsodise on the joys of getting up at what time they pleased, sleeping, swimming and sunbathing, in fact they don't altogether appear to go too much on having to work – still who does for that matter. The weather here is frightfully hot and the hottest part of the year is still to come – frankly it just flakes me out. It must be delightful in England now, green fields, colourful flowers – in fact all the things we never think of but just accept until we have to leave them behind – when I do get home I don't think I'll voluntarily leave England for at least a couple of years. Here life goes on in the same dull dreary way – there are few entertainments and in any case indoor amusement is unpleasant in this temperature.

Sweetest I am missing you so very much – do you realise that it's a year since we first met; the first three months were marvellous but now it irritates me that I should have to spend so much precious time away from you. I love you my darling and you know that I will never change. My one consolation is that you still smile at me from your photographs – I don't know how I managed before you sent them. Incidentally did you manage to get the photograph you wanted from Bacons – Mother told me that she went in to pass the necessary authority but that they knew nothing about it.

Must finish pet but please write as often as you can

All my love angel
Ever your own
Don.

P.S. This green cross label – put it on the air letter card and it receives priority.

Coastal Force Base,
Malta

5th July 1943
Air Letter No 23

Cpl. Linda Russell W.A.A.F.,
R.A.F. Ringstead,
Near Dorchester,
Dorsetshire,
ENGLAND.

My darling

I don't know why it should be but I've just returned from seeing "This Above All" and I feel most horribly depressed. As a film I quite enjoyed it so maybe it's seeing people in W.A.A.F.s uniform - not forgetting that appalling cap - sweet you simply must wear it when I get home just so that I can tell you how awful it really is! Sorry, promise not to make any more nasty remarks about your delightful uniform.

Did you receive my cable? I do get rather worried when the interval between your letters is so great more especially as I hear of odd raids on the South Coast - please wretch do write as often as you can, I feel it's my only link with normal existence.

Life here is as boring as ever and I feel pretty fed up with the place, although I did go to a dance last Saturday. A most enjoyable evening! The girls were frightful and almost fifteen - the drinks were even less mature with the inevitable result that we spent the remainder of the evening in the Chocolate King. I suppose the main reason for my boredom here is that there is no one with whom I have the slightest thing in common. In the 25th I could argue with Dick, drink with Dudley and natter at Gibby (occasionally all three at once) while Peter and I had violent political diversions of opinion - here there isn't a single person I can even argue with; what would you do chum?

And, of course, I miss you as badly as ever. I'd do anything I possibly could to get back home to you, so that we could spend the whole of our time together. Sweetest when that day really does come I just won't let you out of my sight ever again. I suppose I've been fairly lucky in that we have had a fair amount of activity and that rather tends to take one's mind off personal problems - but only for the time. I love you so much Linda - I just want to be with you.

Saw another film t'other night "Hi Gang" and found it most disappointing - these radio shows never come up to expectations when they are filmed.

I must finish sweet - please take good care of yourself and please write as often as you possibly can - it is important. Give my love to Johnnie - I hope she's still keeping out of trouble.

All my love Linda darling
Good night and God bless
Ever yours
Don.

P.S. Hope to send off some snap shots in the near future, assuming they're not as bad as I rather fear.
P.P.S. Have a pint of beer for me and drink to the end of this bloody war.
P.P.P.S. I've just read this letter - sorry it is so depressing but things really aren't as bad as they appear.

Coastal Force Base
Malta

19th July 1943

Cpl. Linda Russell W.A.A.F.,
R.A.F. Ringstead,
Near Dorchester,
Dorsetshire,
England.

My darling Linda

Many thanks for your letter of 30th June and your cable which I received today on my return. As you may imagine things have been quite hectic over the last week or so and I'm terribly tired. I don't propose to write a long letter – simply must get some sleep.

We've had quite an exciting time but there's very little information I can pass on – as usual we were there for the landing – one of the crew has the bright idea that he goes home after two invasions – some hope!

I love you so very much my angel, my thoughts are always with you.

Write lots – all my love
Ever yours
Don.

P.S. I'll write again as soon as I can and let you know about the ring etc.
P.P.S. In case you hadn't guessed, I'm just crazy about you.

Coastal Force Base
Malta

24th July 1943
Air letter No 25

Cpl. Linda Russell W.A.A.F.,
R.A.F. Ringstead,
Near Dorchester,
Dorsetshire,
England.

My darling Linda

Before I give you all the news – and I don't suppose there's much I can say – I must answer your letter of 30th June – sorry about the lack of mail but the reasons are obvious!

It may interest you to know, young Linda, that it is an impossibility to drink too much out here as the ration is about two bottles for officers per month and I certainly can't get very far on that especially as guests consume about half of that. Of course you can get tight ashore but at a price and I certainly can't afford £5 a night!

Gutteridge I gather is engaged to a Maltese girl (he's also been promoted to Wing Com!) but I will nevertheless pass on Chris Watt's love to him next time I see him.

Glad to learn that you've heard from Mother and she told me in her last letter that she had received your reply – I'm sure that you'd like her. Anyway she just can't help liking you (compliment – unveiled!).

This 'ere ring. I think it would be better if you gave me some idea of prices these days and when I can send on the additional amount requested – but please do get something you like – I fear I've just no idea of prices at home. As you suggested I've asked Mother if she does know anyone in the racket but I don't think she does.

You are not the only one with sore back etc as I was misguided enough to sunbathe at sea the other day – the result is that my arms have blisters and after being exposed for the past nine months. I do wish you wouldn't make my mouth water so much. Lobster suppers! Seems like a beautiful dream – actually I'd swap it for a pint of English beer at the moment.

I don't really know what the news is from this end – just go stooging around and hope for the best – one of these days I'll arrive in port and find we haven't captured it after all! Our job in the invasion went off quite smoothly but there was a fair amount of tension in the ensuing days. However we came out safely and that counts quite a lot – although I don't think my nerves are what they used to be.

Darling all I want now is to be with you all the time and the day this b----- war ends just can't come too soon for me. I love you terribly my sweet and spend all my time dreaming and thinking of you. Never in my life have I had these feelings about anyone else – guess it must be love. Please write often my angel – your letters mean so much to me. I'll write as often as I can but I fear we are pretty busy at the moment.

I'll always love you as much Linda darling.

Ever yours
Don xxx

P.S. I think it's time I had some photos from you – what about it?

Coastal Force Base
Malta

30ᵗʰ July 1943
Air Letter No 26

My darling Linda

I was very disappointed to get back and find nothing from you amongst the mail but I'm hoping something will turn up before we move off again. Wretch you do write as often as you can don't you? It is so important as I'm certain your letters do much to preserve my sanity in this awful dump.

Things are still pretty hectic and we've been working rather hard but have been very fortunate and had no casualties. Had one miserable trip in filthy weather when the stove broke down and we lived on corned beef sandwiches and cold water for a couple of days, wasn't at all sorry to get in harbour.

Met a bloke here yesterday whom I haven't seen for over three years, I knew him very well before he was at the office. Now he's a Sub on a destroyer and as it's his first visit to Malta I showed him round the place (or the pubs anyway) last night. In fact as it started at 6.00pm and ended at Lord knows what hour it was a hectic but extremely successful evening. I always find it fun talking about old times, of places and pubs we used to visit and loads of odd incidents. This bloke and I have quite a lot in common and before the war we used to do a fair amount of work together, anyway intelligent conversation is quite a novel experience these days (and don't accuse me of being an intellectual snob – I'm not, in my 'musical' tastes I'm just the lowest of the low – in case you didn't know!). I meet Scarland again on Saturday at the Union Club dance – few actually dance as there's no one with whom to dance but you can drink if you take your hootch with you if you've got any hootch to take with you which I haven't. All of which is very depressing.

Mother told me that she had asked you to come to Liverpool if you can manage it – please do if you can at some time as I'd love you to meet each other.

Linda since I am missing you so frightfully and I do so want to get back home to you as soon as I can – do you realise that it's over a year since we first met and so much of that time has, of necessity, been spent apart. We will make up for it when we can and I won't spend even a minute away from you when this b------ war is over. Anyway the news is heartening and perhaps the war in the Med at any rate won't last above a year – then home sweet home for me as soon as I can and I hope I never see the sea again.

Do write soon my angel. I love you more than I can ever tell you and you know I won't ever change.

All my love darling
Ever yours
Don

P.S. Please spill some beer on your next letter – I've almost forgotten what it's like.

Amos House,
Totland Bay,
Isle of Wight.

30th July 1943

Lieut F. D. Bickerton, R.N.V.R.
Coastal Force Base,
Malta.

My darling Don,

It seems an age since I heard from you, the last air letter was numbered 20 received the beginning of the month. I made arrangements with Ringstead to forward your letters but it is highly probable that they have forgotten. Actually, I'm worried about you, as Malta had one or two air raids last week, please write as soon as possible.

As usual, I'm spending a quiet leave at home. I collected my small nephew from school, Weybridge Surrey and he is spending a few weeks here as my sister is in a nursing home. Coming down the train was packed, Derek and I squashed like sardines in the corridor, one of your men gave him an orange, which kept him quiet from Basingstoke to Southampton. This naval lieut. was on leave, based in Northern Ireland, naturally I told him all about you and said that you were in Gib. last Oct. Apparently he was there then but returning from West Africa.

I received another letter from your mother last week, by this time I expect she is on holiday, enjoying our beautiful summer weather. Darling she is sweet, I'm dying to meet her but I fear she will be disappointed after your somewhat biased description of me! I'm looking forward very much to the photo, which she so kindly asked Bacons to send.

I haven't bought a ring. The £25 is still in my brother-in-law's account in Bournemouth, your mother has seen some rather nice ones in Liverpool. The price of jewellery is high and there is little choice down here – do you mind very much if I wait a little longer until I see something I like and know it be genuine?

My brother-in-law is a dentist, he was called up to the Admiralty last week for an interview, not so good as he has so many patients in Bournemouth. I wish you were here to give him a little advice.

Darling, I love you more than anything in the world, and pray that it won't be long before we are together again. Do you remember this time last year, Tenby, Saundersfoot, etc?

Take care of yourself darling, writing later.
All my love
Ever yours,
Linda

Coastal Force Base,
Malta.

6th August 1943
Air Letter No. 27

Cpl. L. Russell W.A.A.F.,
R.A.F. Ringstead,
Near Dorchester,
Dorsetshire,
ENGLAND

Linda my sweet

This isn't so much a letter as an ultimatum. Since I arrived in Malta over two months ago I've had precisely two letters from you which, quite frankly, doesn't seem to me to be nearly good enough. In that time I've written you at least twelve letters. The figures hardly bare comparison. I haven't the slightest doubt that you are very busy but, in case it had escaped your notice, so am I. What, therefore, I propose to do in the future is to reply to your letters as they are received – in fact an eye for an eye etc.! Darling I'm not being nasty or angry or anything else but I do feel that you're being extremely slack over the whole business. And there's no point in your thinking that my feelings towards you have changed as you know fully well that I love you far more than I can ever tell you. Sweetest please write more frequently as it is so worrying when the silences are as long. Darling are you still as sure of yourself as you were when I left you – I suppose things can change considerably in a year but I can only say that my feelings are exactly the same as they were at that time. Perhaps mail in England is of comparatively little importance but out here it's the be all and end all of existence. Anyway wretch please write as often as you can and if you have changed your mind I'd much prefer to know it.

Received a letter from Mother today from which I gather they are staying in a pub in N. Wales – looks almost as though my careful preparations are at last bearing fruit. At one time I used to consider it an achievement if I could persuade them to have even one drink in a pub.

By the same mail I heard from Richard. He gave me all the local news and he seems to be getting along fairly well – in fact no more fed up than usual. Dudley is still living with that awful French girl (his taste shakes me) while Gibby is still on the water wagon! I only wish I were back with them all.

We've been kept fairly busy and life has had its momentary excitements but I'd still prefer to be home with you. I love you more than ever Linda darling and my one desire is to be with you once more. The news continues to improve so I still have hopes of next year.

Angel please write as often as you can – I do love you so.
Ever yours
Don. Xxx

Coastal Force Base
Malta
12th August 1943
Air Letter No 28

My darling Linda

Many thanks for your letter of 30th July and my truly humble apologies for the remarks made in my last letter – I take back every word of it. You complain that you haven't heard from 1st to 30th July, in fact since letter No 20. After that date I wrote on 27th June, 1st, 5th, 24th, 30th July and 6th August – I also sent you a couple of cables on my return from Sicily to let you know that I was OK. I do hope that they have now all turned up. This end things are just as bad as the last letter I received from you was dated 30th June.

Lucky person being home on leave – I'd give anything to be able to spend the leave with you; I'll try and get the Admiralty to arrange that we spend the next one together. I think it should be spent in some quiet spot where we could do anything we felt inclined to do – and, of course, with a fairly handy pub with lots of English beer – I don't think gin agrees with you!

Mother tells me she is enjoying her holiday and it shakes me very much to find they are staying at a pub – at least the war has accomplished something – certainly far more than I was ever able to do. I am so glad that you like her but wretch have no illusions as I certainly won't build a biased picture of you unless you write many more letters.

Of course I don't mind about the ring – please don't get anything unless you really like it and do let me know as soon as you can how much more you require to get what you want. As I said I just have no idea of prices at home and the £25 was just in the nature of a guess. I feel really thrilled at the idea of us being officially engaged and I only wish we had been married before I left last October.

I fear I don't know what the position of dentists is. I imagine that they are reserved to a certain age but that under that age they are in precisely the same position as any other occupation – I know it's unfortunate but many other people have no doubt felt the same thing. Anyway the Navy is the best service – any arguments?

Yes sweetest I do remember this time last year, I'll never forget the time we have spent together. My angel I love you so terribly and I'm longing for our next meeting, we've so many things to do together – the first and most urgent of which is to get married. I spend my time thinking of you, longing for the time I can next be with you and we can make up for the time we've been away from each other. You know I shan't change Linda darling.

Please write as often as you can – I do, honest chum.
All my love pet
Ever yours
Don xxx

Coastal Force Base,
Malta.

16th August 1943
Air Letter No. 29

Cpl. L. Russell W.A.A.F.,
R.A.F. Ringstead,
Near Dorchester,
Dorsetshire,
ENGLAND

Linda darling

Just returned on board from seeing Mickey Rooney and Judy Garland in "Babes on Broadway" – I've been trying to catch up with it for the past eighteen months and I certainly wasn't disappointed. The two of them are grand together although I thought it not quite so good as "Babes in Arms", however it pulled me out of a very despondent mood.

After the film Stadden, Phyllis (he clings like a leech!) and I had a couple of drinks, much to everyone's disgust, I announced my intention of returning on board – they all appear to be shaken that I have nearly given up drinking, the more so that I had sufficient conviction to leave them to it. I don't know what the change really is. I suppose that in the past it was more the company and the fun that we had together but now we have been split up there isn't anyone in whom I have any interest or with whom I have many common interests. So for the time being I've decided to hibernate.

Last night I ran into MacInnes who used to be at Falmouth and he now has Sheppard as his No 1. – you'd remember him, rather gathered you didn't like him too much. We talked over old times and both regretted that the Greenbanks was so far away. English beer is just a happy memory.

And that's about all I have done since I last wrote principally because there's nothing to do in this dump. I used to get pretty fed up with Algiers but I certainly wouldn't object to returning at the moment. But my main desire is to get home, to be with you and more (it's very nearly a year since I left), see green grass, move about in a temperature that doesn't keep you in a perpetual ooze of perspiration – but principally be with you. I do miss you so very much darling and you may even be aware that I love you rather a lot. Sweetest there are so many things I want to do but to do them by myself would be a mere waste of time – I must be with you.

This time last year I was still able to see you at Haverfordwest to walk with you by the river (pity so many people had the same idea!) to go to Tenby and even to scratch myself to pieces, although the Cambrian had nothing on the mosquitoes in this place.

I do love you Linda darling and I want to spend the rest of my life with you – must have someone who can put me to bed.

All my love sweetheart
Write as often as you can
Ever your
Don.

P.S. The mail situation here is bloody – is mine arriving O.K. D.
P.P.S. I do love you so much darling.

Coastal Force Base,
Malta.

20th August 1943
Air Letter No. 30

Cpl. L. Russell W.A.A.F.,
R.A.F. Ringstead,
Near Dorchester,
Dorsetshire,
ENGLAND

My darling Linda

To my disappointment no mail since I last wrote apart from a letter from Mother about three months' old – there may even now be hope for the arrival of the multitudinous letters you write or are "writing later" (the naval expression is "much later"!) Darling do you realise that I've only received about three letters from you in the past couple of months. I realise that much blame can be laid at the door of the mail situation generally but I nevertheless do feel that you are not writing as frequently as you might. I have tried in the past to explain to you the overwhelming importance that mail assumes in this part of the world. Apparently I was unsuccessful and therefore I will try to be more explicit. In Malta there is nothing to do, nothing of interest, very little with home associations, and therefore no means of forgetting even temporarily how much we miss people at home – consequently we attach an even greater importance to our one link with those people namely mail. I have no doubt that you are busy, so am I but I do find time to write to you usually about twice a week. Believe me wretch I'm not being awkward but I do consider you most slack in this respect. So please write as often as you can. My final plea!

Haven't done much since I last wrote. Last night I saw a very old film, and one I'd seen before, called "The Woman in Room 13" – not particularly brilliant. Today I've been most energetic and started painting the wardroom – actually finished off the deckhead. This evening I went ashore at six pm, had one beer, felt thoroughly fed up and returned to the ship, where I moped through a New Statesman and thoroughly disagreed with everything they said! In fact I'm hardly in the right mood to write a readable letter – yes my sweet I've no doubt that you have already discovered that.

Sorry sweetest things aren't really so black as I paint them – I guess it's just that I feel pretty fed up at not being with the old crowd, or maybe it's because I've stopped drinking and I can't say I feel any better for it.

I am missing you so very much my angel, I'm only living for the time when I can be with you in my arms again – even with Alice to poke her head round the door! I love you with all my heart and you must be quite certain that I'll never change. Sweet I reckon a biggish party would be a good idea when I get home, and then we could stooge off somewhere for the next few months to recover – what do you say?

All my love always Linda sweetest

Ever your
Don. Xxx

P.S. Let me know if all my letters to date have turned up – they're all numbered.
P.P.S. This is a frightful letter – my abject apologies and in case you didn't know I love you a hell of a lot.

Coastal Force Base
Malta

29th August 1943
Air Letter No 32

My darling Linda

Faithful as ever although I haven't heard from you since your letter of 30th July. I hasten to tell you my doing of the past week – actually I'm feeling rather guilty that I haven't written for a week and I fear that for once I have no excuse to offer! 'Smatter of fact I haven't been feeling too well for the past few days, dysentery I guess, but I now seem to be recovering – anyway I went ashore both last night and tonight.

I believe I told you that I had given up drinking? Well last night I went ashore for my usual glass of alleged beer and ran across a bloke who was with me at King Alfred. That unfortunately appeared to give me the taste for Scotch once more and when I left him I pushed off to the dance at the Reunion Club only to discover some RAF types I met in Algiers. Well we talked and drank (seems to be the only occupation at this dance!) and generally enjoyed ourselves – I think we even woke the place up a little. At that time Jack Swift turned up and he proceeded to get things well and truly organised – mind you, I didn't get tight (honest chum) but I certainly didn't feel so good this morning. So I think I will keep off the stuff!

I've seen no more films since I last wrote to you, in fact there doesn't appear to be anything that's worth seeing. I find these days that I only want to go to the cinema to be amused and there are very few films capable of doing that.

Max turned up tonight just before I went ashore; he's much the same as ever and just about browned off with things as I am. However he was feeling pretty tired and I said I'd go and see him tomorrow. I never thought the day would arrive when the sight of Max's face would be so welcome – he, too, misses the old flotilla and if we are to all meet again I certainly won't be responsible for the party that's certain to happen!

Darling I'd no idea that rings were so expensive until Mother wrote and gave me some information so please hold on and I'll arrange to remit some more money. I do hope you'll find something you like and much as I'd like to help there's nothing to be had at this end. It seems to take some little time for remittances to get through but please do not get anything until it does arrive.

Actually wretch I'm rather worried that I haven't heard from you although several airmails have arrived recently. Please, darling, I do love you so very much and your letters mean more than you can ever realise – please write as often as you can. It was just about this time last year that we learned that we were to go abroad. Do you remember the night of our farewell party, waiting ages at Neyland for a boat to turn up, the drive to Tenby and then knocking them up at the Lion. Poor old Johnnie wasn't too well if I remember correctly!

I'm missing you like hell sweet and just longing for the day when I can be with you again. Write lots angel, I'm always thinking of you.

All my love, pet
Ever yours
Don.

P.S. Do keep writing to Mother – she seems to enjoy your letters – so do I when I get them!

Coastal Force Base
Malta

31st August 1943
Air Letter No 33

My darling Linda

I feel like inserting an advertisement in the agony column beginning "All is forgiven etc" but what I really intend to convey is my thanks for your letter of 16th August. However I have no intention of expressing regret that you should eventually have felt ashamed of yourself for writing so little – in fact it all goes double! I accept your promise to write more frequently than you have been doing, and I assume I may confidently expect one letter per month – till the strain becomes too great anyway. Incidentally you say that if you wrote as often as you think about me I would hate the sight of letters – it's a chance I'm more than prepared to take.

I don't know McKevitt but I rather think I know when he was lost – hope you have more success with the ring but I think it would be better to hold on until the other money arrives.

So pleased that your sister and the infant are getting on so well but I must admit that children at that age always appear quite hideous to me – anyway they make such a hell of a noise & I'd like something that didn't remind me of Phyllis all the time.

I hope you are able to get the 48 hours & make Liverpool as I know they are all dying to meet you. A word of warning. I have no doubt that they will very nearly take advantage of my absence to spin you all sorts of quite untrue stories and show you photographs of my infancy (probably faked!). Don't believe a word of 'em. My past is pure & unspotted (almost).

Went ashore with Max last night and had quite a good night. He hasn't changed in fact he can still shoot as big a line as ever – however it is good to see one of the old crowd. I hope to run across Dick, Dudley, Gibby etc in the next few days & then I think sparks really will fly. I'll write and let you know when it happens.

I received a letter from Mother today and she said she was hoping you would be able to get up there – she seemed a little fed up at the time as Dad was fire watching while Les was at Home Guard. I also received a hell of a lecture on the evils of drink principally as far as I can gather because I grumbled at the shortage of beer in this place. Believe me I'm not drinking these days partly because the stuff isn't beer but also because I have too much work to do – perhaps you'll gently explain when you get home.

Darling I am missing you so frightfully and just longing for the day when I'm with you once more. It's been nearly a year now and has seemed far longer – however I'm told that the first year is the worst. I love you more than anything in the world and my idea of perfect happiness is just to be with you and hold you so very tight in my arms. In fact I almost forgive you for your lack of letters.

Please write soon sweet.

All my love angel
Ever yours
Don.

Chapter Eight

SEPTEMBER – DECEMBER 1943

With the invasion of Sicily complete by 17th August 1943, the Allies quickly moved to invade the Italian mainland. On 3rd September, the British Eighth Army launched Operation Baytown, crossing the Straits of Messina to Reggio di Calabria in mainland Italy. The Italian defending troops surrendered and, by the following day, the British had reached Bagnara (see **Map F**, over the page). However, progress became slow owing to blown-up bridges, roadblocks and mines. On 8th September, Italy surrendered and all Italian troops stopped fighting. Two further invasions were launched the following day. Operation Slapstick, executed at short notice following the Italian Government's offer to open the ports of Taranto and Brindisi to the Allies, saw the Royal Navy sail into Taranto unopposed and, later, Brindisi. Initially, the British 1st Airborne Division was held up by German troops but, by the end of September, they had advanced 125 miles to Foggia. The third, and main invasion, was the US-led Operation Avalanche which was also launched on 9th September against Salerno, and this comprised 500 ships and 165,000 US and British troops. They faced fierce resistance from the Germans and the operation could easily have failed. It took the best part of a week for the Allies to get onto the front foot and convince the Germans to withdraw, which they did on 18th/19th September.

In his book, *A Leaf Upon the Sea*, Gordon Stead describes the part played by his ship *ML 126*, and also *ML 121*. He states that eight ships of the 3rd ML Flotilla (including Don's *ML 338*) sailed first to Tripoli to take part in the operations. Of the two MLs that did not go to Tripoli, *ML 168* was left in Malta with engine defects but took part later, while *ML 575* went directly to Bizerte, Tunisia. From Tripoli, *ML 135* sailed a day before the remaining seven MLs, which left on 5th September to Palermo where they refuelled the following morning. MLs *126* and *121* then joined the convoy headed for Salerno where they undertook minesweeping duties. The remaining five MLs (including Don's *ML 338*, although Don's ship is not specifically mentioned in Stead's book), each with landing craft squadron commanders on board, set off for Termini where they joined the landing craft for the final assaults. The MLs were in close contact with the enemy in numerous engagements throughout the area and much more so than in the invasion of Sicily, which had largely taken the enemy by surprise. Apart from the four MLs already identified by Stead, he also mentions MLs *134*, *480* and *565*.

In his paper, *3rd ML Flotilla*, H C Atkinson recalls that, subsequently, the flotilla became divided. Four ships, including Don's *ML 338*, operated on the west coast of Italy, whilst the others went on to the Taranto area and later operated in the Adriatic Sea. The west coast division, after Salerno, was first working out of Naples and then at Ischia, when it was occupied, where a Coastal Forces Base was established. From Ischia, units of the flotilla continued with their minesweeping operations and also took part in other operations including diversionary landings at Civitavecchia and Elba. They then undertook initial minesweeping operations at La Maddalena and operated for a considerable time in mine clearance sweeps, notably at Bastia and Ajaccio (see **Map F**).

The formation of the flotillas is uncertain. In his book *Flag 4*, Dudley Pope notes that, by December 1943, ML strength had increased to 11 flotillas comprising some 90 craft. Pope states that, following a reorganisation, a new flotilla (the 8th) was created. The 3rd was the largest with 13 ships – although other evidence points to the 3rd being reduced to 8 craft, possibly as a result of this reorganisation. However, probably a more reliable source comes in the shape of Sub-Lieutenant L H Nixon's *Private Papers*. Nixon recalls that the 3rd ML Flotilla was split into 3 divisions of 5 ships each. His *ML 554* transferred from the 31st ML Flotilla to the first division of the 3rd, which included Don's *ML 338*, and was deployed to the west coast of Italy. The second division sailed to the Adriatic Sea, and the third operated in the Maddalena and Corsica area.

MAP F

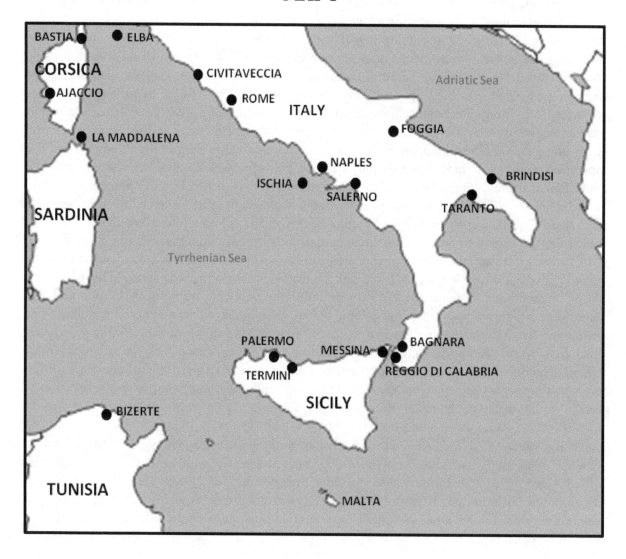

Before examining the next letter in Don and Linda's correspondence, the ongoing story of the engagement ring reaches a conclusion. Linda has purchased a diamond ring with a £25 cheque and £14 cash from S A Fordham, Swanage on 6th September 1943, and she kept the receipt:

Receipt for Linda's engagement ring

R.A.F. Ringstead,
Nr. Dorchester,
Dorset.

12th Sept. 1943.

My darling Don,

It's an age since I heard from you – almost three weeks ago I received your air letters 29 and 30. Frankly, I worried in case there is something wrong, stupid of course but you know how one imagines things.

You must admit that I'm writing more often (as promised) and trust that by this time most of them have caught you up.

Nothing of interest has happened since my last letter. I spent an S.O.P. with my

Page 1 of Linda's letter 12th September 1943

On **12th September 1943,** Linda writes saying she had not heard from Don for three weeks (air letters Nos. 29 & 30 are the last ones she has received). She does not mention the invasion of Italy, although she has probably guessed that Don may have been involved. She says that her mother has been looking after her nephew, Derek, for almost seven weeks, whilst she had spent her SOP (presumably permission to take leave) with her sister in Bournemouth who is not very well. She says that her young nephew, Anthony is a lovely boy and her brother-in-law, Herbert (the dentist), is joining the Navy on Friday. (He was a Lieutenant Surgeon and, according to the *Naval Lists*, was based at *HMS Victory* in Portsmouth. Owing to the severe bombing suffered by Portsmouth,

Victory V was established in Southampton in 1941, so he may have been based there for a time. However, anecdotal evidence suggests that he was mainly attached to the Royal Naval Hospital Haslar at Gosport.) Linda's letter ends with confirmation that she has received Don's photograph from Bacon's of Liverpool, and to say she loves her engagement ring and hopes that Don will.

Don's first surviving letter, after the Italian invasion, is dated **15th September 1943** (air letter No. 34). He apologises for not having written for two weeks because he has not had the opportunity "since this show started". He comments that he has not heard any news for days saying that "the nearer you are the less you hear". He had not realised that the Italians had surrendered until the morning after the landing, which would suggest that he was involved in Operation Avalanche. They had found it hard to believe the Italian surrender because of the intensity of shelling and bombing but, of course, it is the Germans who are resisting. Don is full of praise for his crew. But when he told them that they were on their way to Naples, one of the jokers amongst his crew had made reference to the saying 'See Naples and die'. This is an Italian proverb meaning that after one has visited Naples nothing else is worth seeing, although in the context of the war it could have been imagined to have a more sinister meaning! They must have been worried about dying so often. Don confirms that he had been reunited with Dick, Dudley, Gibby, etc. before he sailed. It may be his former 25th ML Flotilla was also involved in the invasion and that they had met up in Tripoli.

On **28th September 1943** (air letter No. 35) he announces that he has now returned (presumably to Malta) and, amongst the mail, were two letters from Linda dated 20th August (missing) and 12th September. He sarcastically declares that he is impressed with receiving two letters from her in a month. He is glad she has found an engagement ring and says that he will send the rest of the money. He refers to Linda's mention that her nephew, Derek, had put grasshoppers in the bed, saying that his ship is overrun with cockroaches. He tells her that when he returned to harbour he had met Richard and Gibby and a party had ensued.

There is then the unprecedented gap of six weeks before Don next writes, on **8th November 1943** (air letter No. 36). He says that he has been in hospital for a short time, and that it is nothing serious and that he is fully recovered. There is no further mention of this in any of the correspondence, so the nature of his illness will remain a mystery. One wonders whether he was suffering from exhaustion, having been at the fore of two invasions in two months. He has received Linda's letters of 3rd and 20th October (both missing) and hopes that she will soon be able to visit his parents in Liverpool. He remarks that it is a year since their first invasion (North Africa) and admits that he and his crew had been scared. He gives her assurances that all will be wonderful on his return, although he does have some doubt as to how easily he will slot back into his old civilian job. He promises to write again the following day.

In fact, his next surviving letter is dated **12th November 1943** (air letter No. 37). In it, he reports that there are a number of personnel changes pending. Dudley is leaving Coastal Forces to take command of a corvette in the Mediterranean – he is disappointed as he thought he was going home and had informed his wife, Eda accordingly. Gibby has been appointed to take charge of the flotilla (presumably the 25th).

In his book, *A Leaf Upon the Sea*, Gordon Stead notes that he leaves the 3rd ML Flotilla at about this time, and that his place as senior officer of the flotilla is taken by John Peal.

Don says Richard and Dennis are expecting to go home as they have decided to transfer to larger ships. He thinks that Richard is silly as he will just be a duty officer rather than having his own command and, although he will now get some home leave, the large ships will go to the Far East. Don says that he was tempted to grab some home leave but had decided that it was too much of a gamble and he asks Linda for her thoughts. Peter is transferring from MLs (motor launches) to MTBs (motor torpedo boats) and Phyllis has got his own command, much to Don's relief. He is due to sail shortly but does not indicate to where.

So how was Don developing and progressing since his promotions, initially to Sub-Lieutenant and then to Lieutenant commanding his own ship?

In one of his letters (see the letter of 16th August 1943), he had revealed that, after over two months, he was still struggling to settle down with his new colleagues in the 3rd ML Flotilla. In several letters, he talked about missing his old pals of the 25th. He enjoyed excellent relationships and was held in high regard by his colleagues there.

In a report in his service record, dated September 1942, Richard Vick had described Don as a "thoroughly efficient and able officer who handles both ship and men well. Has a good sense of responsibility..." and Don's SO, Lt Cmdr Dudley Arnaud recommended him for a command even though he was only aged 25. However, relationships were not so cosy in the 3rd.

In October 1943, Lt Cmdr Gordon Stead did not produce a totally glowing report, although he did qualify his statement stating that, for operational reasons, Don had not accompanied him in an operation or at sea. He described Don as a "very pleasant personality with a keen sense of humour" and "willing to work with others". However he did not regard him to be "an outstandingly strong character". He pointed out that Don's ship "suffered several minor collisions which were allegedly not his fault, although in that he may well be correct". He also remarked that Don's ship had "more than average engine failures" and criticised his paperwork. He concluded saying that Don was "of sound physique" and "a keen tennis player".

Later, in September 1944, Don's new SO, Lt Cmdr Pearse would describe Don as "reliable" with "a good sense of responsibility", and note that he was "a good mixer". He would go on to say that Don's "maintenance routine needs to be greatly improved. His crew like him but he is too easy going and a more staid discipline needs to be observed. This has been pointed out to him and he has shown more keenness and improvement. He is quick witted and quickly grasps situations. His health is good and he is fond of outdoor sports and literature." Counter-signing the report, Captain Stevens concurs with Pearse's "easy going" description and would note a "somewhat unimpressive appearance". However, he was to conclude: "Lt Bickerton has a latent capacity for producing a surprising performance in emergency."

Having read these reports, it occurred to me that my father's experiences in the Navy had strengthened his character and set him in good stead for his outstanding career in the civil service (see Chapter Fourteen).

His letter of **17th November 1943** (air letter No. 38) begins as the previous one ended, disappointed that he has not received a letter from Linda. He has been ashore and seen an old film, *The Texas Ranger Rides Again*, at an Italian cinema that has been taken over by the army. He says he has re-read some of Linda's letters and looks forward to returning home within a year.

Linda is obviously so worried that she sends a telegram from Bournemouth to Don. It is stamped St George, Sliema, Malta and dated **19th November 1943**.

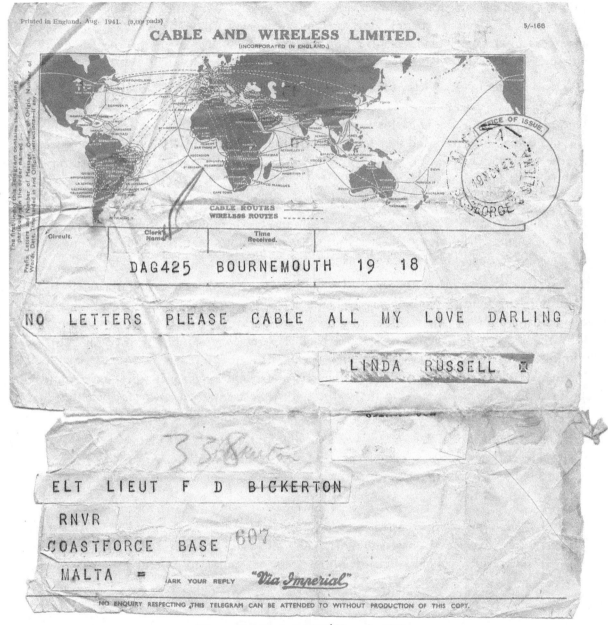

Telegram from Linda dated 19th November 1943

The message seems to indicate that, rather than have him write (as she would wait at least three weeks for a letter to arrive), she would prefer a cable to hear that he is safe. There has been a long period of silence with Don being in hospital, and his letters of 8th and 17th November have not yet arrived.

In the letter she writes two days later, on **21st November** at 04:00 from *RAF Ringstead* (although the sender's address is given as Amos House, Totland Bay, Isle of Wight), she says that Don's air letter of 8th November 1943 (air letter No. 36) is the first that she has received from him for almost two months and she has been worried. She wants to know what has put him in hospital. Unfortunately, as previously mentioned, none of the surviving correspondence throws any light on the matter. At Don's mother's suggestion, she will visit his parents in Liverpool in spring. She anticipates a dull Christmas with her parents on the Isle of Wight, although she considers that better than staying in *RAF Ringstead*.

Don's air letter No. 39 has not been found, but No. 40 is dated **30th November 1943**. He has just received a cable from Linda but is unable to reciprocate. He says no such facilities exist where he is, and he is not in Malta. Presumably he is in Italy. He has got a new suit from Gieves and has come across Max and they had a party ashore. He has a new No. 1, who has taken over from Phyllis, with whom he is getting on well. On the previous evening, McInnes had turned up and they had a party on board.

Don's next letter is dated **6th December 1943** (air letter No. 41). He says that there is not much to report as any time spent in harbour is in places where it is preferable to stay aboard. He again speculates where they might live after the war and notes that she has not responded to his previous suggestions. He has not seen his friends for some time.

Linda writes on **Christmas Day 1943** from *RAF Branscombe* near Sidmouth, acknowledging Don's air letter of 30th November. She had been in hospital for ten days with influenza and bronchitis and, just as she was looking forward to Christmas at home, her new posting came through. She says that she wishes she was back at *RAF Ringstead*. She is to go on a two-week administration course at Wing (*RAF Wing*, Buckinghamshire) on New Year's Eve. She says that Women's Auxiliary Air Force (WAAF) supervisors are no longer being granted commissions and she therefore does not see a future there. In a postscript, she asks Don whether he has received two parcels from her.

Don's air letter No. 42 has not survived, but on **30th December 1943** he writes No. 43, which is a very brief pencil note, owing to a damaged right hand. It is addressed to *RAF Ringstead* but is redirected to *RAF Branscombe*.

Thus 1943 ends with the Allies slowly increasing the pressure on the Axis in the Mediterranean. The Italians have surrendered and Sicily and Southern Italy have been captured. The Germans battle to hold a defensive line, north of Naples, to prevent the total capture of Italy.

Letters:
September – December 1943

2.

that I should visit her in
the Spring. When the evening
are longer and the weather a
little warmer, so, note on the
Spring (and the next 2 years).
Grandma? I'm going home
perhaps what — on Christmas, of course it
will be dearly done but
anyhow to get away from
camps, his well I remember
his and all those
last year to picnic him, and
you may forget. And
coming night march finding
my boot full of empty beer and
whisky bottles. It will be
more than at home having
a few quiet ones with Dad
Mother is not looking.
I can't think of anything
more perfect than spending
a little time with you and poor

Ringstead.
21st Nov. 1943.
4am.

My darling Son,

I am feeling a completely
different person since I received
your air letter 36 (8th Nov), almost
two months without a letter
has been an absolute agony, in point
of fact if it hadn't been for
Mother's comforting words
things would have been too bad.

I'm terribly sorry to hear
you have been in hospital,
somehow it is difficult to imagine
you stopping in bed for any
length of time! Seriously, what
has been wrong? you've an important
hunt you know. I'm glad to
hear you are back on board
again, and do take great care
of yourself.

Your Mother has suggested

Sender: Cpl. L. Russell W.A.A.F.
R.A.F. Ringstead
Nr Dorchester
Dorset

12th September 1943

Lieut F. D. Bickerton, R.N.V.R.
Coastal Force Base.
Malta.

My darling Don,

It's an age since I heard from you – almost three weeks ago I received your air letters 29 and 30. Frankly, I worried in case there is something wrong, stupid of course but you know how one imagines things.

You must admit that I'm writing more often (as promised) and trust that by this time most of them have caught you up.

Nothing of interest has happened since my last letter. I spent an S.O.P. with my sister two or three days ago. Her husband is joining the Navy on Friday, and there is a terrific flap and panic as she is not too well. Young Anthony is a lovely baby, I told your Mother about him and in reply heard about you and Leslie at that age!!

Mother has had Derek for almost seven weeks, and believe me he is a handful. Apparently the other morning his bed was full of grass-hoppers, which he had collected at an early hour. Father's language wasn't too good when he saw the beastly things jumping in the bathroom.

Darling your photo is an absolute Godsend, you have no idea how wonderful it is having you smiling at me and please don't doubt my love for you, surely you must know that I love you more than anything in the world – and each day I love you more and more.

Darling this is a most frightful letter, forgive me but it is 4am and to use an R.A.F. expression 'I'm completely on my knees' I dare not read it through. So write as soon as possible, just a few lines.

More later,
All my love,
As ever
Linda xx

P.S. I do like the ring most awfully and hope you will.

Coastal Force Base,
Malta.

15th September 1943
Air Letter No. 34

Cpl. L. Russell W.A.A.F.,
R.A.F. Ringstead,
Near Dorchester,
Dorsetshire, ENGLAND

My darling Linda

Sorry about my absence of letters over the past couple of weeks but since this show started I just haven't had any opportunity to get them away – however I hope to be able to get this letter posted tomorrow.

As you may guess things have been pretty hectic but they seem to be going fairly well although I haven't heard any news for days – it's always the same, the nearer you are the less you hear. We'd no idea the Italians had thrown in their hand until the morning after the landing and then I didn't believe it as there seemed to be far too many shells and bombs to substantiate such a theory. The crew were rather amusing when I told them we were on the way to Naples and after a long silence I heard someone mutter "see Naples and – well die"! But as usual they were absolute tops and things went with their usual swing. I saw Dick, Dudley, Gibby etc before we sailed and we had quite a party to celebrate the reunion – and felt like death the next day.

Darling I love you such a hell of a lot and just want to get home to you again – maybe it won't be too long now and then we can make up for so much wasted time.

Must finish and try get this away.

All my love my sweetest
I'll never change
As ever
Don xxx

P.S. In case my letter home doesn't make it will you tell Mother that everything is O.K.?
P.P.S. Please write lots and although we've had no mail for several weeks there should be quite a file when we return.
P.P.P.S. I do love you.

Coastal Force Base,
Malta.

28th September 1943
Air Letter No. 35

Cpl. L. Russell W.A.A.F.,
R.A.F. Ringstead,
Near Dorchester,
Dorsetshire, ENGLAND

My darling Linda

It was heavenly to get back and find a whole stack of mail awaiting us including your letters of 20th August and 12th September – not had two letters in under a month – you are improving!

I'm so glad you have found a ring that you like and I'll send the rest of the money by the same means as before (No – I don't agree to the 50-50 – sorry). It sounds pretty good and I think you were lucky to get it.

Sweet please don't worry if there are gaps between my letters, you must surely know that while I write at every opportunity things have of late been fairly hectic in this part of the world and it's quite impossible to post letters at sea. Every time we've been in anywhere I've sent off either a letter or cable – and believe it or not I can look after myself! Honest chum.

I had numerous letters from Mother and I gather you are going up home in the near future. Mother very eagerly says that she's sure I will have no objection to her telling you all my past history – I'd like to know just what line she's going to shoot. I think she'll probably start off by showing you photographs of me in the nude on my stomach at the tender age of six months (keep your children at home by keeping a family album). In addition no doubt you will be told how I used to yell with rage if I didn't get my own way (wonder if it's worth trying these days?) how I used to treat rice pudding and prunes and many other little treats they keep stored up for the unwary visitor – and unfortunately I won't even be there to defend my honour!

I think Derek would enjoy himself onboard as we are completely overrun with cockroaches – whether your father would prefer them to grasshoppers is quite another matter.

When I got in harbour who should I meet but Richard and Gibby – the rest should be painfully obvious. Yes, we had a party including some newspaper blokes I know and today is the day of reckoning.

The last few weeks have been pretty hectic but well worth it and the news continues to be good – one day I'll tell you the story of how I nearly sank a cruiser – one of ours!

Darling I do love you so much and of course I trust you. One year is nearly up (this time last year we were at Falmouth – heaven) and I hope the other doesn't take too long to pass. I'm living for the day when we can be together again – I'll always love you just as much.

All my love angel
Ever your
Don xxx

P.S. Two letters in a month may be an improvement but I can stand many more – please write soon sweetest.
P.P.S. I love you xxx

Coastal Force Base,
Malta.

8th November 1943
Air Letter No. 36

Cpl. L. Russell W.A.A.F.,
R.A.F. Ringstead,
Near Dorchester,
Dorsetshire,
ENGLAND

My darling Linda

I can't tell you how sorry I am about the awful silence over the last month but the fact is I was poked away in hospital for a short time – no, wretch, nothing serious and anyway I've completely recovered now. It's good to be back on board again – I'd no idea a rest could be so boring!

A million thanks for your letters of October 3rd and 20th – in fact one thank for each time I've read them. I certainly don't admit that you are writing much more frequently but unfortunately I'm not in any position to criticise. No doubt I will receive numerous nasty remarks when you reply – but believe me sweet so long as I hear from you nothing else matters.

I do hope you are able to manage a visit to L'pool – incidentally would you drop Mother a line and tell her that I'm perfectly fit as I know she must be worrying – I'll ask her to do the same. She tells me that you like the photo which all goes to show how appalling your taste can be on occasions – your illusions will be sadly shattered when I do return.

It's just a year ago since we did our first invasion and boy were we scared – quite a lot has happened since then and I suppose we have had quite a number of parties – in our own quiet way, of course!

Darling why should you think that I'll be disappointed in you when I return? You must know that I couldn't go on at all if it weren't for the certainty of coming home to you. I think it far more likely that it will be you who will be disappointed as I feel about five years older than I did when I last saw you (I might as well warn you now that it will be no good trying to hold this against me when I get back and thus attempt to avoid any parties!). I do love you so very much my angel and as you say we will always be perfectly happy together. What I'm longing for is for us to go away to some quiet spot in the country stay at its village pub and do nothing but laze and make love to you. Two years is a long time – God knows the past year has been long enough – but it still leaves us quite a number of years together and I intend to enjoy them to the full with you.

You ask if I think I will settle down easily after the war. Frankly I don't know but I'm prepared to have a good shot at it – what really worries me is that I shall be completely incompetent to do my job – no doubt naval flannel will come to the rescue.

I fear that this letter contains almost no news at all but I will be writing to you again tomorrow to give you the lowdown on Dudley, Dick etc.

Good night my darling. God bless and take care of yourself.

I'll always love you as much

Ever your
Don xxx

Coastal Force Base,
Malta.

12th November 1943
Air Letter No. 37

Cpl. L. Russell W.A.A.F.,
R.A.F. Ringstead,
Near Dorchester,
Dorsetshire,
ENGLAND

My darling Linda

So much seems to have happened that I fear I didn't keep my promise to write on the 9th but perhaps you'll forgive the extra three days – just this time please.

Every one seems to be breaking away. Dudley is leaving coastal forces to take command of a corvette - and therein lies a tale. In the first place he actually had orders to go home and to his disgust it was cancelled and he was appointed to one in the Med. It really was bad luck as he had cabled to Eda telling her to expect him before X'mas. Now of course he's feeling pretty fed up with things although we've cheered him up a little with a few quiet parties - one of them was quite good in fact! Gibby has taken over the flotilla to everyone's delight although he unfortunately hasn't got his half stripe for the job. Richard is expecting to go home together with Dennis as they have both decided to throw in their hands so far as C.F. are concerned and have a shot at larger ships. Personally I think Richard is very silly, as I informed him, and I've no doubt he won't enjoy being a duty stooge in a large ship after having his own command. Actually I imagine he did it to get back home but although I considered it very carefully I don't agree with him. What he won't realise is that the larger ships are certain to go to the Far East and that if he serves his time on Med. Station he will be due to go home and stands a reasonable chance of not going abroad again. Either way it's a gamble but I believe I'm right but you've no idea what a temptation it was to grab at any chance which meant seeing you again. Darling do let me know what you think about it because I don't suppose it's too late to change my mind.

Peter too is going out of ML's into MGB's - God knows why.

I've been hoping so much for a letter from you before I sail but it seems I am unlucky. I love you my angel and without the thought of you waiting for me this life would be completely unbearable - as it is I do know that in a year I will be coming home to you - I think we'll spend that X'mas together anyway!

I don't think I told you that Phyllis has got his own command at last thank God and I don't get the gnattering from morn to night. I haven't got a permanent new No 1 yet but I'm hoping he's an improvement - he can't be worse.

Darling do write lots and please think about me sometimes

All my love sweetest
Ever your
Don xxx

P.S. How about a photo for X'mas?
P.P.S. I love you

Coastal Force Base
Malta
17th November 1943
Air Letter No 38

My darling Linda

Still hoping for a letter from you and, as usual, I fear, still disappointed by its absence. And I'm afraid I haven't very much to write about except the inevitable reiteration that I love you, and that, I imagine, you fully realise. This sounds a horribly formal beginning but it isn't intended to be – fear I'm a little fed up with things generally tonight so perhaps you'll forgive me if and try and work it off!

Went ashore to the local cinema this evening – was Italian but the Army have taken it over – to see an old but quite amusing film "The Texas Rangers ride again" – Wild West up to date.

I've been reading through some of your old letters tonight. Do you realise how frightful we thought it when I went as far away as the Bristol Channel for a couple of weeks with the certainty of return to you at the end of that time. Now I've been stuck out in this bloody place for over a year and not a hope of seeing you for a further year. – all very depressing. Darling we will make up for it after that time. I'm never going to even let you out of my sight and there are so many things that we must do together – how about starting off with a tour of old English pubs – or wouldn't you approve?

To help things along there aren't even any Wrens or nurses in this dump – don't get the wrong idea as you've no conception of my righteousness since I've been abroad! Honest chum. But their company makes a pleasant change and I find myself becoming so churlish that I'm incapable of making myself pleasant to or of putting myself out at all for any of the girls I've met recently. It all sounds awfully bad but I shan't be like that when I return home. Perhaps you won't recognise me when I do get back – I'm told I look older and more serious (believe it or not!). But the others have changed. Dudley has lots of grey hairs and looks a good ten years older, Richard looks about 33 Gibby much the same but perhaps even redder faced. This all reads like a confession but it isn't. We've worked hard and honestly believe we have done a good job of work – anyway three invasions and follow ups isn't too bad.

I've just reread the letter this far – it sounds foul so I won't continue in that strain.

Linda darling you know how much I love you – it will always be the same and I just hope that you won't change your mind at any time. So far the only personally useful object the war has achieved is to help me meet you and even so I can't believe that, war or no war, we wouldn't have met anyway. It has made an unpleasant gap in our lives at a time when we should have been enjoying ourselves but fortunately we won't like some unfortunates, be too old to make up for it afterwards. Sweet I do love you more than anything in the world and I'm just living to come back to you.

All my love wretch
Write soon
Ever yours
Don xxx

P.S. The perfume and stockings have turned up again so I'll send them off once more.
P.P.S. Don't forget the photograph.

Sender: L. Russell
Amos House,
Totland Bay,
I.O.W.

Ringstead.
21st November 1943
4 a.m.

Lieut F. D. Bickerton, R.N.V.R.
Coastal Force Base
Malta

My darling Don,

I am feeling a completely different person since I received your air letter 36 (8th Nov), almost two months without a letter has been an awful worry, in point of fact if it hadn't been for your Mother's comforting words things would have been far worse.

I'm terribly sorry to hear you have been in hospital, somehow it is difficult to imagine you stopping in bed for any length of time! Seriously, what has been wrong? Quite an important point you know. I'm glad to hear you are back on board again, and do take great care of yourself.

Your Mother has suggested that I should visit her in the Spring, when the evenings are longer and the weather a little warmer, so, roll on the Spring (and the next 2 years). Guess what? – I'm going home for Christmas, of course it will be deadly dull but anything to get away from 'Camp do's', how well I remember last year and all those parties at the Picnic Inn, and coming off night watch finding my bed full of empty beer and whisky bottles. It will be much more fun at home having a few quick ones with Dad when Mother is not looking.

I can't think of anything more perfect than spending a lifetime with you, and soon after you arrive home a quiet holiday at a country pub is a terrific idea; I'm hoping it will be less than two years.

Darling you asked why I thought you'd be disappointed in me when you return, I was afraid that you were building me up in your mind as something big and wonderful, that's all chum. Looking forward very much to your letter and the lowdown on Dick, Gibby etc: - you might give them my love, any news of dear old Spotless?

Much love my darling,
Ever yours
Linda xxx

Coastal Force Base,
Malta.

30th November 1943
Air Letter No. 40

Cpl. L. Russell W.A.A.F.,
R.A.F. ~~Ringstead,~~ Branscombe
~~Near Dorchester,~~ Nr Sidmouth
~~Dorsetshire,~~ DEVON ENGLAND

My darling Linda

I've just received your cable and I fear that I can't cable a reply as no facilities exist where I am at the moment. However I imagine that you have now received the letters and cable I sent when I was last in Malta and that I'm forgiven – I hope. Wretch you are naughty to worry about me as you know that there are times when it's impossible to write – please sweet don't as you know, in spite of your nasty insinuations to the contrary, that I can take care of myself. And of course it was rather a shock to find that in spite of the cable there was no letter from you in the pile of mail we received. Darling I know that I've been bad recently but I do write as often as is possible so please <u>please</u> <u>please</u> write as often as you can, your letters make life worth living.

There doesn't seem to be much that's worth recording. Got a new suit from Gieves the other day just in case I go home in the reasonably near future otherwise you'd wonder who the scarecrow was when you saw me (and I don't want any cracks!).

I ran across Max the other day and had quite a party ashore and then went on to a dance where we found exactly two other people – both males! Good thing there was a bar. Max is much the same as ever and his tendency towards exaggeration shows no apparent sign of decreasing – still I always divide by ten.

I had a letter from Mother in which she said she had heard from you – she seems to feel much better these days and is quite optimistic about the nearness of the end of the war in Europe – I wish I could believe it.

My new No 1 has now turned up and is a very good type quite different to Phyllis fortunately. We seem to have quite a number of things in common so that life on board has taken a turn for the better. MacInnes turned up last night and we had quite a party although with the present shortage of hootch they don't compare with the old days at home. Did I hear you say "Thank God for that"?

Sweetest the only thing I really want to say in my letters to you in that I love you more than anything in the world. The time when I will come home to you is getting closer but I begrudge every moment that I spend away from you. Darling I do so want to be with you and promise never to leave you again when I do get back. But promise me one thing. Don't ask me to go for a cruise in the Med. after the war – I've had it!

Do write lots Linda darling just the three words I love you is all I want. I miss you like hell pet but as you say we can and will make up for it – in fact you'd better get in training for it now (don't let that low mind of yours place the wrong interpretation on that).

I'll write again as soon as I can and if there are gaps please don't worry darling as I promise you I'll be O.K. – I have to be as I've quite made up my mind to come home to you.

All my love Linda sweetest
I'll never change
Ever your
Don xxx

P.S. Don't forget the photo.

Coastal Force Base,
Malta.

6th December 1943
Air Letter No. 41

Cpl. L. Russell W.A.A.F.,
R.A.F. ~~Ringstead,~~ Branscombe
~~Near Dorchester,~~ Nr Sidmouth
~~Dorsetshire,~~ DEVON ENGLAND

My darling Linda

No word from you since you last wrote but for that matter we haven't had any mail at all – should be quite a collection when it arrives (I always get that idea and it usually turns out to contain one or less from you!)

I haven't done much since I last wrote (seems to be a lot of repetition) as any time in harbour has been spent in places calculated to make one stay on the ship, which from most points of view is quite a good thing. Neither have I had any parties, in fact just the sort of existence of which you approve. All right chum I ain't being nasty but life has been and still is dreadfully dull. What annoys me even more is that all this time might have been spent together – as it is God what a waste. It's all very well to speak and write of the time we'll have together in the future, what I want is to be with you now as well as then. I hope I'm not being too dreadfully dismal but I do love you so very much that any time spent apart from you seems quite valueless. I know now that I should have taken the chance that was offered and stayed at home – I certainly won't have the same qualms in the future. My time here is occupied thinking of you and dreaming of our next meeting – darling it's so difficult to put into words but it all boils down to the fact that I love you so very much. I'd give anything to be able to put the clock back to September 42 and keep it there permanently – I've never been so happy as I was then but next time things will be even better as I shan't have to leave you to go abroad and you, I hope, will have finished with uniform – especially that too, too divine cap! No wonder you usually carried it.

I've often asked you where you would prefer to live after we're married but I don't think you have replied to date. So far as I know my job will be in London although that depends largely on developments in the M of H in the latter stages of the war. Personally I like London but that is principally, I think, because most of my friends are there. Anyway I leave it to you for bigger and better ideas.

It shakes me to think that X'mas is almost here and that for once it's going to be a pretty dry one – nary a drop of whisky or gin on the ship. Anyway it looks as though it will probably be spent at sea so I suppose it really couldn't matter less.

I haven't seen Dick or Gibby or anyone else for some little time now and I must admit that I miss their cheerful company. Dudley should by this time have joined his new ship and is probably engaged in knocking down every quay between the Atlantic and the Red Sea!

Sweetest do write soon and <u>please</u> try and write more often – your letters mean everything to me.

There may be a short gap in my letters but I promise to write again as soon as I can.

All my love my darling
I'll never change
Ever your
Don xxx

P.S. xxxxxxxxxx for X'mas.   P.P.S Don't forget the photo.   P.P.P.S. I love you xxx D.

R.A.F. Branscombe
Salcombe Regis
Nr Sidmouth
S. Devon
25th December 1943

Lieut F. D. Bickerton, R.N.V.R.
Coastal Force Base
Malta

My darling Don,

Very many thanks for your air letter dated 30th November and I'm hoping there are a few more on the way. Sorry about the cable but as I hadn't heard for 2 months, I had every right to be anxious (consider yourself squashed).

I've been in hospital for 10 days with influenza & bronchitis and, just as I was recovering and looking forward to my Christmas leave at home, my posting came through. This place doesn't compare with Ringstead, I would give almost anything to be back there, darling you have no idea how miserable I am, no more S.O.Ps home and to my sister's home in Bournemouth. Here I am complaining and you, poor dear, have been away for fifteen months. Now I have just heard I'm to go on an admin course (2 weeks) at Wing on New Year's Eve!

Darling, I will let you have a photo as soon as I can get to Exeter, as apparently there is not a decent photographer in Sidmouth. We are on a three watch system (which is killing me) and I haven't had an opportunity to get away. Can't you possibly let me have some snaps (just want to make sure you haven't grown a beard!) please do if there is a chance. I'll try and send you snaps as they are more natural than the other things – how I loathe posing.

I hope you are having a lovely Christmas, lots of dances, parties etc. – but not too much to drink, please write soon and tell me about it. I wonder what you'll be doing New Year's Eve, last year you were out at sea.

Poor old Mr Dudley Arnaud thinking he would be home for Christmas, what a shocking disappointment. Nice work Gibby taking his place, please give him my love (I bet old bad type Gibby is not enjoying life without wrens and nurses!!), and I hope his other ring will be up the next time I see him. By the way, have you received the letter in which I told you that A.M. are not commissioning W.A.A.F supervisors in this racket, apparently they have enough – so there ain't no future in it.

All my love darling
Linda xxx

Cont'd on next air letter
I'll never change

P.S. Have you received my two parcels?

H.M.M.L. 338
c/o G.P.O.

30th December 1943
Air Letter No. 43

CPL. LINDA RUSSELL W.A.A.F.,
R.A.F. ~~RINGSTEAD,~~ BRANSCOMBE
~~NR DORCHESTER,~~ NR SIDMOUTH Devon
~~Dorsetshire,~~ S. DEVON
ENGLAND

Linda darling

No I'm not tight it's just that I've damaged my right hand and I can't write with it –
don't laugh! Many thanks for your letter of 21/11 and your airgraph but I hope you
won't mind me not replying properly until I can do rather better than this.
This year is nearly over and next year with any luck I hope to be with you again.
Please don't be angry if I finish now as I just can't compete.
Sweet I do love you so very much – please write often.

All my love angel
I'll always be your
Don
xxxxx

P.S. Happy New Year for us together.
P.P.S. Will you use the boat as address as mail seems to be going adrift.

Chapter Nine

JANUARY – MAY 1944

Following the successful Allied invasion of Italy in September 1943, American and British forces advanced in a north westerly direction towards Rome but the Germans set up a number of defensive lines. Eventually, they forced their way through the first of these, the Volturno Line, in mid-October and, in early November, they broke through the Barbara Line. In early December, the German troops fell back to the Bernhardt Line in the west and the Gustav Line in the east. Bad weather and fierce German resistance resulted in heavy casualties on both sides and it was not until mid-January 1944 that the Germans retreated in the west to the Gustav Line, which was in the vicinity of Cassino (about 85 miles from Rome). There then ensued a stalemate.

In an effort to break the stalemate, a plan was hatched by the Allies to launch a seaward invasion behind the Gustav Line to break the German defences. It was decided that the location for Operation Shingle would be at Anzio just 40 miles south of Rome and an attack took place on 22nd January 1944. Initially there was little resistance and, by midnight, 36,000 men landed and secured a beachhead 2-3 miles deep. Rather than press their advantage, the invading force dug in to protect the beachhead from attack. This delay gave the Germans the time they needed to regroup and, although the Allies then made additional advances inland, in early February the Germans were able to launch a counter attack with superior forces. Fighting through February resulted in heavy losses for the Allies and a stalemate again as the Germans set up the Caesar Defensive Line between Anzio and Rome (see **Map G**, over the page).

The first surviving letter of 1944 is Linda's, dated **2nd February 1944**, from *RAF Branscombe* near Sidmouth, saying that it is weeks since she has received a communication from Don. She has heard about his damaged right hand from his mother, so his letter to her of 30th December 1943 has obviously not yet arrived. She asks whether he can get someone to write and let her know what has happened. She is worried that he has changed his mind about their relationship.

Don writes on **5th February** (air letter No. 45, so air letter No. 44 has not survived). He announces that his hand is much better and he thanks her for the writing case and her letter of Christmas Day 1943, but he can only confirm receipt of one of the two parcels she sent. He says he is jealous of Dudley who is home on six weeks' leave before taking up a posting as training commander at Fort William. It is not until the third paragraph of his letter that Don mentions that he has been involved in the Anzio landings, and he points out that his ship (*ML 338*) is the only Coastal Forces vessel to take part in all four major landings (North Africa, Sicily, Salerno and Anzio). He finishes his letter by reporting that he had a quiet Christmas but there had been a New Year's party ashore. He spent the evening dancing with an English girl who was married to an Italian. He hastily adds that he cannot raise any enthusiasm for another as he just wants to be with Linda, although he warns her not to suggest a Mediterranean cruise for their honeymoon or foul murder might ensue!

MAP G

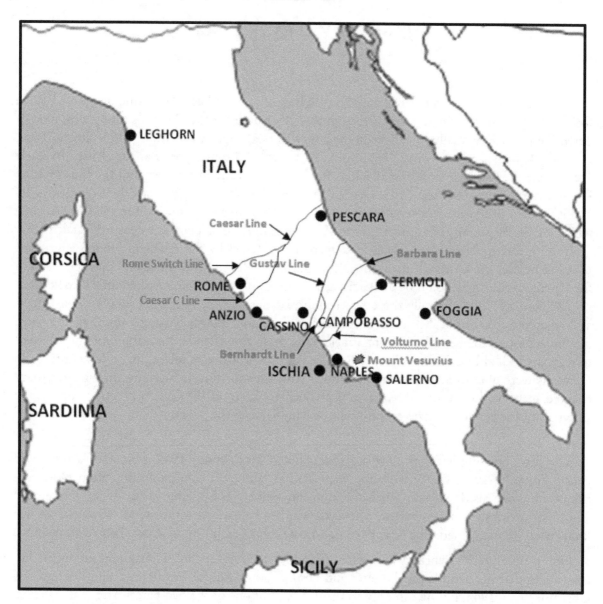

He next writes on **12th February 1944** (air letter No. 46). He comments that he had not thought that it would be a week before he would be able to write again, and he has no idea how long it will be before he is able to post it. The weather has been so bad that he had thought that they might capsize. He acknowledges that reports on the land fight from Anzio are not encouraging, although his old ship *HMS Mauritius* has been bombarding the enemy. He says that, at the time of writing, they are "in a harbour of sorts" (possibly a temporary harbour established as part of the invasion). He completes the letter two days later, saying that they had to leave the harbour temporarily and they are due to go out again that night – but not before having dinner in the mess that they have set up in one of the local hotels. He says that the "base wallahs" initially had not wanted the crews in their mess but that they have subsequently decided that the crews' mess is better. His letter ends in a familiar way saying how he yearns to be with Linda and how they should get married as soon as possible upon his return.

Don writes a few lines on **14th February**, enclosing photographs of a local spot he has visited. He says it is not as pleasant as the images suggest, stating: "give me England every time".

His next proper letter is dated **17th February 1944** (air letter No. 47). In it, he acknowledges receipt of Linda's of 2nd February (see above) and scolds her for thinking he might change his mind about their relationship. He reveals that he has just returned from the most unpleasant job he has had to undertake all through the war, as it entailed being only about a mile off the enemy shore batteries by themselves and in broad daylight. Although under fire, fortunately they did not take any direct hits. He says that the main topic of discussion on board is how to devise ways and means of getting home, after Dudley's success. He suggests that Linda should meet up with Dudley to get "the lowdown on everything".

Three days later, in his air letter No. 48, he reports that things have been pretty quiet. That afternoon he has watched a game of football between his crew and the local team but, after he had left, the locals walked off in a huff after a penalty was awarded against them.

Sub-Lieutenant Nixon describes an incident that occurred on 22nd February 1944, during the Anzio operation when *ML 565*, his own *ML 554* and Don's *ML 338* were carrying out an H formation exploratory sweep up the coast from Anzio. Initially helped by a smoke screen laid by the destroyers, they made their way up the coast towards the Tiber. As they turned for the last leg of the sweep, a shell landed just alongside Don's *ML 338*. She was immediately observed to increase to full speed, the sweeps leaping from the sea and dancing on the surface. She sensibly dropped a smoke float. As *ML 554* then altered course another shell landed in the water a little way away and she cleared out at full speed. Nixon reports that *ML 565* nonchalantly maintained her progress before coming under the German gunners' sights. They were then ordered back to Naples and moored next to two destroyers for two days. During the second evening (23rd February), there was a vicious air raid and Sub-Lieutenant Nixon was hit in the leg by shrapnel and had to be carried across the other MLs and destroyers, which were lying alongside one another, before being transported to hospital where he underwent an operation. The hospital was bombed in a previous raid and a sister had been killed. Nixon describes seeing Army battlefield casualties being brought into the hospital and deciding that he had been right to volunteer for the Navy.

He was still in hospital a month later when Mount Vesuvius erupted (see Don's description in his letter of 21st March). Subsequently Nixon went to Ischia to recuperate, during which time his promotion to Lieutenant came through with the relevant increase in pay.

Don writes on **23rd February 1944** (air letter No. 49) and makes no mention of either incident. Even if he wanted to worry Linda, he would have been unable relate these events owing to censorship. He has spent the last couple of days in harbour (Naples) and, although he has had a quiet time, tonight is guest night at the mess and he plans to enjoy himself. His coxswain managed to get permission to keep another animal, which is only a month old and rather sweet. He says that, judging by the papers he receives, people at home are confident that the war in Europe will end in 1944. Although he does not disagree, he thinks that they overlook the fact that there will be a lot of fighting and casualties. He predicts that: "when we actually invade Northern Europe they will face realities and indulge in a little less wishful thinking." He says that where he is, whilst people are confident of eventual victory, Anzio has shown them that, even after initial success, setbacks can occur. Their main worry is whether they will get any leave before being sent to the Far East. On that serious note, there is a two-day pause before he completes the letter as he had been persuaded to go ashore to the mess. He regards the evening as amusing because there were two ENSA (Entertainments National Service Association) girls there with a dozen naval officers dancing attendances on each of them and a new paymaster Lieutenant who was debagged. Since then he has been at sea but has had to return owing to the inclement weather.

Don (2nd row, 4th from left) on *ML 338* with crew

Linda writes from *RAF Branscombe* on **26th February 1944**, having just received Don's letter of 12th February together with a photograph which has cheered her enormously. She has recently returned from her usual nine days leave. She says that, when on shift, activities include lectures, gardening and drill. She does not enjoy the latter because, as a corporal, she is expected to shriek at her female subordinates. She wonders if Don remembers nearby Sidmouth, as his mother tells her that they once holidayed there. She says that fortunately the town has two cinemas, but on her next 36-hour off-duty spell she is hoping to visit Exeter and look for a decent photographer.

She speculates that the war will not last much longer as the Germans are having a "darned good hiding" and it is just a matter of time before their collapse.

Don sends photographs of himself on **1ˢᵗ March 1944** and writes just a few lines to accompany them.

On **14ᵗʰ March 1944** (air letter No. 51), Don acknowledges receipt of her letter of 26ᵗʰ February and responds to comments she made about his photograph. He jokes: "yes we have no bananas" (a song from the 1920s). He mocks her for complaining that she only has 36 hours off every eight days, saying that she should consult her solicitor – and for having to take squad drill. He says he has not visited Sidmouth with his parents, only passed through, and he prefers North Devon. He again ends with dreams of a quick end to the war and marriage.

With a short note to be sent by air, he encloses a photograph of himself with his crew on **19ᵗʰ March 1944**. He promises to write properly that evening.

However, in his letter dated **21st March 1944** (air letter No. 52) he admits that (contrary to what he had promised two days earlier) he actually went ashore to see the film *Reunion in France*, showing at a hotel taken over by the Americans as a rest camp. He said some of the "yanks" then insisted on them having numerous sidecars (cognac or bourbon based cocktails) and eventually they had a 3-mile walk back to the boats.

Despite filthy weather with gales and wind, he describes the eruption of Vesuvius (17ᵗʰ-23ʳᵈ March) as being a magnificent sight. Smoke is pouring from the crater some hundreds of feet into the air, and at night it is vividly red with streams of lava pouring down the mountain. However, he speaks of the poor unfortunates who live on the slopes and has heard that several villages have been evacuated and one already engulfed. (In fact some 20 people died, either as their houses were crushed by the weight of ash or through asphyxiation. Vesuvius is some 5 miles to the south east of Naples, which is about 150 miles down the coast from Anzio.)

Mount Vesuvius erupting in 1944 by unknown member of 12th *USAAF*, 340th bomb group [public domain], via *Wikimedia Commons*

Considering the detailed description Don gives of the eruption then perhaps, two months after the Anzio landings, he is now based considerably south of Anzio. He pointedly says that he has received several letters from his mother but none from Linda. He again suggests that she should overcome her shyness and visit his parents in Liverpool. He thinks it a good idea that she should go to Exeter and have her photograph taken.

Don next writes on **10th April 1944** (air letter No. 53) apologising for not having written for three weeks and saying he has been patiently awaiting a letter from Linda, the last being dated 26th February. He says he is so worried. He is currently spending a week in a rest camp on the island of Ischia (about 15 miles south west of Naples) and enjoying both the relaxation and the delightful lack of responsibility. It is his first break in the 18 months since he had left Britain. His thoughts then drift to the week he had spent with Linda in Tenby and he repeats how he longs to be home with her. Over half of his original crew have already returned home and a further two are awaiting reliefs. He jokes that maybe someone is pushing his relief around in a pram. He has been out walking, but they are unable to play tennis owing to a shortage of balls. He asks whether she has received the additional £14 for the engagement ring.

S Angelo, Ischia by *ischiahotel.net* [public domain], from *Wikimedia Commons*

He writes again, from the rest camp, on **12th April 1944** (air letter No. 54). He says that Ischia is famed for its mineral baths, so he and Dickie have tried them and then four of them visited a hotel run by a Swiss. In the evening they had gone to another hotel on the front, also run by a Swiss, but they did not take to the RAF crowd there. That night is to be their last there and, being Dickie's wife's birthday, that gives them an excuse for celebration. He asks Linda to write as often as possible and to go to Exeter for a photograph.

Linda writes on about **22nd April 1944** (the removal of the stamp when the air letter was folded has left a number of holes and the date is not fully legible) acknowledging that she has received Don's letters of 10th and 12th April, written from Ischia. As requested by him, she has forwarded the photographs of him and his crew to his mother but says that it will not be possible to visit Liverpool just now. She comments on his mineral bath and is pleased he is getting some rest. She assures him that she is missing him and, on his return, will never leave him. However, she has not received the £14.

Don corresponds next on **30th April 1944** but seems to have abandoned his numbering system. Her letter of 22nd April had arrived on the previous day. Ken is in hospital and will be returning to the UK. His relief, whom Don has not yet met, is a brand new Sub-Lieutenant from home. After abstaining from parties for a while, one developed in the mess two evenings earlier and he suffered a hangover the next day. He reminds Linda of the parties during their last week in Falmouth. He finishes by saying that he is hopeful of returning home later in the year and that they will marry as soon as possible. (His assumption was wide of the mark as he would not return until July 1945.)

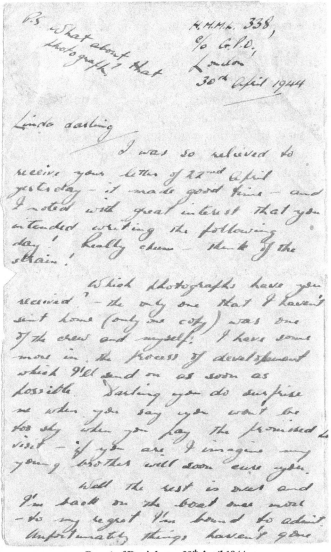

Page 1 of Don's letter 30th April 1944

Since the Allies had repelled a German counter attack near Cisterna (13 miles inland from Anzio) at the end of February, the stalemate would continue until May 1944. However, on 11th May the Allies launched Operation Diadem. As part of this major offensive two further plans were devised, with Operation Buffalo commencing on 23rd May 1944, followed by Operation Turtle. Lack of coordination allowed large elements of the enemy to retreat north but, by 2nd June, the German defences had completely collapsed, and on 4th June the Allies entered Rome. Although casualties were high – with 7,000 Allies killed and 26,000 wounded or missing; and with 5,000 Germans killed, 30,000 wounded or missing and 5,000 captured – the initiative could not prevent deployment of German troops to repel the Normandy landings, which commenced on D-Day, 6th June 1944.

These operations, being inland, do not require significant naval involvement, and Don's next surviving letter (letters no longer numbered) is dated **27th May 1944**, whilst these battles are ongoing. He acknowledges Linda's mailing of 10th May (missing). He is back in the rest camp on the island of Ischia, which he says is the only place in the Mediterranean that he would care to visit after the war. He says that the puppy in the photograph of his crew that he had sent her (not the photograph on page 174), had become sick and had to be destroyed. He admits he would love to have Spotless (*ML 280*'s original dog) with him. The weather is perfect, but he is covered in insect bites. He says that he has heard from Dudley, who never secured command of a corvette. Instead, he is in charge of another flotilla (presumably MLs) on the South Coast. He says the letter had been re-censored – "must be that invasion feeling". He says that his colleagues are wondering whether they will be doing anything at the same time as the "push across the Channel". From his comments, it sounds as though D-Day (6th June 1944) is widely anticipated. He also reports that Richard has gone home.

Letters:
January – May 1944

Sender: Linda Russell
Amos House,
Totland. I.W.

R.A.F. Branscombe,
Nr Sidmouth
S. Devon

2nd February 1944

Lieut F. D. Bickerton,
R.N.V.R.
H.M.M.L. 338
c/o G.P.O. London

Darling,

What has happened to you? It is weeks since I've heard and now your mother has told me that you have hurt your hand, and a change of address. Can't you possibly ask someone to write and tell me what has happened. Also, I suggest at least three months' leave! Darling I do want to see you very soon just to make certain you haven't changed. If you have changed your mind for heavens' sake write and tell me.

Your mother is most frightfully worried about you. I only hope that you are not hurt badly and I've told her that if it were serious the Admiralty would have informed her by this time. It is so difficult to know what to think when you are so far away.

Did you have a pleasant Christmas & New Year? I'm longing to hear what you did and all about the parties - that is if you can remember!?! Are the old crowd still with you, apart from Dick & Dudley Arnaud? Don darling I am missing you so frightfully and I do want you to get back home soon - do you realise that its 15 months since you have been away, we will make up for it one day, won't we? And please don't leave me again.

Do write soon and tell me you haven't changed & please what about those photos you promised? I'll send some as soon as I can get away. All my love,

Yours as ever
Linda xxx

P.S. Excuse scribble but I'm writing in bed.

H.M.M.L. 338
c/o G.P.O.,
London

5th February 1944
Air Letter No 45

Cpl. Linda Russell W.A.A.F.,
R.A.F. Branscombe,
Salcombe Regis,
Nr Sidmouth,
South Devon,
England.

My darling Linda

As you can see the hand is now heaps better so perhaps I can write a proper letter once more instead of a peculiar looking pencilled note. Many thanks for the marvellous writing case and also for your letter of 25th Dec (No – only one parcel has turned up so far). Darling it was awfully sweet of you to take so much trouble and I do really appreciate it but you know quite well you shouldn't especially as things are so frightfully expensive these days. I feel very guilty at not sending you anything but unfortunately there's nothing here except a lot of cheap trash that's of no use to anyone – I'm hoping for better things from Rome!

Sweet please do take care of yourself – you seem to catch cold so easily – only wish I could get home to look after you.

You don't sound very pleased at your move to Salcombe Regis – I've never been there & imagine it must be rather quiet but I'd cheerfully swap it for this place. Still time marches on and now at the end of sixteen months I'm still trying to discover ways & means of getting home – thought my hand might be useful! – with no apparent success. Incidently Dudley didn't catch up his corvette and is now at home with six weeks leave and an appointment as training commander at Fort William – some people have all the luck.

As you may have guessed we were in the Anzio landing and I've just discovered that this is the only Coastal Force boat which has taken part in the four major landings – but I don't suppose they'll send me home on those grounds.

Phyllis has managed to get some photos developed and he has promised to let me have some copies next time I contact him. I'm sorry it's been so long but it's rather difficult to get things done when you don't know how long you're going to stay in any one place.

Christmas was quiet, in fact I stayed on the ship but I had rather a good New Year's party ashore – spent most of the evening dancing with an English girl who is married to an Italian – but frankly wretch I just can't work up any enthusiasm for anyone or anything at the moment. You know that all I want is to be with you again – I love you so very much my darling; don't dare suggest a Med. Cruise for our honeymoon or there will be foul murder done in the family forth with.

Write as often as you can please sweet – I miss you so much.

All my love
Ever yours
Don xxx

H.M.M.L. 338
c/o G.P.O., London

12th February 1944
Air Letter No 46

Cpl. Linda Russell W.A.A.F.,
R.A.F. Branscombe,
Salcombe Regis,
Near Sidmouth,
South Devon,
ENGLAND.

My darling Linda

I'd no idea that it would be a week before I was able to write to you again and even now I've no idea when I'll be able to get this one away. I'm longing to get back to base to see if there are any letters from you and in the remote possibility of me being disappointed there's going to be more trouble than that!

The weather here has been filthy (thought we were about to turn over the other night) and the news from Anzio is not encouraging. However I hear on the radio tonight that my old ship "Mauritius" has been bombarding – we never quote facts, purely hearsay!!!

Actually we are in a harbour of sorts at the moment, in fact it was so miserable outside that I had horrible visions of hitting the rocks in the driving rain that I thought that we might not make it at all – as usual we made it!

My motor mechanic has just been down to tell me in no uncertain terms just how he feels about the sunny Med. – and I can't help but agree with him.

Darling this letter is horribly full of complaints and I don't feel that way at all. I suppose it's just that I want to be home with you again – I do miss you so much sweetheart.

<u>14/2/44</u>
I'm afraid we had to go out and that was as far as I could get and, unfortunately, we are away again tonight. I was hoping when I arrived in harbour this morning to receive stacks of mail but I fear we were all disappointed. Do please write as often as you can wretch as your letters cheer me incredibly.

I'm away to have dinner at the Mess before we sail. We've taken over one of the Hotels here, as the base wallahs didn't care to have us in their Mess (we're too noisy!) and find we can enjoy ourselves rather more without them. Now, of course, they find it far better than their own and want to come into ours.

Sixteen months away from you darling and it seems more like sixteen years – I'm just living for the day when we can be together once more and I reckon the first thing we do is get married as soon as possible, preferably without the presence of Coastal Force types otherwise I can see it degenerating into what has been misnamed a party. Sweetest I love you more than anything in the world and I intend to make up for the time we have been forced to spend apart. Please don't ever change my angel – I want you to be just as you were when we were together last (although not quite so bad tempered as one night I remember in Falmouth).

All my love my darling
Ever yours
Don xxx

P.S. I won't get a chance to write home tonight – would you let them know I'm O.K.

14th February 1944

Cpl. Linda Russell W.A.A.F.,
R.A.F. Branscombe,
Salcombe Regis,
Near Sidmouth,
South Devon,
ENGLAND.

Linda darling

One spot we visited and found quite pleasant but not so pleasant as the photos suggest.
In fact give me England every time.

All my love,
Ever your own
Don xxx

H.M.M.L. 338
c/o G.P.O.,
London

17th February 1944
Air Letter No 47

Cpl. Linda Russell W.A.A.F.,
R.A.F. Branscombe,
Salcombe Regis,
Near Sidmouth,
South Devon,
ENGLAND.

My darling Linda

Your letter of 2nd February arrived this morning. Sweetest why do you keep asking if I've changed my mind? You must surely know by now that it's quite impossible for my feelings to alter at all and that I'm wholly and completely yours. I spend all my time thinking of you and of the day when we will be together once more. Please don't ever doubt me angel – I know there are sometimes gaps between my letters to you but that is circumstance and not choice (talking of gaps incidentally, 2nd Feb is quite some time from Dec 25th – or does this racket only work one way?)

We've just got back from the most unpleasant job I've had to do this war as it entailed being only about a mile off enemy shore batteries by ourselves and in daylight at that. Jerry didn't like it much and opened up with an accuracy which was quite shaking. Fortunately we didn't get any direct hits but sister were my knees shaking! Next time I imagine they'll want us to sail up the Tiber and capture Rome singlehanded.

Did you not receive the letter I attempted to write when my hand was damaged? – I wrote at the same time as I wrote home. And you haven't told me if the photograph arrived.

I'm not sure that I altogether like the remark "if I can remember" what happened over Christmas and the New Year. However, as I have already given you the dope, I trust you are duly penitent!

Do I realise that it's sixteen months since I saw you? Darling it seems even longer than that and I promise that when I do get back I'll never leave you again. It is so heartbreaking to think that this is time that could have been spent together instead of which I'm stuck out here and feeling pretty miserable about it. Our main topic of discussion these days is devising ways and means of getting home – Dudley is the only one to have met with any success to date.

Why don't you drop a line and arrange to see him – he can give you the lowdown on everything (but behave yourself – I'd trust that guy only as far as I could see him!).

Sweet do write lots as your letters are so very important. You know I love you terribly and that I'll never change except perhaps to love you even more – if that were possible.

All my love Linda darling
Ever your
Don xxx

P.S. I do miss you so much pet.

H.M.M.L. 338
c/o G.P.O.,
London

20th February 1944
Air Letter No 48

Cpl. Linda Russell W.A.A.F.,
R.A.F. Branscombe,
Salcombe Regis,
Nr Sidmouth,
South Devon,
England.

My darling Linda

Nothing really to write about but I seem to get such awful bother if I don't write every time I'm in harbour that I just don't dare take the chance!

Actually things have been pretty quiet since I last wrote and in spite of my threats to go ashore and get tight on that evening I had a most sedate evening. I did go to the mess for dinner and although things began to develop, I suppose I just wasn't in a party mood so I came back on board and read N.S. & N. – mental uplift!

This afternoon I've walked and also watched an alleged game of football between my blokes and the local team – now I hear that after I left a penalty was awarded against the locals so they walked off the field in a huff. We live and learn.

I've today received a letter from Mother in which she tells me she hasn't heard from me for a month. Are you receiving my letters? – if not will you please let me know which numbers are adrift and I'll try and make inquiries from this end. I intend writing home again tonight but nevertheless I should be grateful if you would inform them that all is well.

I am missing you so much my darling, I only wish I'd had Dudley's good fortune and landed a shore job at Fort William – perhaps I should write and suggest that he needs officers with plenty of operational experience (too much in fact!) on his staff and that I would be admirably suited to fill the bill. I hear that one of your bright suggestions to account for my apparent lack of correspondence was that I was on my way home. I hate to disillusion you but I fear that, for the moment at any rate, it has no basis in fact. You know quite well how much I love you angel and I'm living for the day when I can again be with the sweetest girl in the world and the only one I can ever love. I promise you my angel that I'll never change and believe it or not will be quite faithful to you – and I don't want any cracks.

Please write as often as you can pet as there are invariably gaps of a month or more between your letters.

All my love my darling, I'm always thinking of you

Ever yours
Don xxx

H.M.M.L. 338
c/o G.P.O.,
London

23rd February 1944
Air Letter No 49

Cpl. Linda Russell W.A.A.F.,
R.A.F. Branscombe,
Salcombe Regis,
Near Sidmouth,
South Devon,
ENGLAND.

My darling Linda

I was hoping to hear from you with this mail but no luck so far – darling please write more often as it's ages since I heard from you and your letters do mean so much.

I've spent the last couple of days in harbour but nevertheless have had a very quiet time – actually stayed on board and we ain't got us hootch on board either! Tonight however it's guest night at the mess and I think some relaxation is indicated – that doesn't mean, as I've no doubt you're thinking, that I'm going to get tight – very sober type these days!

We seem to be acquiring dogs these days. The cox'n has just been down to get permission to keep another animal that might be almost anything – however he's only a month old and really rather sweet.

Judging by the papers I receive people at home are very confident that the war in Europe will end this year. I don't disagree with them but they seem to forget that there is quite a lot of fighting to be done yet and that quite a number of people will be killed – perhaps when we actually invade Northern Europe they will face realities and indulge in a little less wishful thinking. Out here we I suppose are also confident of victory this year but we have also seen how sticky things can become even after initial success viz Anzio. Perhaps our main worry is whether or not we will get home for leave before going on to the Far East – I hope we shall but I'm not too sure that everyone will.

25/2/44

Well that was as far as I got as all the bods came down and whistled me away to the mess. It was quite amusing, for example there were two Ensa girls there with at least a dozen naval officers dancing attendance on each of them (not including me I may say!) and a new paymaster lieutenant who was debagged during the course of the evening. Since then I've been at sea but the weather was too filthy for words so I've come in.

Linda darling I miss you so very much but perhaps it won't be too long before I can come home to you. Sixteen months at this time in our young lives makes quite a gap but fortunately we aren't too old to make up for it. I love you a hell of a lot wretch and when this miserable business is all over I promise never to leave you again – you must know that life without you would be completely unbearable. Please write soon and tell me that you still love me as much as I do you.

All my love angel
Ever your
Don xxx

<u>Sender</u>: Cpl. L. Russell W.A.A.F.
Amos House,
Totland. I.W.

Nr Sidmouth
S. Devon

26th February 1944
Night watch

Lieut F. D. Bickerton,
R.N.V.R.
H.M.M.L. 338
c/o G.P.O. London

My darling Don,

Your air letter dated 12th February arrived yesterday afternoon, also a photo of 31st December (43) which has cheered me enormously, what fun! Are there any bananas in the basket and are you holding a cauliflower? I imagine you were wearing much lighter clothes.

I returned from leave a few days ago and at the moment 'life ain't too bright'. As usual I spent a quiet 9 days at home and lots of early nights. Life here is so different from Ringstead, one free 36 every eight days instead of four, during our working 36 we have lectures, gardening and horrid drill, (which I loathe & detest & unfortunately have to take - can you imagine me shrieking at women!) – I usually take them for a walk instead.

Your Mother told me that she spent a holiday down here years ago, which possibly meant that you were with her. Perhaps you remember Sidmouth? a tiny little place with two cinemas, fortunately. I'm hoping to go to Exeter on my next 36, and I'll look for a decent photographer. In the meantime I must find, someone with a camera; you must ignore the uniform though! Darling, surely this war can't go on much longer. The Germans are having a darned good hiding. I suppose now it is just a matter of time before the final collapse!

It is almost eighteen months since you have been away, and as you say more like eighteen years but just wait until you come back, you'll be seeing <u>too</u> much of me. I'm dying to meet your Mother. If I can't get up to see her before you come back then I suggest we both do so immediately you arrive in England. You must meet my parents, they have seen your photos, and were amused at the latter!

Darling, I love you so much, please come back as soon as you've finished your job. I swear I'll never change.

Write soon,
Ever yours,
Linda xx

H.M.M.L. 338
c/o G.P.O.,
London

1st March 1944

My darling Linda

You asked for it – so now you can see the worst! I know they're perfectly appalling but facing into the wind isn't conducive to a happy smile. Denton has some better ones taken during the summer & I'm still awaiting copies.

All my love sweet
Ever yours
Don.

H.M.M.L. 338
c/o G.P.O.,
London

14th March 1944
Air Letter No 51

Cpl. Linda Russell W.A.A.F.,
R.A.F. Branscombe,
Salcombe Regis,
Near Sidmouth,
South Devon,
ENGLAND.

My darling Linda

I was greatly relieved to receive your letter of 26th February today – first for a month. Glad you liked the photos – yes it is a cauliflower and yes we have no bananas out here – you're getting mixed up with West Africa.

You are a lucky person managing to get home on leave, I wish I could have been with you – might have made it a little more hectic I reckon. You poor little thing – only 36 hours off every eight days. I should imagine that the best thing you can do is get your solicitor to write a strongly worded protest to the Air Ministry pointing out that should an immediate change not be effected questions will be asked in the House. Frankly my sweet I love the idea of you taking your dear little girls at squad drill – do you march in threes or fours?

No I wasn't with Mother when she visited Sidmouth but I remember that she quite liked the place. I have passed through but personally I prefer North Devon. Please don't forget the photograph darling, I am so looking forward to receiving it. I too hope the war won't go on very much longer as I'm more that fed up at being away from you for so long. My only hope is that when I do get home I shan't be sent out to the Far East. Precious do you _really_ think I can ever see too much of you? Please believe me when I say that you are the only girl I've ever fallen for in this way – and I've been around in my time! However I promise to be very faithful and in case your horrid mind thinks other things may I tactfully point out that I _have_ behaved for the last eighteen months. I miss you so much darling all I want in the world is to be back with you and never leave you again. As soon as I do get home we are going to get married and away to some small spot where there's no sign of the ocean. Or perhaps it would be more amusing to go to a port and leer at the blokes as they slip to go to sea!

Please write again soon my darling. All my love – I'm always thinking of you.

Ever your own
Don xxx

H.M.M.L. 338
c/o G.P.O.,
London.

19th March 1944

Linda darling

Here's a rather better snap of the crew and myself taken some little time ago. I'd be grateful if you could pass it home as it's the only copy I've been able to get.
I'm writing by air mail to you tonight.

All my love angel
Ever your
Don xxx

P.S. They are not quite the crowd of ruffians they appear.

HMML 338,
c/o G.P.O.,

21st March 1944
Air Letter No 52

Cpl. Linda Russell W.A.A.F.,
R.A.F., Branscombe,
Salcombe Regis,
near Sidmouth,
South Devon,
ENGLAND

Linda darling

'Fraid I didn't write the other night as I promised in my sea letter but someone inveigled me into going ashore to see a film. We actually got that far too - it's a hotel taken over by the Americans as a rest camp - and saw "Reunion in France" (Joan Crawford); it wasn't particularly good or bad. Then, of course, some of the Yanks insisted on us drinking numerous side cars - then we walked the three miles back to the boats! Still it was quite a change as we rarely go ashore these days and we haven't a drop of hootch on the ship (I wish you wouldn't cheer quite so loudly).

The weather is filthy, blowing a gale with a heavy sea running and in addition it's raining like hell. Vesuvius is a magnificent sight. Smoke is pouring from the crater for some hundreds of feet into the air, and at night it is vividly red with streams of molten lava pouring down the mountain. However I don't suppose the reaction of those unfortunates who live on the slopes is the same as mine as several villages have been evacuated and one already engulfed.

Had several letters from Mother the other day (none from you of course!) and everyone at home seems to be pretty fit. Why don't you go up and see them? They'd be delighted to meet you and I have explained what a shy little girl you are and that you probably need me there to give you the moral courage! All right chum I won't be sarcastic any more.

I've been considering going ashore tonight as I understand that there is a dance at some place or other although as dances they are usually a washout - 50 males per female or thereabouts.

What do you do with yourself in Sidmouth? - may I suggest that in your next 36 off you take yourself away to Exeter and have that photograph taken. - please

Darling I do miss you and the last eighteen months have been just so much a waste of time. Promise you'll never leave me when I do get home and I only hope that it won't be long now. I love you more than anything in the world wretch - without your photographs I don't know what to do. Please don't ever change my angel - I want things to be always as they were during the time we did spend together.

Write soon Linda darling

All my love - you are always in my thoughts

Ever yours
Don xxx

H.M.M.L. 338,
c/o G.P.O.,
London

10th April 1944
Air Letter No 53

Cpl. Linda Russell W.A.A.F.,
R.A.F. Branscombe,
Salcombe Regis,
Near Sidmouth,
South Devon,
ENGLAND.

My darling Linda

Sorry I haven't written for so long sweet but I've been patiently awaiting a letter from you – the last I received was about 26th February. Darling what is the trouble – I feel so worried please write as soon as you can. Mother tells me that she hasn't heard from you for some time. If you can send a cable please do so.

I'm spending a week at a Rest camp and really enjoying both the relaxation and delightful lack of responsibility – it's the first time for over eighteen months so I intend to make the best of it. The place itself is a hotel we have taken over and although it apparently specialised in taking invalids in peace time the cooking is far from good although we supply our own rations. However the villa and the island (Ischia) are wholly delightful and I'm thoroughly enjoying life – and, incidentally, trying desperately to catch up with my correspondence. There are several blokes with me whom I've known for some time so we've all decided that this is to be a rest – all parties are taboo. We've actually succeeded to date!

Darling I do miss you so and getting away from the boat and staying in a place like this reminds me so much of the marvellous week we had in Tenby. If you were here with me this place would be equally marvellous – although I think that goes for any place where we could be together. I love you more than everything else in the world put together and I still only live for the day to come when I can return home to you. It's quite incredible really that over half my original crew has already returned and a further two are awaiting reliefs – maybe someone is still pushing mine around in his pram!

We've been trying to organise some tennis so far with no success as balls are difficult to come by. Still I'm doing a fair amount of walking – not so pleasant as Tenby to Saundersfoot – and feel better than for months.

Please wretch write soon and don't forget the photograph – I'm trying to organise another one down here. I do so want you to tell me you still love me and that you'll never change – you know that I shan't.

All my love my sweetest
Ever your own
Don. xxx

P.S. Have you received the £14 – I don't think you've mentioned it in your letters.

H.M.M.L. 338,
c/o G.P.O.,
London

12th April 1944
Air Letter No 54

Cpl. Linda Russell W.A.A.F.,
R.A.F. Branscombe,
Salcombe Regis,
Near Sidmouth,
South Devon,
ENGLAND.

My darling Linda

Still at the Rest camp and still doing nothing except lie in bed most of the morning and sleep in a deckchair in the sun during the afternoon – in fact an ideal occupation!

The island is apparently famed for its mineral baths and, if one is to judge by its brochure, they cure anything from the common cold to (almost) anxiety neurosis. Dickie and I tried them yesterday with the result that today I have a cold and he has a hangover that can't even be put down to drink – maybe we'll sample the mud baths this afternoon and be sent home.

Before lunch we visited the hotel on the hill for a quick snifter. The proprietor, a Swiss, is a good type and insisted upon us trying his speciality which he aptly calls "Secret Service". It consists of very good pre-war Vermouth and few drops of something he makes himself but will certainly not tell us what it is – anyway the effect is innocuous. The folk staying there are a fairly surly bunch as our four very polite "Good Mornings" were completely ignored – or maybe we just look suspicious characters. Still we seem to get by!

Last night was just as quiet. We went to another hotel on the front, also run by a Swiss, in the hope of crashing a party of some sort. Instead there were a dreary crowd of R.A.F. blokes who just sat around and looked as the world were due to end – so negative party, instead another distressingly early night. I admit that this is a Rest camp but there is such a thing as carrying it to extremes. Tonight however is our last night – it's also Dickie's wife's birthday – so I think we must do something about it, in fact we're even skipping Guest Night at the Mess just to ensure that a good time will be had by all (they probably wouldn't approve of my new found passion for lemonade!).

Darling I do so wish you were here with me and life would again be quite perfect; I'm sure you'd love this spot, in fact the only one I've struck I'd care to visit after the war with you. I miss you more every day darling and I'll never leave you again once I can get home even if it means living in the wilderness of the Highlands. Please write as often as you can – I promise that I will and please don't forget that visit to Exeter for the photograph.

Incidentally wretch I should be grateful if you could send the photo of the crew etc on to Mother as I can't get another copy.

All my love my angel
Ever your own
Don xxx

P.S. I love you.

Cpl. L. Russell
Branscombe

22nd April 1944
[date not fully legible]

Lieut F. D. Bickerton,
R.N.V.R.
H.M.M.L. 338
c/o G.P.O. London

My darling Don,

I've just received your two letters dated 10th & 12th April which came as a great surprise as it is sometime since I've heard from you.

Have written to your Mother enclosing the photographs you mentioned, actually, I intended forwarding them to her – she will be thrilled. It isn't possible to get away just now but I will slip up and see her later, and I might mention that I'm really too shy!

Darling, I'm so pleased you are enjoying your rest somehow I can't imagine you're (without me!) spending such a lazy time. Damn funny about your mineral baths, I really mean about catching cold so easily, I imagine you either stopped in too long or you are slightly out of practice! Anyway, I don't advise a mud bath!

The island sounds perfect – it <u>must</u> be nice if you would care to visit it after the war – how I'd adore to be with you, wouldn't it be heavenly?

I'm thankful that you have all decided to have a rest and no parties, very sensible. Quite frankly I don't know how you manage to cope with so many parties. Remember our last week together consisted of numerous excuses for celebration – nearly killed me!

Darling, I do miss you so much and when you come home <u>I'm</u> not leaving you. So please hurry back so that we can settle down & live a normal life.

All my love darling
Ever yours
Linda xxx

P.S. I haven't received the money you mentioned, perhaps you should make enquiries soon.
P.S. Writing again tomorrow [illegible]. I'm a little [illegible] night watch.

H.M.M.L. 338
c/o G.P.O.,
London

30th April 1944

Cpl. Linda Russell W.A.A.F.,
R.A.F. Branscombe,
Salcombe Regis,
Nr Sidmouth,
South Devon,
England.

Linda darling

I was so relieved to receive your letter of 22nd April yesterday – it made good time – and I noted with great interest that you intended writing the following day! Really chum – think of the strain!

Which photographs have you received? – the only one that I haven't sent home (only one copy) was one of the crew and myself. I have some more in the process of development which I'll send on as soon as possible. Darling you do surprise me when you say you won't be too shy when you pay the promised visit – if you are I imagine my young brother will soon cure you.

Well the rest is over and I'm back on the boat once more – to my regret I'm bound to admit. Unfortunately things haven't gone too well as Ken is in hospital and will probably return to the U.K. His relief, who hasn't yet put in an appearance, is a brand new Sub from home so it looks almost as if I shall have to do some work.

Well I kept my resolution to have no parties until the night before last when what had every appearance of a quiet night in the Mess developed for no apparent reason, into a really hectic party. It was pretty fair while it lasted but my head next morning suggested that it lasted rather too long. So now I'm back on orange juice again amongst howls of mirth from some of my so called friends. However we certainly haven't come up or do you prefer descended to the standard of the parties during our last week in Falmouth – when, incidentally, I stayed remarkably sober apart from that first night. Alright chum I wouldn't make cracks at you!

Angel all that I want to hear is that you miss me as much as I'm missing you and believe me you won't get a chance to leave me – my middle name will be leech from now onwards. I love you so very much darling and I'm feeling quite hopeful about returning to you this year – I can at any rate bank on leave when I do get home and so that we waste no time I think marriage is indicated as soon as possible.

Must finish now my precious

All my love
Ever yours
Don xxx

P.S. What about that photograph?

HMML 338,
c/o G.P.O.,

27th May 1944

Cpl. Linda Russell W.A.A.F.,
R.A.F., Branscombe,
Salcombe Regis,
near Sidmouth,
South Devon,
ENGLAND

Linda darling

Many thanks for your air letter of 10th May – I was relieved to receive it as it is some time since I last heard from you.

You ask me how I'm feeling after my week's rest – as a matter of fact I'm back again at the rest camp and feeling on top of the world but as you say I should much prefer spending the time at home with you. I'm sending by sea mail some photos of the island, the only place in the Med. I'd care to return to after the war, and it would be even more perfect with you here with me.

Yes the puppy in the photo did belong to the crew but unfortunately she was sick and has since been destroyed. I'd love to have Spotless here, he was always good for a laugh if nothing else.

The weather is absolutely perfect at the moment but I fear it has yet to become much warmer and I'm not so keen on that. The flies and mosquitoes are becoming pests and as usual I'm covered with bites – I seem to have some uncanny attraction for them.

I've just received a letter from Dudley. He never made the corvette and now has another flotilla on the South Coast somewhere – his letter has been recensored – must be that invasion feeling. Out here we're all hanging on wondering whether we will do anything at the same time as the push across the Channel but your guess is as good as mine! Dudley tells me he has run across John Bick and Ken Morley once or twice – they still manage to hang on at home.

Anyway time passes and I hope to be home in time for X'mas – incidentally just heard that Richard is going, or has gone, home – I'll write and ask him to look you up if he can.

There's no need for me to tell you that I'm still missing you like hell my darling and longing to come home and hold you in my arms again and tell you that I love you more than anything in the world and always will.

Take care of yourself sweetest – I hope it won't be too long now.

Ever your own devoted
Don xxx

Chapter Ten

JUNE – AUGUST 1944

Don writes on **8ᵗʰ June 1944** (again, the letter is not numbered and he comments that he has lost his list) saying that his holiday is over and he has just returned from a filthy trip. He remarks that the "big show" has started (clearly a reference to D-Day which was launched on 6ᵗʰ June) and that progress seems to be reasonable despite the weather. He guesses that Dudley and other ex-colleagues are involved and declares that he would sooner be in Italy. He has not heard from his mother or Linda and thinks that the mail situation is deteriorating. He considers that the war is going well on the Italian front and is hopeful that he will be home for Christmas and a Christmas wedding will ensue. He has not seen any of the old crowd, apart from Phyllis, who has become unbearably cocky since he has been given his own command.

MAP H

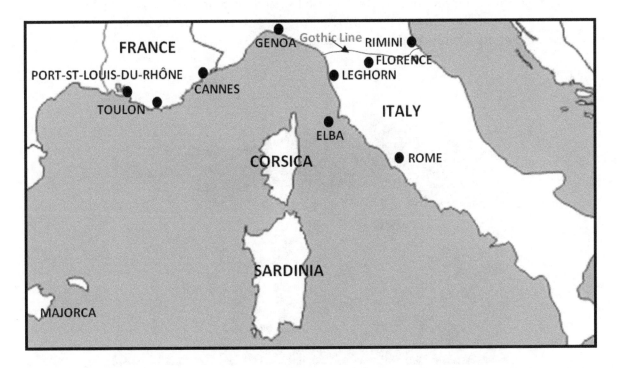

Linda writes on **16ᵗʰ June 1944** saying her note will be short as she has not heard from Don recently and she has no uncensorable news. She is being kept busy and things are likely to become busier. She has not heard from Dudley and imagines that he is having a hectic time and that it must have been a thrill landing on the French coast.

Meanwhile on the night of 16ᵗʰ/17ᵗʰ June 1944, following pre-invasion bombing, Free French troops invade the island of Elba (see **Map H**, on the previous page). They included Goums, who were native North African units led by French officers. In Operation Brassard they were supported by the American and British navies and Royal Navy commandos. Elba is further up the Italian coast, some 180 miles north west of Rome. In the days leading up to the invasion, unusual German naval activity between the island and the mainland is mistaken by the Allies as an evacuation. In fact the Germans are reinforcing their hold on this strategic island and their forces are instructed by Hitler to hold the island, to their last man. As the waters around Elba are shallow, only smaller naval craft can be used, and they are split into three groups:

> Group 1 comprises British MTBs (motor torpedo boats) and American PT boats (a similar fast attack torpedo craft) to create diversions and land French commandos on the north side of the island.
> Group 2 comprises five LCIs (landing craft, infantry) and eight MLs (motor launches) each towing an LCA (landing craft, assault) to attack four beaches on the south coast.
> Group 3, which is the main force, is to land on two beaches in three waves. The first wave comprises nine LCIs, four LSTs (landing craft, tank) and three MLs towing Landing Craft Support (Medium), the second another 28 LCIs and the third 40 LCTs, bringing in heavier equipment.

French 9th Colonial Division landing on Elba, 17 June 1944 from *Wikimedia Commons*

The French lose around 250 men with about 635 wounded, and the British 38 dead and nine wounded. The Germans lose 500 men with a further 2,000 captured. To avoid further loss of life, the Germans are allowed to evacuate 400 men on 20th June 1944.

After his hospitalisation in Naples and recuperation in Ischia, Lieutenant Nixon (awaiting his own command) returns to *ML 554* in time to partake in the invasion of Elba. He describes the MLs towing landing craft to the beaches.

During the operation, *HDML* (Harbour Defence Motor Launch) *1301*, having released its assault craft of French Colonial troops, including Goums, spots the 'flak lighter', *Köhn*.According to *Wikipedia*, the Marinefährprahm, known to the Allies as a 'flak lighter', is the largest German landing craft and over twice the length of an HDML. *HDML 1301* does not move hoping that (a) *Köhn* would not see it and (b) *Köhn* would not spot the assault craft. (b) was achieved but not (a). In the ensuing encounter, the CO of *HDML 1301*, Lt F L Carter is killed and his No. 1, Sub Lt Goddard is seriously wounded. At least five other crew members are also injured. They return, under the command of Lt Peter Spencer, RN to the LCT-HQ which acted as a hospital ship and exchange the injured men for a fresh crew. Royal Navy commandos are despatched and successfully capture *Köhn*.

Right:
***HDML 1301* in Malta (Photograph taken by Lt F L Carter RNVR)**

**Far right:
Lt F L Carter RNVR in Malta**

(Both photographs kindly provided by David Carter)

Nixon reports that the landing at Campo Bay on Elba is difficult as the Germans are anticipating a probable landing and have sited anti-tank guns on the hills overlooking the beach. Mortar shells land under the stern of another HDML, temporarily disabling her steering. In fact the operation is faultering until a rocket ship is deployed and a party of commandos manages to attack the German positions from the rear. During the next two days the MLs sweep mines around the island, although navigation is difficult owing to iron ore mines interfering with the ships' compasses. Next, they return to Bastia (see **Map F**, on page 152).

Once there, Nixon is given command of the damaged *HDML 1301*, which he describes as having become dirty with an ill-disciplined crew. Lt F L Carter had been well liked by his crew and *HDML 1301* had been described as a 'happy ship' with high morale. The replacement of over half the complement clearly had a devastating effect.

After a month, Nixon is not sorry to transfer to *HDML 1246* to replace her sick CO. HDMLs (Harbour Defence Motor Launches) were smaller craft than the MLs. They were just 72-foot long, with a laden displacement of 54 tons, and powered by diesel engines with a speed of 12.5 knots. In addition to two officers, they typically had a crew of ten and their primary role was to maintain harbour navigation. Although designed for harbour defence, HDMLs were frequently used alongside MLs carrying out similar tasks, as in the invasion of Elba. Throughout this book, it should be borne in mind that, where references are made to MLs, this may include HDMLs.

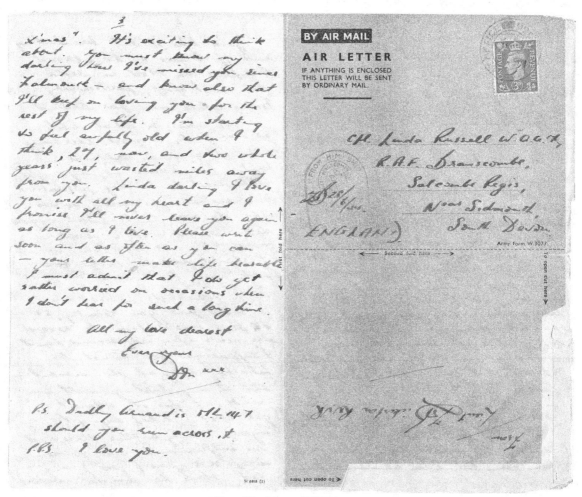

Part of Don's letter 28th June 1944

In his letter of **28th June 1944**, Don apologises for not having written but he surmises that Linda will guess the reason. He informs her that they are still frantically busy. At the time of writing they are at anchor and rolling in a heavy sea. He pointedly, not for the first time, stresses that he has received a letter from his mother but not one from Linda. He says that, whilst his birthday (he was 27 on 22nd June 1944) was spent at sea, they had quite a party later but without the old gang. He comments that the news, or what little they have heard, is good: "Cherbourg,

Elba(!) and the advance in Italy." Clearly (!) is his code to tell Linda that he had been part of the Elba invasion, although whether his *ML 338* was in Group 2 or Group 3 (see page 198) is unknown. However, the evidence points to *HDML 1301* being part of Group 2 and *ML 338* being attached to Group 3. Don assumes that Linda is also busy. Being on the radar at *RAF Branscombe*, she would have had heavy involvement in the Normandy landings. He again anticipates that he will be home by Christmas. In a postscript he says that Dudley Arnaud is in command of *ML 147*.

On **8th July 1944,** he again notes that he has received a letter from his mother but has still not heard from Linda. His parents are staying in North Wales (a country he loves) and seem to have a variety of food which he envies. He has no potatoes, no fresh vegetables or meat, just the same old stewed steak for lunch and dinner, and they have run out of tinned vegetables. He hopes to stock up when he reaches a base of sorts. The weather has changed and it is blowing a gale and raining heavily. He is feeling fit and cheerful with life. Whilst he misses Linda, perhaps the experience has taught him how much he loves her. In a postscript he comments that there has been a hitch over the £14 but that she should receive it soon.

The tone of his next letter, dated **29th July 1944,** is more desperate as he has not heard from Linda or his mother for over two months. The mail situation is bad and some of his crew are worried, especially those with relatives in London.

The first V-1 bomb had been launched on 13th June, a week after D-Day. These self-propelled rockets (known as doodlebugs or flying bombs) were 27 feet long with a wingspan of 17 feet and carried a payload of nearly 2,000 lbs of explosives. Initially they had a range of 150 miles, which was increased to 250 miles. They were inaccurate and indiscriminate. 10,500 of these bombs were launched at Britain, and they presented a serious threat to London and south-east England.

Although not mentioned in my parents' correspondence, it is worth noting that the more deadly V-2 rockets were launched by the Germans between September 1944 and March 1945 at targets in England and in liberated territories on the continent. Over 1,400 were targeted mostly on London killing nearly 2,800 people. Many landed in unpopulated parts of Kent as a result of British Intelligence leaking falsified accounts of rockets, overshooting their targets, but some strikes were devastating – one killing 160 people in a Woolworth's store in New Cross, south-east London.

Continuing with Don's letter, he says they have been working hard and spending much time at sea and the hot weather has been blistering his face. Although he is feeling fit, there are too many parties to maintain a healthy lifestyle. He now has a new No. 1, who has recently taken over from Ken. (He had mentioned the arrival of Ken on 30th November 1943 in air letter No. 41 – see Letters appended to Chapter Eight.) Ken had replaced Phyllis much to Don's relief, and now he has another new man. He regards his latest recruit as too green. He is only 20 years old and is straight from UK and basic training. He says that, although he means well, he is about the last person he would choose to live with. Apart from Phyllis he has not been in touch with the old crowd, although he has heard that Gibby has an MID (Mention in Despatches). Don has been ashore for the first time in a week to visit the local officers' club. They drank wine and discussed the usual topic: when they are likely to return home. He was impressed with the RAF band.

He writes two days later, on **1st August 1944**, asking Linda to cable to confirm that she is safe. He is again bothered that he has not heard from her, although he has now received a letter from his mother. Instead of going ashore the previous evening, he had a blitz on cockroaches. At the time of writing, the weather is beautiful. He is planning to take the jeep down to the beach to read and laze. Although he is unable to reveal his whereabouts, he says that he has been too lazy and too busy to contact the locals but some of the crew have enjoyed making contact in some of the hill villages. The locals are far cleaner and better clad than those on the mainland. This indicates that possibly he is still on the island of Elba or perhaps La Maddalena (See **Map F**, on page 152). He says that there is a lot of squalor in the Italian towns. His one regret is not visiting Rome, which he has heard from others has been quite untouched by war. He reports that Dickie Durstan has turned up. Don then finishes with the same, recent optimism that he will be home for Christmas.

On **6th August 1944**, Don's concern at no word from Linda has reached fever pitch. He has still not heard and admits that he is worried stiff, especially as other mail is getting through and he has received three or four letters from his mother. He feels certain something is wrong and again wonders whether she has changed her mind about their relationship. If so, he would rather know – if she is ill, perhaps someone else could write and explain. He has not been ashore since he last wrote, as there is no incentive to do so and the area is bleak and mountainous. It is hot and the flies are a bother. Quite a number of the personnel in the flotilla have nearly completed two years and they are all fairly confident that they will be home for Christmas. He speculates that, as the war is going so well in Russia and France, it might be over by the end of October. Although they have been kept busy, things are quiet where they are.

On **7th August 1944**, Linda acknowledges receipt of the two photographs and says she has also heard from his mother, who is worried about the hall floor rotting, and has received photographs taken with Don's father, Les (his brother) and his latest girlfriend who is a ballet dancer. Linda is still on a three-watch system, with no leave, and she is not allowed to travel more than 20 miles. She too thinks Don will be home by Christmas, and she is nervous about meeting him again. She assumes that Dudley Arnaud is still in the English Channel and asks whether Don has heard any news from him. She is one of the few WAAFs who has not volunteered for France as the minimum time scale is two years.

She writes again on **15th August 1944**. Although there is no news, she intends to keep writing until some mail catches up with him. She says his letters are arriving in record time, about a week, but she wonders whether there is a better address she could use for him. Her crew is preparing to perform a camp show and her supervisor is to be compere, which she anticipated will be better than ENSA. The weather is lovely and she is looking forward to a swim. She asks whether he knows Francis Coleridge (*ML 568*), a friend of LACW Jane Seymour.

Operation Dragoon commences on 15th August 1944 and involves the invasion of Southern France along a 35-mile stretch of coast between Toulon and Cannes. There is little resistance as the Germans are expecting an invasion at Genoa. There is minimal British involvement and the main invasion force comprises the American navy and US and Free French troops.

A relieved Don writes on **16th August 1944**, having at last heard from Linda (although her letter of 30th July is missing from the collection). He reports that he did not take part (in Operation Dragoon), although they were down to go in the original orders. He is delighted that Linda has not volunteered for posting to France; he has also received her letter of 7th August. He is hopeful of an end to the war in Europe within two months but he is concerned that he will be sent to the Far East. However, he looks forward to coming home and reminisces about their time in Tenby, Saundersfoot and Falmouth. It is still very hot and the mosquitoes are a problem.

Contrary to what he had told her, in Don's next letter (see Letter appended to Chapter Eleven) he confirms to Linda that they had, in fact, taken part in the operation. Pope reports in *Flag 4* that four ML flotillas were involved, the 3rd, 24th, 29th and 31st, the latter having been reinforced by three ships of the 8th Flotilla. The minesweeping gear of the 3rd and the 31st had been overhauled, whilst the 29th had been fitted with new Bofors guns at Algiers, and the 24th were equipped with special radar devices at Ischia. The force had assembled at, or passed through, La Maddalena (see **Map F**, on page 152). The operation was a complete success, with Allied shipping losses negligible – although *ML 563*, which went to try to save survivors from a ship which had hit a mine, herself fell victim; the SO (Senior Officer) of Don's 3rd ML Flotilla and a rating were severely hurt; moreover, *ML 562* was damaged by shellfire from a shore battery; *ML 559* was damaged by two mines exploding close ahead; and three American PT boats were also mine victims.

PT-9 by Harris & Ewing, photographer [public domain], via *Wikimedia Commons*

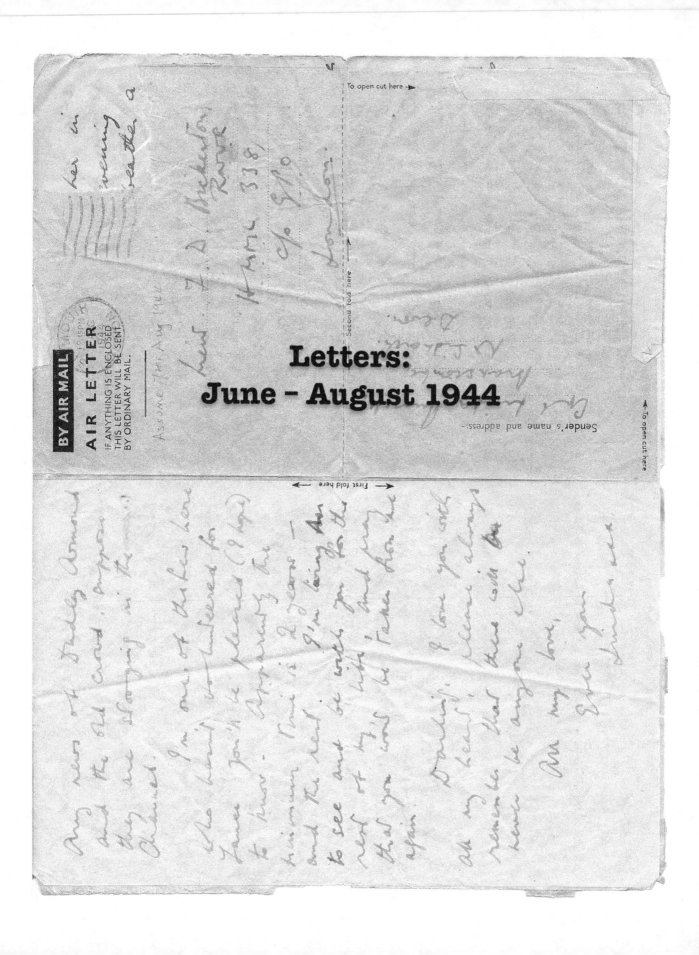

Letters: June – August 1944

BY AIR MAIL

AIR LETTER

IF ANYTHING IS ENCLOSED THIS LETTER WILL BE SENT BY ORDINARY MAIL.

Sender's name and address:-

To open cut here →

Second fold here

First fold here

← To open cut here

H.M.M.L. 338
c/o G.P.O.,
London

8th June 1944
Air Letter No ?
I've lost my list!

Cpl. Linda Russell W.A.A.F.,
R.A.F. Branscombe,
Salcombe Regis,
Nr Sidmouth,
South Devon,
England.

Linda darling

The holiday is unfortunately over and I've just got in from a particularly filthy trip – can't imagine why I wasn't sick!

Well the big show has started at last and the progress seems to be reasonable notwithstanding the weather – I imagine that Dudley and the rest of them are in the thick of it and probably not enjoying it too much either. Personally I'd sooner be out here for the moment.

I haven't heard from you or Mother for some little time, in fact the mail situation out here seems to become worse instead of better. I know I'm pretty slack about writing but please believe me that it doesn't mean I love you or miss you any the less; it's just I suppose that writing to you is so far less satisfactory than holding you close to me and telling you that, to me, you are the most precious person in the world. The longer I'm away from you the more I miss you and the more desperate I become to go home to you. Darling these words on paper are so futile and yet you must know how very true they are – perhaps the simplest thing to say is just that, I love you with all my heart.

The war seems to be going quite well on this front and at the moment we are still undecided as to whether the Casino at Monte Carlo will make a good mess or not. I haven't seen any of the old bunch except Phyllis and that hardly fills me with enthusiasm – since he got his own command he's become unbearably cocky.

I imagine that you must be horribly busy at the moment but please don't forget the photograph and please, please take good care of yourself.

Even if I don't get home before I have hopes of being home for X'mas and a X'mas wedding will suit me as well as any – unless it happens to be earlier.

My darling you are always in my thoughts and I do love you so very much.

Write as often as you can.

Ever your own
Don xxx

H.M.M.L. 338,
c/o G.P.O.,
London

16th June 1944

Cpl. Linda Russell W.A.A.F.,
R.A.F. Branscombe,
Salcombe Regis,
Near Sidmouth,
South Devon,
ENGLAND.

My own darling Linda

This, I fear will be only a very short note as it's ages since I heard from you and I haven't any uncensorable news I can pass on. Life goes on in its usual routine way and unfortunately we're being kept busy and are going to be even busier.

I haven't heard any more from Dudley and I imagine he must be having a very hectic time – I'm still glad I'm not there even though it must have been a hell of a thrill running into the French coast on a stunt of that magnitude.

The only real purpose that this letter serves is to tell you that I'm still absolutely crazy about you, that I love you more than anyone in the world, and that my time is spent thinking of you and the day on which I will return to you. Darling I do love you so very much.

All my love my angel
Ever your own
Don xxx

H.M.M.L. 338,
c/o G.P.O.,
London

28th June 1944

Cpl. Linda Russell W.A.A.F.,
R.A.F. Branscombe,
Salcombe Regis,
Near Sidmouth,
South Devon,
ENGLAND.

My own darling Linda

Sorry I haven't written for the last week but you will be able to guess the reason – and we still are frantically busy. Actually we're at anchor at the moment, rolling like hell, hence the appalling writing. One of the other boats brought up some mail but while there was one letter from Mother, in which, incidentally Mother said she hadn't heard from me for six weeks, though naturally I have written, there was unfortunately no letter from you. However I'm hoping there are some on the way.

Of course I spent my birthday at sea but we made up for it later – no I didn't pass out but it was quite a party, unfortunately none of the old gang were there.

It's been blowing quite a lot recently but, apart from today, it's been very hot and as usual I'm peeling particularly on the forehead.

You'd like it out here darling and if I have to be abroad I suppose the Med is better than most spots, particularly Ischia which is now far behind.

The news, or what little we hear of it, is good. Cherbourg, Elba(!) and the advance in Italy. But, believe me, my angel you'll need to be very persuasive to coerce me into going to sea after the war. It's been suggested that I should write a book called "No more Sea time" – it should have a large sale with Ex Coastal Forceites!

Mother tells me that she has heard from you recently, so it's some consolation to receive the news even at second hand. I suppose you, too, must be hellishly busy at the moment but oh my darling will we make up for it when I get home. I keep saying to myself "Only another three and one half months and you've done two years (God!), my lad. Home to Linda before X'mas". It's exciting to think about. You must know my darling how I've missed you since Falmouth – and know also that I'll keep on loving you for the rest of my life. I'm starting to feel awfully old when I think, 27, now, and two whole years just wasted miles away from you. Linda darling I love you with all my heart and I promise I'll never leave you again as long as I live. Please write soon and as often as you can – your letters make life bearable. I must admit that I do get rather worried on occasions when I don't hear for such a long time.

All my love dearest
Ever your
Don xxx

P.S. Dudley Arnaud is M.L. 147 should you run across it.
P.P.S. I love you.

HMML 338,
c/o G.P.O.,
London

8th July 1944

Cpl. Linda Russell W.A.A.F.,
R.A.F., Branscombe,
Salcombe Regis,
near Sidmouth,
South Devon,
ENGLAND

Linda darling

I'm disappointed – still no letter from you. Honest, wretch, I'm hoping for at least six when the next lot of mail eventually turns up.

I had a letter from Mother a few days ago – they're staying at some small place in North Wales (a country I love!) and seem to be enjoying it very much judging by Mother's comments on the variety of food. Wish I could say the same about our food; no potatoes, no fresh veg., no fresh meat – just the same old stewed steak for lunch and dinner, and to cap it all we've now run out of tinned vegetables. Browned off - proper! Nevertheless we seem to get by and I hope to be able to stock right up if and when we get to a base of some sort. We've been working pretty hard, but fortunately it's been nearly all day work which is an excellent thing. Things are pretty quiet and Jerry hasn't bothered us since the last op. when some of his shells were too close for my tender state of health.

The weather has changed today and instead of the usual blazing sun (see my back for evidence) it's now blowing a gale and has been raining like hell most of the day. But it's pleasant. No dust, the air is fresh and cool, and my shirt is quite dry.

As you may have guessed I'm feeling pretty fit and today, for no apparent reason, taking a particularly rosy view of life. Maybe it's the change in the weather, maybe the thought that soon I'll be coming home to you again my darling. If the last couple of years have done no more, at least they have taught me that life without you is both unbearable and unnatural and that I do love you more than ever I thought I was capable of doing. You mean the world to me Linda – in fact the essential difference between life and existence. To that extent at any rate I suppose the time has not been wasted, 'though I groan inwardly when I consider how much better it would have been spent with you, and the many things we could have done together. Each day brings us nearer once more hence, as said, the optimism of my present mood.

Linda my angel I do love you – no words can express it.

All my love always darling
Ever your own
Don xxx

P.S. Understand there's been some hitch over the forms for the £14. You should get it soon.

HMML 338,
c/o G.P.O.,
London

29th July 1944

Cpl. Linda Russell W.A.A.F.,
R.A.F., Branscombe,
Salcombe Regis,
near Sidmouth,
South Devon,
ENGLAND

Linda darling

I'm getting quite worried – over two months since I heard from you and much the same time since I heard from home. God knows what has happened to all our mail as the ship's company is in the same state and some are rather worried particularly those with homes in London.

We've been doing lots of hard work recently and so much time at sea in this particularly fiendish climate has not done my face any lasting good as I tend to blister rather too easily – the agony of that! However I must admit that I'm feeling pretty fit, far fitter in fact than when I'm refitting then there are too many parties which is not a good thing.

I believe I told you that I had a new No 1 – but perhaps not that I've had him in a big way. He's young, only twenty, straight from UK and training, and although I've no doubt that he means well he's just about the last person I should choose to live with. I'd far sooner Ken were back and, even at a pinch, Phyllis. Haven't seen any of the old crowd except Phyllis but I hear that Gibby has got an MID – nice going tho' I don't know quite what it's for.

Went ashore last night for the first time for a week with some of the bods to visit the local officers' club. It's a dreary place reminiscent of a tenth rate night club with prices much in the same sphere. However there was an RAF band which was quite good so we sat back drank the local wine, listened, dripped and discussed the prospects of our return to the UK. Wherever you go the main topic of conversation invariably is "when are you due to go home?" I must admit that it's always uppermost in my mind and that I'm just longing to be with you again. Two years in October and tho' it seems so long many happy memories of days spent with you remain as fresh as ever. Promise me darling that you won't change and that we'll always be able to do lots of crazy things together. The time we had together was so short yet in that time we seemed to do so much that time passed all too quickly. I love you my sweet and you know that I always will – at any rate it does take a war to keep me away from you – I can think of nothing else that could do so.

Write soon and as often as you can my angel.

Good night pet, I'll dream of you.

All my love
Ever yours
Don xxx

HMML 338,
c/o G.P.O.,
London

1st August 1944

Cpl. Linda Russell W.A.A.F.,
R.A.F., Branscombe,
Salcombe Regis,
near Sidmouth,
South Devon,
ENGLAND

Linda darling

Some mail actually arrived last night, my sum total was one letter from Mother and not a thing from you. I must admit that I'm getting rather worried about it as it's such a hell of a time since I heard from you and far too many things are happening at home for my peace of mind. Please write or better still cable if you can.

Didn't go ashore last night but instead had a blitz on the cockroaches with a special insecticide bomb which brought them out literally in their hundreds – they just fell on the deck, until it was quite thick, and expired. Today we are more or less clear tho' the odd one puts in an occasional appearance.

It's quite beautiful today. The sun is very hot but a pleasant breeze does something to counteract it – and as I'm in the harbour I feel at peace with the world. I don't yet know what to do this afternoon but I think I'll take the jeep and go down to the beach to read and laze. I wish you could be here as I'm sure you'd enjoy it tho' perhaps not quite so much as Saundersfoot!

So far I've been far too lazy – and too busy to contact any of the locals and I see no reason for going out of my way to do so. Some of the blokes have made contacts in the hill villages and appear to enjoy themselves (the energetic ones anyway!). The people here look far cleaner and better clad than those on the mainland and in any case it's a relief to get away from the squalor one finds in the Italian towns. My one regret to date is that I have been unable to get to Rome and from the blokes who have been I hear that it appears quite untouched by the war with, apparently plenty of attractive well dressed women (that, incidentally, is not my reason for wishing to go there!).

Dickie Durston turned up last night full of the joys of spring and righteous living, informed me that he is a reformed character and has completely given up drink. I suspect the reason is that he has run out of liquor.

Darling I do love you so very much and I am feeling rather worried so please write soon and as often as you can. I miss you as you know full well and I feel happier when I realise that I should be home by Christmas – perhaps earlier.

All my love my angel and don't forget the photo.

Ever yours
Don xxx

P.S. Do you hear from Johnnie these days?

HMML 338,
c/o G.P.O.,
London

6ᵗʰ August 1944

Cpl. Linda Russell W.A.A.F.,
R.A.F., Branscombe,
Salcombe Regis,
near Sidmouth,
South Devon,
ENGLAND

Linda darling

I'm worried stiff - a pile of mail arrived yesterday but not a word from you. It's so long now since I heard from you that I feel certain something must be wrong. If it is that you have changed your mind about us then I'd much sooner know - if you are ill then please get someone else to drop me a line. I feel so damned helpless being so far away from you, there doesn't seem to be anything I can do to relieve the uncertainty. You know that I love you more than anyone in the world and it has been the thought of my return to you that has made the last two years bearable.

There isn't much to tell you as I've not been ashore since I last wrote to you, principally because there's no incentive to leave the ship in this place. It's bleak, mountainous with barely a sign of green foliage and not a pub, club or anything else ashore - in fact reminiscent of Scapa at its worst. It's hotter today than ever and flies are a perfect pest - everyone's looking washed out and looking forward to the cool of the evening.

I received three or four letters from Mother yesterday and they appear to have enjoyed their holiday - apparently they had good weather and rather more variety in food than they expected. My brother is also on holiday and from all accounts spends his time either chasing or running away from ballet dancers - I'm not sure which!

Quite a number of us in the flotilla have nearly completed our two years and are eagerly discussing our prospects of returning home. We are all fairly confident that we should be home for X'mas. Personally the war is going so well both in Russia and France that I quite expect it to be over by the end of October - I hope!

Things are quiet out here although we've been kept fairly busy - no excitements thank God.

Darling please write as soon as you can as I really am hellishly worried. You know that I'll always love you my sweet - nothing can ever change that. And it won't be too long now before we are back together.

All my love my angel
Ever your own
Don xxx

Cpl Linda Russell
Branscombe
Nr Sidmouth
Devon

7th August 1944

Lieut F. D. Bickerton,
R.N.V.R.
H.M.M.L. 338
c/o G.P.O. London

My darling Don,

Many thanks for the two photos. I like them immensely and can't see that you look any older, you look exactly the same to me.

Heard from your Mother today, she seems very well but is worried about the hall floor which is rotting and has to be taken up – sounds rather like our house! She enclosed two very nice photos, one taken with your father and the other with Les and his latest girl friend – possibly the ballet dancer! Anyway she is darned attractive and I admire his good taste. Les looks very pleased with life and has taken to smoking cigars!

Life goes on in much the same old way. We are still on a three watch system, no leave and not allowed to travel more than 20 miles. I'm having 24 hours off duty from lunch time today until 1 o'clock tomorrow & then its 1 – 6 & all night again. I can hardly call this a free 24 as I'm duty N.C.O!! – what a life.

Darling, I really think you will be home by Xmas. I'm feeling a wee bit nervous about meeting you again, hope they will let me have some leave otherwise I'm walking out!! Any news of Dudley Arnaud and the old crowd, suppose they are stooging in the Channel.

I'm one of the few here who hasn't volunteered for France you'll be pleased (I hope) to know. Apparently the minimum time is 2 years – and the rest. I'm living to see and be with you for the rest of my life, and pray that you won't be taken from me again.

Darling, I love you with all my heart, please always remember that there will never be anyone else.

All my love,
Ever yours
Linda xxx

Branscombe
Nr Sidmouth
Devon

15th August 1944

Lieut F. D. Bickerton,
R.N.V.R.
H.M.M.L. 338
c/o G.P.O. London

My darling,

I have a few minutes to spare during maintenance so here I am again with absolutely no news as nothing has happened since my last letter, but I'm afraid you will be receiving plenty of these as I intend writing until some mail eventually catches up with you.

Can you suggest a better way than c/o G.P.O? Can't I have your present address or are you moving around rather a lot? Your air letters are reaching me in record time, usually from 6 – 8 days.

My crew are putting on a camp show next week, we have already advertised the fact but haven't much idea what we are going to do, of course it will be screamingly funny as there is very little talent amongst us. I've roped in our supervisor, an amusing P/O, as compere, who has suggested wearing our WAAF sgts cooks' uniform – which is somewhat out-size! Anyway however bad it is, I feel confident that it will be an improvement on ENSA, at least the ones that I have seen.

It is a marvellous afternoon, I'm longing to get off watch at 6 and have a swim. How are the blisters, not too painful I hope – you have my sympathy as I have had them on my arms and back.

By the way, do you know Francis Coleridge? (HMML 568) a friend of L.A.C.W. Jane Seymour.

Must close now dashing with white apron tomorrow. Please drop a line when you have time.

I'll always love you.
Linda xxx

H.M.M.L. 338,
c/o G.P.O.,
London

16th August 1944

Cpl. Linda Russell W.A.A.F.,
R.A.F. Branscombe,
Salcombe Regis,
Near Sidmouth,
South Devon,
ENGLAND.

Linda darling

Received your letter of 30th July a few minutes ago and I'm feeling somewhat relieved – I've been imagining all sorts of horrible things over the past month. Darling I hate to lecture you but please remember that mail really is important when you are so far away.

We didn't take part in the S. France invasion tho' how they got along without us I can't imagine – especially as we were down to go in the original operation orders. It appears to have been fairly easy going but I must admit that I wasn't sorry to be out of it.

I'm more than pleased that you didn't volunteer to go to France – if I got home only to find that you had gone abroad for two years it would be just the end. I still feel hopeful that another couple of months will see the end of the war in Europe and we've been trying (unsuccessfully) to find out what will happen to Coastal Forces in the Med. The MTB's have just about had it especially in view of the recent landings as the Germans have now no important sea routes open to them. Whether the boats will go out to the Far East I don't know – my main concern is that I don't go with them!

Mother told me that there were some photographs on the way out but I didn't realise that my sweet young brother was posing as the super film magnate with his latest starlet – however Mother doesn't appear to be worried so it must be platonic!

Angel I'm just living to be with you again; two years has been a hell of a long time but at any rate it makes me feel sure that you are the only girl in the world for me – without the certainty of returning to you life wouldn't be worth a bean. And as for leave when I get home – well I just want to go to some quiet spot to be alone with you and attempt to make up for the lost time. I love you Linda darling as I never believed it were possible to love. I have, too, the many happy memories of Tenby, Saundersfoot, Falmouth (although the gin was a little strong on one occasion!) and they are memories which I can never forget. But they are things of the past and the future must hold even better times together.

It's still as hot as hell out here and I'm my usual repulsive shade of red all over – the mosquitoes are a pest (had one under my net last night) – in fact I've had the Med. in a big way.

Darling must finish – you know I'll always love you.

All my love
Ever your
Don xxx

P.S. Have you yet received the £14 – my receipt has now turned up. Glad you like the photos – wish I were with them.

Chapter Eleven
PORT-ST-LOUIS-DU-RHÔNE

PORT-SAINT-LOUIS-DU-RHÔNE (B.-du-R.) — Les Quais

Port-Saint-Louis-du-Rhône. Image provided by José Valli

On **30th August 1944,** Don reports that, soon after his last letter (dated 16th August 1944 – see Letters appended to Chapter Ten) and the invasion of Southern France, *ML 338* has been sent there and that, although they are working hard, he is enjoying himself. They had arrived at one place (Port-St-Louis-du-Rhône) a day before the Army (see **Map H,** on page 197). Port-St-Louis-du-Rhône is some 80 miles west of the landing beaches of Operation Dragoon. There, a lifeboat had transported the local Maquis (French Resistance) who boarded *ML 338*. The Maquis brought gifts of wine and grapes and their chief had written a 'pact of friendship' (see later in this Chapter). Don explains that collaborators are hanged by the Maquis, and the women who have anything to do with the Germans have their heads shaved. They hate the Germans who, before retreating, burn everything.

Don has also run across Dennis Venning, who was in the 25th ML Flotilla with him and one of the signatories of the Rock-Hotel menu in Chapter Five. Don goes on to report that they have had a few unpleasant encounters with the Germans' shore batteries but they have survived, and he looks forward to the war being over by the end of October. (This is optimistic as, in fact, their enemy's surrender would not happen until May 1945.)

Don refers to Linda's comment about being nervous to meet him after two years, and he reminds her of some of the "lectures" she gave him in Falmouth. He considers that he is more sober these days, and his enforced absence has convinced him that he will always love her. He looks forward to marriage and dreams of them being together to make up for the lost years.

Nearly 70 years later in 2012, four years after my father's death, whilst sorting his papers including all these letters, I found a note written by 'Andy' from an address in Devon. On making contact I found that 'Andy' was Philip Andrews, who was mentioned in Gordon Stead's book *A Leaf Upon the Sea*. Philip Andrews joined Gordon Stead, in mid-1943, on *ML 126* as his No. 1. This was at about the time that Don left the 25th ML Flotilla in North Africa to join the 3rd, just prior to the invasion of Sicily. However, in November, *ML 126* ran into an expired, circling torpedo which blew her bows off back to the wheelhouse. Fortunately half the crew were ashore on leave and there were no casualties. Reference to the *Navy Lists* shows Sub-Lieutenant Philip Andrews was still officially attached to *ML 126* until April 1944, although she would never sail again. Then from April 1944 he was serving on *ML 575* and, later, on *ML 131* as No. 1. In 2012, Philip was 90 years old (Don would have been 95) and some memories had become hazy with time. However, when I raised the subject of the Maquis boarding *ML 338*, he declared that he was there and told me he had kept the 'pact of friendship', which he subsequently found amongst his wartime memorabilia. He kindly let me keep the original:

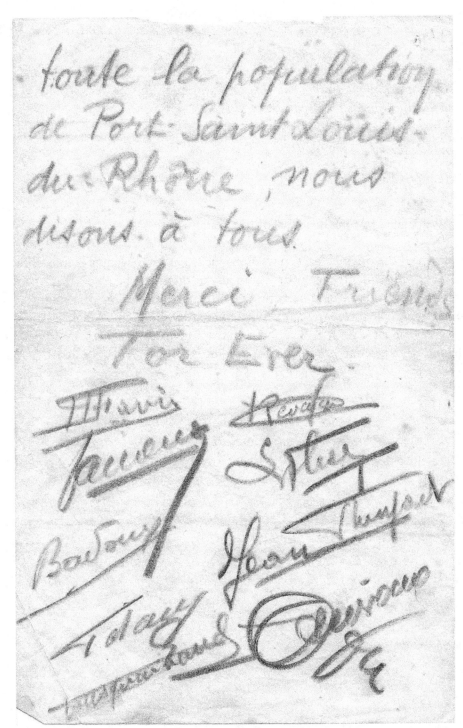

Pact of Friendship (written by the Maquis)

This translates as follows:

We are glad to have been able to pass some time with the valiant crew of his British Majesty.

We have been very touched by the welcome that we have received. We found the assurance that Great Britain and France will find the means to realise the wish of our two countries: an eternal friendship to the service of World Peace.

We will never forget our courageous allies and in the name of the whole population of Port St Louis du Rhône, we say to all

Thank you Friends For Ever.

The 'pact' was signed by nine members of the Maquis.

Having recovered the original 'pact', I was intrigued that nine Maquis members had signed it. What did they go on to do after the war? Could any of them still be alive? Whilst I thought this to be unlikely, perhaps there would be families of the next generation who might be as excited. So I decided to undertake further research to try to identify these nine Maquis.

On the suggestion of a French neighbour, I first wrote to the Mayor's Office at Port-St-Louis-du-Rhône and received a response to my letter on 15th October 2012. It translates as follows:

Sir

Following your letter dated September 24, 2012, my office has tried to decipher the names behind the signatures of nine people who made this pact of friendship with your father and his crew.

Despite the absence of first names, four of them have been approximately recognized FAVIER, REVALOR, BADOUIX, BOUSQUAINAUD and after research in the civil registers, it turns out that these people died.

I cannot give you information about their respective families. However, I shall not fail to send your mail and the pact to any person presenting himself at the town hall to search for this period.

I beg you to accept, Sir, the assurances of my highest consideration.

Paule Mazella

SERVICE E.E.P.
POPULATION
PM/FR

Port-St-Louis du Rhône,
Le 15 octobre 2012

Madame Paule MAZELLA
Responsable du service Population

A

Monsieur David BICKERTON

Angleterre - UK

Monsieur,

Suite à votre courrier du 24 septembre 2012, mon service a essayé de déchiffrer les noms derrière les signatures des neuf personnes ayant conclu ce pacte d'amitié avec votre père et son équipage.

Malgré l'absence des prénoms, quatre d'entre elles ont pu être approximativement reconnues, FAVIER, REVALOR, BADOUIX, BOUSQUAINAUD, et après des recherches dans les registres d'état civil, il s'avère que ces personnes sont décédées.

Je ne peux non plus vous donner d'informations sur leur famille respective.

Toutefois, je ne manquerai pas de transmettre votre courrier ainsi que le pacte conclu à toute personne se présentant à la mairie pour effectuer des recherches concernant cette période.

Je vous prie d'agréer, Monsieur, l'expression de mes salutations distinguées.

Paule MAZELLA

HÔTEL DE VILLE - PORT SAINT LOUIS DU RHÔNE
3, Avenue du Port - BP 142 - 13518 PORT SAINT LOUIS DU RHÔNE Cedex
Téléphone : 04 42 86 90 00 - Télécopie : 04 42 86 21 31 - wwww.portsaintlouis.fr

Letter dated 15th October 2012 from Port St Louis du Rhône

No one did present themselves to the town hall, and direct approaches by me to French historical museums were unsuccessful. I just receive polite replies saying that a copy of the 'pact' would be filed for the benefit of future historians. In 2015, I sent speculative letters to nine individuals bearing one of the identified surnames and who lived in the locality and I received three responses. Two of the replies are worth summarising:

> **Eric Revalor** of Marseille wrote, on 6th October 2015, declaring that one of the signatories was his grandfather, **Jean Revalor,** who was a teacher and then Professor of Italian and English at a school in Port-St-Louis-du-Rhône. He retired to Aubagne, where he died of cancer on 1st August 1982. Eric said that the English liberated Port-St-Louis-du-Rhône and that his grandfather had always been grateful to the British. This recognition, he said, lasts forever in France to this day.

> **Fernand Revalor** of Ventabren replying, on 27th September 2015, did not believe that one of his direct relatives was amongst the signatories. However, he went on to explain that his father had died in 1935 but his late brother, Albert (born 1922) was deported to Germany from 1942 until 1944. This, he said, gives a good hint that the Revalor family were definitely against the Nazis and were honest "résistants". Albert had escaped from the camp in Austria, in which he was interned, and tried to reach Italy and then France by travelling through Yugoslavia. Ironically, he was then interned by the Americans in Naples and did not reach France until 1945. He died at the age of only 50. Fernand expressed his gratitude to Don for helping to liberate his country, saying: "Thanks to persons like your father France kept being France and this is thanks to the English." He finished: "Please excuse my lyricism but those words are sincere."

As I re-read the letter, I could not help but think of Albert Revalor, taken from his home and family at the age of only 20 to a far away country, escaping and then embarking on a hazardous journey back to his homeland. Albert, Don and Linda were but three ordinary young people caught up in the chaos of war, separated from loved ones, at times fearing for their lives but being survivors and rebuilding their lives. Millions more would have had their own stories to tell. Tragically, over 60 million people died as a result of the Second World War and never had a future.

Also, in 2015, through the efforts of the father of my French neighbour, I made contact with Monsieur José Valli, a local author who had written a book entitled *Le Docteur Colonna et Port-St-Louis-du-Rhône.* On pages 42 and 43 of this book, he describes how the Maquis met Don's ship:

> *En août 1944 Simon a donc contribué à la libération de Port-Saint-Louis. Son homologue, le docteur Nougaret, sera nommé president du comité local de libération puis il sera désigné maire pour le plus court des mandats, du 22 août au 13 septembre 1944.*

> **In August 1944 Simon has therefore contributed to the liberation of Port-Saint-Louis. His counterpart, Dr. Nougaret, will be appointed Chairman of the local Committee of liberation, and then he will be appointed mayor for the shorter of the mandates, from August 22 to September 13 1944.**

> *De par sa situation géographique proche de l'embouchure du Rhône, Port-Saint-Louis etait un point stratégique car il suffissait aux pilotes de l'aviation de chasse de repérer la ville pour ensuite*

remonter le fleuve jusqu'au coeur de la France. Dès leur arrive sur les côtes Méditerranéennes, les allies ont donc voulu reconquérir Port-Saint-Louis.

Due to its geographical location close to the mouth of the Rhône, Port-Saint-Louis was a strategic location because it enabled the fighter pilots to pinpoint the city then go up the River into the heart of France. Upon their arrival on the shores of the Mediterranean, the allies had therefore wanted to reconquer Port-Saint-Louis.

Dans son livre, "Quand la mer n'etait pas calme", le Port-Saint-Louisien Daniel Guiraud revient sur un des rapports de sauvetage consigné par son père, Xavier Guiraud qui, au moment de ces jours historiques de la libération de notre ville, était le Patron canot de sauvetage de la SCSN (Société Centrale de Sauvetage des Naufragés) qui deviendra en 1967 la SNSM (Société Nationale de Sauvetage en Mer).

In his book, 'When the sea was not calm', Port-Saint-Louisian Daniel Guiraud reviews one of the rescue reports recorded by his father, Xavier Guiraud who, at the time of the historic liberation of our town, was the lifeboat master of the SCSN (Central Society of Rescue of the Shipwrecked) which became in 1967 the SNSM (National Society for Rescue at Sea).

Voici ce que Xavier Guiraud écrivait:

Here is what Xavier Guiraud said:

"Le 26 août 1944 sur l'ordre du Comité de Libération de la résistance, le1er Maître Guiraud Xavier avec le matelot des Douanes Galaup Antoine, patron mécanicien du canot de sauvetage de Port-Saint-Louis-du-Rhône accompagné de monsieur Cat Agent administratif de l'Inscription Maritime et de monsieur Penhuat Syndic des Gens de Mer, prenaient la mer vers 11 heures à bord du canot de sauvetage 'Commandant de Coligny' au milieu d'un champ de mines magnétiques et autres pour aller prendre contact avec l'escadre anglo-américaine qui patrouillait en vue de la côte.

"On August 26, 1944, on the order of the Liberation Committee of the resistance, skipper Guiraud Xavier with the deck-hand of the Customs boat Galaup Antoine, chief mechanic of the lifeboat of Port-Saint-Louis-du-Rhône accompanied by Monsieur Cat, Maritime Administrator, and Monsieur Penhuat, Trustee of Seafarers, set sail around 11 o'clock on board the lifeboat 'Commandant de Coligny' amidst a field of magnetic and other types (of mines) to make contact with the Anglo-American flotilla patrolling the coast.

La navigation était des plus périlleuses par la présence de nombreuses mines dans le bassin et dans le canal, la sortie était au trois quarts barrée par un navire coulé en travers.

Navigation was more perilous owing to the presence of many mines in the basin and in the channel, the exit was three quarters obstructed by a sunken ship lying at an oblique angle.

Le pavillon national hissé, le canot de sauvetage navigue avec beaucoup de précautions. Monsieur Penhoat reste debout sur l'avant afin de prévenir le patron d'un danger éventuel. L'escadre croisait au large et l'armement du canot fut heureux d'accoster vers 14 heures le premier bateau de guerre anglais, puis alla accoster plus au large le chef d'escadrille.

With its national flag hoisted, the lifeboat sails very cautiously. Monsieur Penhuat remains standing on the front to warn the master of possible danger. The flotilla was cruising in open

waters and the boat's crew was fortunate to dock around 14:00 hours, the first English war ship then went out to sea to rejoin the flotilla.

Après avoir donné quelques renseignements utiles au commandant du patrouilleur, ce dernier délégua son adjoint à se render à Port-Saint-Louis-du-Rhône pour prendre des renseignements plus détaillés et vers 17 heures le canot de sauvetage rentrait au port transportant un officier anglais et son escorte.

After giving some useful information to the commander of the patrol vessel, the latter delegated his deputy to go to Port-Saint-Louis-du-Rhône to gather more detailed information and just before 17:00 the lifeboat returned to port carrying an English officer and his escort.

Les chefs responsables du Comité de Libération prévenus, en la circonstance, reçurent l'officier au bureau de la mairie. Une foule nombreuse acclamait avec joie nos premiers libérateurs en chantant la Marseillaise et l'hymne anglais.

Leaders of the Liberation Committee, having been forewarned and because of the circumstances, received the officer at the Town Hall. A large crowd acclaimed our first liberators with joy by singing the Marseillaise and the English anthem.

Le Comité de Libération donna à l'officier de précieux renseignements tandis que Galaup et Guiraud lui remirent une carte marine de la côte qu'ils avaient dérobée, avant la liberation, à un officier de marine allemand.

The Liberation Committee gave the officer some vital intelligence, while Galaup and Guiraud handed him a chart of the coast that they had stolen, before the liberation, from a German naval officer.

À la suite d'un examen sommaire l'officier déclara que cette carte était d'une grande importance puisqu'on pouvait y repérer divers champs de mines.

Following a brief examination, the officer declared that this chart was of great importance since it could identify various minefields.

Vers 19 heures, ayant recueilli tous les renseignements nécessaires pour un dragage efficace de la côte, l'officier regagna son navire à bord du canot de sauvetage, accompagné du Docteur Nougaret, du Capitaine Favier et de monsieur Vallon du Comité de Libération, de monsieur Colomp, receveur des douanes, du Lieutenant des Douanes Apine, Président du Comité de Sauvetage et de monsieur Revalor instituteur, comme interprète."

Around 19:00, having gathered all the information necessary for an effective coastal sweep, the English officer returned to his ship on board the lifeboat, accompanied by Doctor Nougaret, Captain Favier and Monsieur Vallon of the Liberation Committee, Monsieur Colomp, Collector of Customs, Monsieur Apine, Lieutenant of Customs, the Chairman of the Lifeboat Committee and the teacher, Monsieur Revalor acting as interpreter."

Le Patron du Canot de Sauvetage. Signé: Guiraud Xavier

The Master of the Lifeboat. Signed: Guiraud Xavier

When Monsieur José Valli read the 'pact of friendship' and Don's letter of 30th August 1944, he realised that it all fitted with the events he had described in his book. He asked permission for Don's letter to Linda to be incorporated into the 2nd Edition of his book. This was published at the end of 2015, with the help of the translational skills of Monsieur Hubert Guillois (my neighbour's father), who was instrumental in finding the author. From the evidence that has been unearthed, it was certainly Don's minesweeper *ML 338* that was intercepted by the lifeboat. Whether Don was the English officer who accompanied the lifeboat back to port, and who was handed the chart that had been stolen from the German naval officer and which showed the minefields, will probably never be known for certain but, from the evidence, it seems that may well have been the case.

In the 2nd Edition of his book, the author inserted the following passage near the bottom of page 43:

À bord du HMML 338, le patrouilleur dragueur de mines que le canot de sauvetage de la SCSN de Port-Saint-Louis venait d'accoster vers 14 heures le 26 août 1944, le Lieutenant Commandant se dénommait Frank Donald Bickerton. Né en juin 1917 à Liverpool, pour ses amis et pour sa fiancée Linda il etait "Don", c'est ainsi qu'on le surnommait.

On board the minesweeper HMML 338, that the SCSN Port-Saint-Louis lifeboat came to meet at 14:00 on 26 August 1944, was its commander, Lieutenant Frank Donald Bickerton. Born in June 1917 in Liverpool, he was known to his friends and his fiancée Linda as "Don".

Son fils, David Bickerton, m'a fait parvenir le pacte d'amitié signé entre les résistants de Port Saint Louis et l'équipage du HMML 338. Il a aussi retrouvé plus de 150 lettres que les deux fiancés se sont échangées pendant la guerre.

His son, David Bickerton, sent me the 'pact of friendship' signed by the resistance members of Port Saint Louis and the crew of HMML 338. (In fact, it was just signed by the nine members of the Maquis.) **He also found more than 150 letters that the two fiancés exchanged during the war.**

Voici quelques extraits de la letter que son papa avait addressée le 30 août à Linda Ruby Russell de Totland sur l'île de Wight, sa future épouse.

Here are some excerpts of the letter that his dad had sent on 30 August 1944 to Linda Ruby Russell of Totland Bay on the Isle of Wight, his future wife.

In fact Don's letter was then published in French in its entirety. A copy of the original letter is appended to this Chapter. Valli then continued:

Frank Donald Bickerton avait recontré Linda Ruby Russell en 1942 au Pays de Galles. Lui servant pour la Royal Navy et elle travaillant sur les radars de la Royale Air Force. Au départ de Port-Saint-Louis le bateau du Lieutenant Bickerton fut ensuite envoyé à Gibraltar et c'est seulement en juillet 1945 que les deux fiancés purent être enfin réunis. Ils se marièrent quelques jours plus tard.

Frank Donald Bickerton had met Linda Ruby Russell in 1942 in Wales. He was serving in the Royal Navy and she was working on the radar for the Royal Air Force. After departing from Port-Saint-Louis, Lieutenant Bickerton's boat was then sent to Gibraltar and it was only in July 1945 that the two fiancés could be together at last. They married a few days later. (Subsequent evidence points to ML 338 and the flotilla returning to La Maddalena and not Gibraltar. On 8th September 1944, the officers of the flotilla, including Don, were photographed there – see Chapter Twelve.)

Le pacte d'amitié est aujourd'hui de retour dans nos murs. Il a été signé, entre autres, par messieurs Favier, Revalor, Badouix, Bousquainaud; d'autres signatures sont difficiles à reconnaître, comme certainement celles du docteur Nougaret et celle de Xavier Guiraud.

The 'pact of friendship' is now back in our town. It was signed by, amongst others, Messieurs Favier, Revalor, Badouix and Bousquainaud; the other signatures are difficult to read, but certainly include Dr Nougaret and Xavier Guiraud.

Sa famille mise à part, bien peu de personnes savaient à ce moment-là que le patron Guiraud avait été blessé par l'éclatement d'une bombe aérienne une semaine plus tôt. C'était arrivé le 17 août, lors du bombardement de la ville par un avion allemand alors qu'il prêtait son concours dévoué et courageux au sauvetage et à l'extinction d'un incendie à l'entrepôt des pétroles.

His family aside, very few people knew at that time that the rescue master, Guiraud, had been wounded by an aerial bomb a week earlier. During the bombardment of the town on 17th August by a lone German aircraft, it was the result of his commitment and courage in extinguishing the ensuing fire that the petroleum depot was saved.

Voilà donc encore un héros ordinaire de notre ville. Les dictionnaires définissent le mot "héros" par: "Toute homme qui montre de la grandeur d'âme, de la noblesse et de la force de caractère, qui excelle en quelque matière."

Yet another ordinary hero of our city. Dictionaries define the word "hero" as: "Any man who is admired for his courage, outstanding achievements and noble qualities in any situation."

Monsieur José Valli sent me a copy of the 2nd Edition of his book in which he had inserted the following dedication in both French and English:

Cher David, "l'empreinte d'un homme sur un autre est éternelle, aucun destin n'a traversé le nôtre impunément!" En souvenir du Docteur Colonna et de Frank Donald Bickerton.

Dear David, "the imprint of a man on another one is eternal, no fate crossed ours with impunity!" In memory of Docteur Colonna and of Frank Donald Bickerton, your dad – Friendly, José Valli

Port St Louis du Rhône, le 30 Decembre 2015.

He dedicated a second copy of his book in similar fashion to my three children.

Letter:
30th August 1944

H.M.M.L. 538,
c/o G.P.O,
London
30th August 1944.

HMML 338,
c/o G.P.O.,
London

30th August 1944

Cpl. Linda Russell W.A.A.F.,
R.A.F., Branscombe,
Salcombe Regis, near Sidmouth,
South Devon, ENGLAND

My darling Linda

I might have guessed I was being too optimistic for no sooner had I finished my last letter to you than we were whisked away to S. France and although we're working harder than ever (no shore leave!) I'm rather enjoying things.

There have been one or two amusing incidents and of course one or two which didn't amuse at all. We arrived at one place a day before the army (I didn't know it at the time, believe me) and out came the local lifeboat, full of bods in gorgeous uniforms, to greet us. I had the chief of the local Maquis on board and he was feeling pretty pleased with life. They brought us grapes and wine (I got the stomach ache) and wrote a long screed on the necessity of closer relations between our two countries. Ashore they had hanged the sold collaborators and also shaved the heads of all the women who had had anything to do with the Germans. Anyway we enjoyed meeting them and there's no doubt that they hate the Germans and with good reason. Jerry, of course, before he leaves destroys everything he can – and looks for his next line of defence. I also ran across Dennis Vanning, who was with me in the 25th and we had the odd noggin to celebrate.

I haven't heard any news for some time – the nearer you are the less you know – but the war generally seems to be going well and I still have hopes that it will be over by the end of October – I'm due to go home then anyway. But I must admit the Germans fight hard and we've had one or two unpleasant encounters with their shore batteries recently – their shooting is good but they don't seem to have the luck – thank God!

God, darling I am so looking forward to coming home to you soon – tho' I don't quite understand why you should say you are almost frightened to meet me again – especially when I remember some of the lectures you gave me in Falmouth. Still I don't think two years has changed either of us so considerably, I certainly love you as much as ever and the only change I notice in myself is that I'm a much more sober type these days (there just isn't the liquor to be had!). Seriously darling the enforced absence has done at least one good thing; it has shown me that you are the only girl in the world for me and that I love you and always will love you with all my heart. There'll be so many things to do together when I get back but first I want to have you and only you to myself in some quiet place where we can laze and talk and make up for the two lost years. And of course there's the question of the marriage, anything formal would scare me stiff and I rather dread to consider parents' ideas on this subject! However I'm prepared to be a martyr – if you desire it.

Darling I love you and think of you so much – please don't ever change, I never will.

All my love my sweet
Ever your own
Don xxx

P.S. Wot about them there photos?

Chapter Twelve

SEPTEMBER – DECEMBER 1944

It can be assumed that in September 1944 the 3rd ML Flotilla had some sort of a base on the small island of La Maddalena (see **Map F**, on page 152), off the North coast of Sardinia. Less than two weeks after their encounter with the Maquis at Port-St-Louis-Du-Rhône, Don was having his photograph taken there with the other 15 officers of his flotilla, confirming eight ships in all.

Officers of the 3rd ML Flotilla - La Maddalena, 8th September 1944

Back Row (left to right): Munns, Bannister, Rothwell, Pickles, Dugdale, Cdr Simpson, Osman-Jones, Barfield, Bickerton, Irens
Middle Row: Carter, Denton, Dugdale, Nicol, Gwynn, Andrews
Front Row: "Salerno" Sally (the dog)

On **10th September 1944,** Don sarcastically remarks that, at his age, he struggles with the shock of finding three letters from Linda awaiting him! He has also received a telegram. Over the months and years his tone is always upbeat when he has just received word from her, whereas during weeks of silence his mood grows progressively gloomier. The forces must have realised the importance of maintaining an efficient postal service, in difficult circumstances, on the morale of their troops. With the often-indiscriminate bombing in UK, it must have been as much a relief to the servicemen abroad to hear that all was well as it was to their loved ones back home. For Don and Linda, in their circumstances, having only had intermittent liaisons over a few short months, it would come as added relief to read the words of love and devotion.

In response to one of Linda's letters, he jokes that perhaps she had given a jitterbug exhibition at her WAAF concert. The jitterbug was popular in the early 1940s – it combined energetic dance with acrobatics. In her letter of 15th August (see Letters appended to Chapter Ten) Linda had asked whether Don knew Francis Coleridge, an RNVR and friend of LACW Jane Seymour; Don confirms that he has run across him recently. Don also mentions having heard from Dudley, who had brought him up to date on mutual friends: Richard, Sheila, Max, etc. Dudley Arnaud, who had been SO in charge of Don's original 25th ML Flotilla, had returned to the UK soon after Don transferred to the 3rd. He had gone on to lead the 20th ML Flotilla, of which he was also SO, in the Normandy landings. Don relays how Dudley had told him he had not lost any ships but that the invasion was "mighty unpleasant". It is estimated that some 120,000 Allied troops and nearly as many Germans were killed or wounded during the landings and the subsequent two weeks.

Don has been to the cinema and seen the film *Footsteps in the Dark*. Either this could have been aboard one of the bigger ships in an Allied-occupied port or he may have returned to either Malta or Gibraltar as he says: "since we got back". Wherever it is, he describes it as the most depressing dump ever and, on a "filthy" night, both their engines have broken down and they are now rolling in 40-foot seas. It is also evident that his flotilla is no longer required in Southern France as the Germans have retreated with minimal fighting. He is still awaiting an up-to-date photograph of Linda. He optimistically says he will cable her when his relief arrives, although he accepts that it might be several months. In the event, it was to be ten more months before he would return to the UK.

On **15th September 1944**, Linda is spending some leave in bed with a cold at her parents' home in Amos House, Totland Bay, Isle of Wight. She has had some mail forwarded from *RAF Branscombe,* but nothing from Don. She hopes to be better at the weekend to enable her to visit her sister in Bournemouth and see her 13-month-old nephew (Anthony). She is delighted by the latest war news, and she is inclined to agree with Don's father's prediction that Germany will collapse by 22nd October 1944.

In his letter dated **17th September 1944**, Don apologises for the lack of a stamp. He endorsed the rectangle on the air letter, reserved for a British stamp to be affixed, with the words "NOT AVAILABLE". Clearly it still reaches its intended destination. One wonders if, like today, Linda would have been charged double the required 3d postage charge. Don says he is feeling "thoroughly browned off" as he has not taken to his new colleagues in the 3rd ML Flotilla and parties are conspicuous by their absence. His ship is undergoing a refit, which again might imply that he has returned to Gibraltar or Malta. He reports that Phyllis has been relieved. Don says he would like to sail *ML 338* home now but realises that this is just wishful thinking. He is nearing the point of two years away from home and will then shout for his relief. He has met someone who was based at Fishguard and who remembers the old pubs and his "dear friend" Captain Diggle.

On **24th September 1944** Linda writes again, having found two letters from Don awaiting her on her return to *RAF Branscombe*. She tells how her mother had waved her off at Yarmouth on the ferry. The trains were packed, and she had travelled mostly in the guard's van. The total journey time to Sidmouth was nine-and-a-half hours. She says that, apart from their RAF supervisor getting drunk, the concert had gone well. The CO took a dim view of the male supervisor then dressing as a WAAF. She is glad to hear that Don is not drinking and warns him that, if he does drink heavily, there will be many lectures. She reminds him of the time she waved him off at Falmouth on 8th October 1942 and he was angry because she said that she could not wait for him longer than ten years. In a postscript, she says that the photographs will be another month.

Don corresponds **on the same day**, saying he has just received a sea letter from his mother with photographs enclosed. He reiterates being in the "same dump", having a refit. The cinema has now closed down. The weather is grim and he yearns to be back home.

He refers to the recent White Paper (announced in September 1944) on discharge from the forces at the end of the European war, declaring that he has reached the stupendous age of 54. It makes him hopeful that he will not be required in the Far East, despite attractive rates of pay. He is eager to leave the Navy and resume his career at the Ministry of Health. He wonders what has become of other colleagues who have joined up. Several he knows have been killed and more are POWs (Prisoners of War).

The White Paper to which he refers was drawn up by Ernest Bevin, the Minister of Labour in the wartime coalition government. It was widely regarded as a fair way to demobilise the troops once the war had ended. Troops were categorised into two classes. The majority fell into class A, and the order in which these troops would be demobilised was based on their date of birth and when they joined up. Two months of service equated to a year of age; hence Don's calculation that he was 54! (He was in his 28th year and had served nearly 52 months: 52 divided by two gives 26 which, when added to 28, comes to 54.) Upon release, they were entitled to eight weeks leave on full pay. Workers key to post-war restoration, such as construction workers, coal miners, etc. would be released more quickly, although these troops would only receive three weeks' leave on full pay.

Returning to Don's letter, the men are all wondering what will happen to them now that the Gothic Line has been successfully challenged with the Allies breaking through to Rimini on 21st September. The Gothic Line was the defensive line to which the Germans had fallen back – following the capture of Rome in early June 1944 and other successes the Allies had won in their slow but steady progress northward (see **Map H**, on page 197). The Germans had been preparing the Gothic Line through the Apennine Mountains, approximately 25 miles north of a line from Leghorn (on the Mediterranean Sea in the west), through Florence, to Ancona (on the Adriatic Sea in the east). There were about 3,000 fortifications constructed, in a 10-mile deep band, mostly by 15,000 Italian slaves. These Italians were no fans of the Germans and ensured that the concrete used and the workmanship undertaken were both of substandard quality.

The Allies eventually launched attacks against the Gothic Line in Operation Olive, commencing with the British and Canadians on the Adriatic coast side on 25th August 1944. This was followed by a US Army push through the centre, north of Florence. Fighting was heavy with attacks and subsequent counter-attacks. The decisive Battle of Rimini (see **Map H**) took place between 13th and 21st September 1944. It was probably news of this success that had filtered through to Don and his colleagues and had prompted him to comment that the Gothic

Line had been successfully challenged. He goes on to speculate that it is unlikely that the Germans will hold any Mediterranean coastline for any length of time and, hopefully, the ML crews will be sent home.

Damon Runyon from *Wikipedia*

Don writes again on **7th October 1944**, acknowledging receipt of Linda's letter of 15th September. He casts doubt on his father's grasp of the political situation to predict that the war in Europe would end on 22nd October 1944. He reports that things have slowed down in the Mediterranean and the weather has been "pretty filthy". They have moved again and, although their new base is not up to much, it is better than the previous location and there are three cinemas and frequent ENSA shows. He has been passing his spare time reading, principally Damon Runyan and Thane Smith. Damon Runyan was an American author who wrote short stories mainly about Broadway and New York in the 1920s and 1930s. The musical *Guys and Dolls* was based on one of his books. Archive information on Thane Smith, however, seems to have faded with time.

Don remarks that the mail situation has worsened; his mother has not heard from him for five weeks, despite him writing to and cabling his parents and Linda regularly. He confirms that he has received a receipt for the £14 transmitted but has had no acknowledgement from Linda. Don's letters invariably conclude with a long paragraph saying how much he loves her and he reveals that the first thing he always looks for in her letters is confirmation that the sentiments are reciprocated. As his two years is now up, he eagerly scans the signals file to see whether his relief has been appointed.

Although he has not received any more mail by **10th October 1944,** he nonetheless writes to give Linda his address, which is Mess 276, c/o Coastal Forces Base, Leghorn in Italy. Presumably he had not been at liberty to mention that fact three days earlier. As it is about 25 miles south of the Gothic Line, this really confirms that the Allied advance beyond the Gothic Line has consolidated and that Leghorn (Livorno) can be protected from enemy bombardment – it had suffered badly from Allied air attacks before it fell. Don says he enjoyed watching *Girl Crazy* at one of the three cinemas. The weather is still bad, with strong winds and heavy rain. He reckons that he had a lucky escape from a party the previous evening, held to celebrate one of their No. 1s getting his own command. He is planning to go to the cinema again that evening with a couple of friends.

On **16th October 1944,** he again reports that no mail has arrived. He hopes to visit Florence in the next week or so (which is about 55 miles inland from Leghorn), as it will be good to see a town free from damage. Some personnel have already been and found plenty to do and plenty of drink available.

Don would have observed the destruction on Leghorn, which, being an industrial port, was an Allied bombing target. As an Axis power, the bombing of Italy was never as controversial as was that of France. However, the Allies did come under pressure not to bomb Rome, as it represented the heart of the Christian faith. Other cities and towns which were considered of outstanding architectural merit, such as Florence, were also avoided as much as possible.

However, Florence was a major rail junction and strategically situated about 25 miles south of the Gothic Line. Therefore the Allies used their most accurate bomber squadrons. Also, after the Italian surrender in September 1943, the Germans were effectively occupying part of the country and there was a fine balance between bombing strategic targets and protecting civilians, which was not always achieved. The fact that ML crews were able to visit Florence was a good indication of the control that the Allies had south of the Gothic Line.

Two evenings earlier, they had watched an ENSA performance before bringing the company down to the boats, and Don had spent the previous evening having a quiet game of poker, which he invariably won. That day, he had planned to play tennis but decided to write letters instead. He has obviously grown fond of *ML 338*, which they have recently painted, and again comments that he would like to take her back to UK but does not expect to get the opportunity. He is beginning to come around to the likelihood that he will not return home until 1945 but, by comparison, many in the Army are serving abroad for four years. His fear is that eventually he will be deployed to the Far East. They have been organising a dance for the following Saturday but, despite acceptances from the male faction, they have no women.

On **14ᵗʰ November 1944** Don writes, still from Leghorn, acknowledging Linda's letter of 25ᵗʰ October and her cable (both missing). He apologises for not having replied earlier but, without any explanation (probably owing to censorship), he says that he has been away for a short time. He comments that she is lucky to be granted leave over Christmas; his hopes of spending that time with her are rapidly fading. They have had an easy time recently, principally owing to bad weather. They have not had many parties, and Hugh and he have been spending their time cheering up some of the "confirmed pessimists" who want to go home – even though they have not been there as long as they have.

This is the first mention of Hugh Gwynn who became Don's best friend – the following year he was to be the Best Man at Don and Linda's wedding. From the *Naval Lists*, Hugh was appointed Lieutenant on 11ᵗʰ December 1942, three months after Don. In August, October and December 1943 his entries show him in command of *HDML 1237*; in February and April 1944 in command of *ML 483*; and in March 1945 in command of *ML 462*. Although there is no record of flotillas in these publications, it is a reasonable assumption that in November 1944 Hugh was with Don in the 3ʳᵈ ML Flotilla. This is borne out by the photograph on the first page of this chapter.

Returning to Don's letter, he says they spent one afternoon collecting chestnuts but in that area there are few walks other than through blitzed muddy towns. Most evenings are spent either at the cinema or on the boats, with the probable date of arrival of their reliefs the main topic of conversation. They have had one good evening, not in Leghorn, partying at someone's flat. When the girls had gone and they had cooked and eaten dinner, they went on to visit the American Club. Don then tells Linda he has had a letter from Dudley Arnaud who now has a shore job in London.

Don writes on **26ᵗʰ November 1944** saying the weather is again cold, wet and windy. His spare time has mostly been spent quietly with Hugh, although they did have a party at the American Club. It now looks as though his relief will not arrive until the New Year. He comments that, under the demobilisation scheme, all married women will be released from service – implying that, once married, Linda will fall into this category.

Linda replies from *RAF Sennen*, Lands End (rather than *RAF Branscombe*, Sidmouth) on **4th December 1944**, having just received Don's letter of 26th November. She comments that it is her usual luck to be posted there just before Christmas, as changes are always unsettling. She has been billeted in a largish hotel overlooking the sea, with 100 steps leading up to the building. She has sent a photograph by sea.

Don sends Linda a 1944 Christmas card:

1944 Christmas card from Don

Don writes again on **31st December 1944** with apologies for not having written for over a week, owing to hard work and Christmas parties. He responds to Linda's letter of 26th November and says that he had felt dejected on Christmas Day, as he had had visions of spending it with her. He had a party on board with his crew in their mess. On Boxing Day evening, the "dinner at the local Officers Club thrown for us by our Big White Chief" had been a disappointment and he and Hugh had left early. He had been ashore the previous evening to see *Ministry of Fear* which he enjoyed. He says his mother told him that they have received Linda's most recent photograph, which he is still awaiting. At midnight he plans to drink a toast to the two of them for "one quick, long and happy marriage".

So 1944 closes with the prospect of Germany collapsing within a few months and the war in Europe finally ending. One interesting fact that appears in the book *Flag 4* is that during the year of 1944 the 3rd ML Flotilla had swept a total of 177 mines.

Letters: September – December 1944

now and I believe a
rather mischievous young
monkey, almost as bad as
you were at his age!

Isn't the news magnificent.
I'm sure this business will be
over sooner than we expect –
you _____ Germany will
_____
I am inclined to agree.

Darling I love you so
very much and I won't
change. Please write soon.
More later.

All my love,
Ever yours
Linda

H.M.M.L. 338,
c/o G.P.O.,
London

10th September 1944

Cpl. Linda Russell W.A.A.F.,
R.A.F. Branscombe,
Salcombe Regis,
Near Sidmouth,
South Devon,
ENGLAND.

My darling Linda

You should know that at my great age I can't stand such shocks – I got back and found three letters from you awaiting me! Darling I'm so relieved to know that all is well as I was thinking the most horrible things. Believe me I do trust you and know that you love me but when I don't hear from you for so long I can't help feeling that something must be wrong – but I promise to be very good in future if you keep writing as frequently.

How did your concert go off – one assumes that you gave a jitterbug exhibition, or perhaps you thought it might not appeal to the majority tastes. Do let me know.

Yes I know Francis Coleridge – he's quite a good type and I ran across him again only a short time ago. I also had a letter from Dudley who appears to be getting worked to death but apparently found time for a hectic party with Richard, Sheila, Max etc. From his rather vivid description I'm not sorry I wasn't able to be there! He tells me that he hasn't lost any boats in the Channel affair but that it was mighty unpleasant.

I went to the cinema tonight for the first time for God knows how long – "Footsteps in the Dark", Errol Flynn in a Thin Man type of story which at any rate whiled away a couple of hours. This really is the most depressing dump ever – haven't even had a drink since we got back, almost TT now!

We had a pretty filthy night at sea, both engines broke down and we lay and rolled in 40 foot seas – how I loathe the sunny Mediterranean.

Darling I miss you so much and not even a more recent photograph to help me out of my misery; however perhaps it won't be long before I won't have any need of such things and I'll be able to hold a real live you in my arms once more. When I left I didn't believe I'd be able to face two whole years without you but it's amazing what you can do when you have to. I think of you all the time and the whole flotilla must be rather fed up with hearing about you (one of the blokes was at Falmouth when we were there and remembers you).

I'll cable you as soon as I get definite news of my relief although it may of course be several months yet. Still I have the feeling of suppressed excitement as the time approaches and God knows how I'll feel when I actually see you again – the day can't come too quickly.

All my love my angel, please write as often as you can
I'll always love you as much

Ever your own
Don xxx

P.S. Your telegram arrived at the same time – many thanks.

Miss Linda Russell,
Amos House,
Totland Bay,
I.O.W.

15th September 1944

Lieut F. D. Bickerton,
R.N.V.R.
H.M.M.L. 338
c/o G.P.O. London

My darling,

I'm afraid there is nothing in the way of news since yesterday. Unfortunately, I'm in bed with a temperature – suppose I caught a cold changing into civvies - & feeling sorry for myself.

Mother has been fussing around with hot milk and filthy medicine, and I fear is coming up to rub my chest with camphorated oil. (It is rather nice really, I'm quite enjoying myself!!). I had some mail from Branscombe but nothing from you. Hope to hear within the next few days, no doubt there is some on the way.

Surely you are due for leave? Have just been looking at those photos you sent of Ischia - what a heavenly place; almost as beautiful as this funny little Island!

I'm hoping to be fit this weekend to spend a few days with my sister in Bournemouth. It is ages since I saw my young nephew, he is thirteen months old now and I believe a rather mischievous young monkey, almost as bad as you were at his age!

Isn't the news magnificent? I'm sure this business will be over sooner than we expect – your Father says Germany will collapse by October 22nd, and I am inclined to agree.

Darling I love you so very much and I won't change. Please write soon.
More later.

All my love,
Ever yours
Linda xxx

HMML 338,
c/o G.P.O.,
London.

17th September 1944

Cpl. Linda Russell W.A.A.F.,
R.A.F., Branscombe,
Salcombe Regis,
near Sidmouth,
South Devon,
ENGLAND

My darling Linda

I think the Admiralty must have forgotten of our existence as far as mail is concerned as we have had none since our return – apart from the back mail which was awaiting us. I must be in a nostalgic mood as I have just reread it all including Dudley's description of the party with Richard and Max – wish we could both have been there. At the moment I'd give a lot to run into old Gibby as I'm feeling thoroughly browned off – none of the types in this flotilla interest me and parties are conspicuous only by their absence.

I'm still doing my refit but there is no relaxation or amusement in this dump and even the cinema has now closed down. It's even worse for the troops and none of us will be sorry to get away.

Phyllis has just been relieved but no one seems to know quite why and it doesn't appear that he's going home. Personally it would suit me very well to bring the boat home but that is probably only wishful thinking.

At the moment I'm just lying at a buoy and ditching all the water I was given in the petrol and feeling pretty fed up with the whole business. However rather less than a month to go to the two years and then I'm going to start shouting for my relief.

Darling I do wish I was with you now and I promise I shouldn't be grumbling about anything – not even the lack of beer! You know that you are the only girl in the world for me and we'll have lots of fun together to make up for the past two years. I suppose it's going to be quite difficult to settle down when I do get home but so long as I can get based near you I don't mind what happens.

I met a bloke the other day who was based at Fishguard and remembers all the old pubs and my dear friend Captain Diggle – I wonder if he's still there.

This is a horribly incoherent sort of letter and its only purpose is to tell you that you are the sweetest person in the world and that I love you with all my heart.

Please write soon and don't forget the photograph.

All my love my angel
Ever your own
Don xxx

P.S. Sorry about the stamp (or lack of it) but there just aren't any here.

H.M.M.L. 338,
c/o G.P.O.,
London.

24th September 1944

Cpl. Linda Russell W.A.A.F.,
R.A.F. Branscombe,
Salcombe Regis,
Near Sidmouth,
South Devon,
ENGLAND.

My darling Linda

No more mail has arrived except for some old sea mail which included a letter from Mother enclosing the photographs. Les' taste seems to be improving and neither Mother or Father look any older – in fact I'm not sure that I'll look young enough to claim them as parents by the time I get home.

I'm still stuck in the same dump doing my refit but I hope to be away shortly tho' quite where I don't yet know. I believe I told you that now even the cinema has closed down so there just isn't anything to do except write and of course I'm getting through enormous numbers of books.

The weather too is pretty grim as it's been blowing hard, plenty of rain and also quite cold – in fact I've had the Med. I'd love to be at home in cold weather, a warm cheering fire, the cheerful company of the real pub and last, but hardly least, you. Last night I even dreamed that my relief had arrived but as I'm no fortune teller I wouldn't know what interpretation to place upon it. To think that this time two years ago I was on leave almost makes me weep – still it shouldn't be long now.

I see that according to the recent White Paper on discharge from the Forces at the end of the European war I have achieved the stupendous age of 54 – makes me feel hopeful that I shan't have to go to the Far East in spite of the more attractive rates of pay. All I wish for is to get out, return to the Ministry of Health and become a stodgy civil servant. I often wonder what has become of the blokes I knew there; several I know have been killed and more are P.O.W. but that, of course, was before the invasion and I suppose one must expect rather more to become casualties.

Not even any parties to tell you about I'm afraid – everyone is sitting quietly on board although there was some talk earlier of a poker party, nothing seems to have materialised.

We are all wondering what will happen to us now that the Gothic Line has been forced as it seems unlikely that the Germans will hold any coast line on this side for any length of time (I hope!). Maybe they'll even send us home.

Darling I'm feeling all excited at the prospect of seeing you again in the not very distant future – there are so many things to tell you, so many things to do together. I love you very, very much my darling and the sooner we can settle down to a normal life the happier I shall be. That is the day to which I've been looking forward ever since I met you.

Please write as often as you can – your letters are the only joy in a dreary present.

I'll always love you my sweet

Ever your own
Don xxx

P.S. What about that photo?

Cpl L. Russell
Branscombe
Nr Sidmouth
S. Devon

24th September 1944

Lieut F. D. Bickerton,
R.N.V.R.
H.M.M.L. 338
c/o G.P.O. London

My darling,

I got back last night and found two letters awaiting me, which saved me from bursting into tears.

Mother saw me off at Yarmouth smiling as she waved the beastly top heavy ferry out of sight, and then huge lumps came into my throat – you know how it is, and I wanted to jump over the side and swim back to her.

The trains were packed and I travelled mostly in the guard's van; people, as usual, were kind but I felt miserable and unsociable and pretended to read – nasty spoilt girl!! I left home at 10 and arrived at Sidmouth about 7.30. Well, it is good to hear that you have had some mail from me. I suppose it was a shock! Anyway it is a relief to know that all is forgiven.

The concert went off quite well, apart from our R.A.F. supervisor getting drunk. He insisted on telling low jokes and appeared on the stage when he wished. However we persuaded him to change into a W.A.A.F. uniform, which kept him quiet for some time and then there was no holding him back. Needless to say a week later his posting came through (the C.O. took a dim view!).

No I did not jitterbug. A. I can't and B if I could I wouldn't because I think it looks grim – consider yourself squashed! It is good to hear that you are almost T.T. I am serious too as I couldn't bear the thought of you always drinking heavily. If you start again there will be many lectures I promise you.

Darling I am quite sure that I love you more each day, very soon it will be impossible to love you any more and then what are you going to do?

Two years on October 8 I left you at Falmouth – what an age? Remember how angry you were when I said I couldn't wait for you longer than 10 years! Perhaps within six months we shall be together again and the fighting in Europe, anyway, will be over [illegible].

All my love darling
Ever yours
Linda

P.S. the photo will be another month – sorry. Just a small one.

H.M.M.L. 338,
c/o G.P.O.,
London.

7th October 1944

Cpl. Linda Russell W.A.A.F.,
R.A.F. Branscombe,
Salcombe Regis,
Near Sidmouth,
South Devon,
ENGLAND.

Linda darling

So pleased to receive your letter of Sept 15th but not nearly so pleased to learn that it was written from your bed - do hurry up and get better darling, it's so miserable being so far away from you. Yes, I am due for leave but you know how uncertain reliefs are out here and I may, therefore, do several months over my two years. Trust you enjoyed your visit to your sister at Bournemouth tho' I'm not sure I like the comparison drawn between your young nephew and myself at the age of thirteen months - in fact precisely what has Mother been telling you? Anyway it's a lie!

Much as I admire my Father's grasp of both the political and military situation in Europe, I find it a little difficult to believe that his inside knowledge surpasses that of Churchill and I am therefore a little sceptical of his date of Oct 22nd - much as I hope it will prove correct. Things have slowed down considerably out here and believe me the weather is pretty filthy.

We've moved again and although this place is not up to much nothing can be worse than our last base - at any rate there are three cinemas and fairly frequent ENSA shows, which help to keep the troops happy. I've been doing a fair amount of reading - principally Damon Runyan and Thane Smith both of whom I like immensely.

The mail situation has deteriorated and Mother informs me that she hasn't had a letter for five weeks - I simply can't understand it as I write to you both very regularly and send cables whenever an opportunity presents itself. Incidentally you haven't yet told me whether or not you have received the £14 - the receipt from the accounts section has turned up at this end.

Darling the thing I always look first for in your letters is to see if you say you love me still and, when I see it, I can then settle down happily and read the rest of the letter. I love you with all my heart darling and always will - for keeps. Two years is quite a lot of leeway to make up but I think we can do it without much difficulty. Now that the time draws closer I grow more and more impatient day by day and eagerly scan the signal file to see if my relief has been appointed - as yet without luck.

Please remember Linda angel that I'll always love you as much - I just couldn't change

Please write soon

All my love darling
Ever your own
Don xxx

Lieut F.D. Bickerton R.N.V.R.
Mess 276
c/o Coastal Force Base,
Leghorn,
Italy.

10th October 1944

Cpl. Linda Russell W.A.A.F.,
R.A.F. Branscombe,
Salcombe Regis,
Near Sidmouth
South Devon,
England.

Linda darling

No more mail yet but I thought I'd better write and give you the above address – I hope it will hasten things.

Nor have I much news for you – did go to a cinema the other night where I saw Mickie Rooney and Judy Garland in "Girl Crazy" which I quite enjoyed. This place is almost the end, it's badly damaged principally, I imagine, by Allied air attack before it fell – but at any rate there are three cinemas and an ENSA show. The weather, too, is hardly contributing to our happiness at the moment as it's raining hard and blowing quite a lot – still I think we can get by!

There was quite a party last night (which I didn't attend) as one of the No 1's has got his command. I was on one of the other boats when I heard rather frightful sounds coming from the quay, guessed the reason and decided to make myself as inconspicuous as possible. I learned this morning from one of the wan faces that they were on their way over to drag me out, according to them under the impression I'd say "It couldn't matter less" and join them. Quite a lucky escape!

Tonight I'm off with a couple of the blokes to the cinema tho' I've no idea what the film is – anyway it's better than sitting on board with nothing to do except read (My dear, not a drop of hootch on the ship!!!).

My crew are wondering whether their reliefs will turn up in time to enable them to get home by X'mas – I sincerely hope so but I'm not at all confident that it will be so. However I suppose the longer we stay out here the less will be our chances of being sent out to the Far East and, believe me, I've not the slightest desire to leave you ever again once I get back.

Darling I do love you so very much and I can think of no new words with which to express my feelings. But you must know that my only wish is to get home, marry you and never leave you again. There are many things we must do together and I feel appalled that we are forced to spend so much valuable time away from each other. Just keep on telling me that you love me and the separation is almost bearable.

Write soon Linda my sweet

All my love always
Ever your own
Don xxx

Mess 276,
Coastal Force Base,
Leghorn,
Italy.

16th October 1944

Cpl. Linda Russell W.A.A.F.,
R.A.F. Branscombe,
Salcombe Regis,
Near Sidmouth,
South Devon,
ENGLAND.

My darling Linda

The inevitable day – still no mail! tho' I think we should get some in the next couple of days. And there isn't very much to write about but I hope to visit Florence in the next week or so, it will be a change to see a town free from damage. Some of the blokes who spent a couple of days there thoroughly enjoyed themselves as there is plenty to do and, apparently, plenty to drink which will be quite a change.

Last night we spent quietly on one of the boats playing poker – I won as usual, my luck seems to be good out here – and then sat back and talked shop for a couple of hours, ventilation of more drips than chat.

The night before we went to an ENSA show, the best I've seen, and then brought the company down to the boats. They were a good bunch and I think everyone enjoyed themselves.

Today I don't know what to do with myself. As it wasn't raining I had decided to play tennis but I now feel far too lazy so instead I'll just bore you. We've just painted the ship and the old boat is looking very tiddley – I'd love to take her home but I don't suppose I'll get the opportunity. It's now just two days over two years since we left U.K. and I have a horrible suspicion that I shan't see it again until next year – it's a hell of a long time but nothing can be done about it, in fact I'm glad I'm not in the Army where they appear to do over four years.

We've been organising (more or less, anyway) a dance for next Saturday and to date we got everything except women. The unfortunate part is that we have already sent out all the invitations and have been inundated with acceptances from the male faction – now we're almost at the stage where we send out revised invitations to a party with lots of hootch. I'll let you know how it goes if I don't get kicked to death in the meantime!

Darling I miss you very much and I was hoping to be with you before X'mas but I fear the chances are not very good. But please believe me when I tell you that I love you with all my heart and that you are always in my thoughts. The only thing that scares me is that I might go home, get leave, and then be sent out to the Far East – just the last thing I want to happen as I couldn't bear to leave you again. Maybe I'm just rather depressed at the moment and nothing of the sort will happen.

Please write as often as you can Linda darling and please take care of yourself and don't catch any more chills or colds.

All my love always sweetest
Ever your own
Don xxx

P.S. What about the photograph?

Mess 276,
Coastal Force Base,
Leghorn.

14th November 1944

Cpl. Linda Russell W.A.A.F.,
R.A.F. Branscombe,
Salcombe Regis,
Near Sidmouth,
South Devon,
ENGLAND.

My own darling Linda

I've received your letter of 25th October together with the cable – sorry I haven't replied earlier but I've been away for a short time. You are a lucky person to have drawn the X'mas leave ticket, my own hopes of spending it with you fading rapidly i.e. X'mas 1944 anyway.

We've had a pretty easy time recently principally because the weather has been so filthy, rain, wind and icy cold especially in the mornings, when it should be time to get up – I get lazier day by day and of course think of Tenby when the temptation was irresistible! Parties just don't seem to happen these days and Hugh and I spend our time attempting to cheer up some of our confirmed pessimists who are gnattering about going home tho' they have been out far less time than either of us (How can anyone attempt to write coherently with the radio blithering alleged "jazz"?).

We spent one afternoon collecting chestnuts which we took back on board and roasted – big eats! But as you can guess in this place there are few walks, I don't find walking through blitzed muddy towns particularly attractive, and most evenings are spent either at the cinema or on the boats discussing the probable date of entry into the Navy of our reliefs.

However we spent one good evening, not in Leghorn, at a flat belonging to one of the shore bods, dancing and drinking oodles of beer. When the girls had gone we cooked our dinner (quite domesticated these days!) and, having seen off the beer, went on to an American Club – well we weren't thrown out, not quite anyway.

Had a letter from Dudley the other day; he now has a shore job in London and seems to be enjoying life. I might add that he promises some frightful parties when we get home, but I've told him that I rather fear my leave may be filled with other more important matters! What say you my sweet?

'Fraid the photograph has not turned up yet my darling but sea mail seems to take up to six weeks still – however I'm looking forward immensely to receiving it.

Exactly two years and one month today since I sailed from U.K. – a hell of a long time but it won't last much longer and when I come home I'll be with you for keeps. I adore you my angel and just want to be with you always, nothing can ever change my feelings for you. Keep writing as often as you can and just tell me that you'll always love me, that's all that matters to me – darling these words are so futile I want to be with you and tell you then you couldn't possibly doubt it.

All my love always Linda my darling
Ever your own
Don xxx

Lieut F.D. Bickerton R.N.V.R.
Coastal Force Base,
Leghorn,
Italy.

26th November 1944

Cpl. Linda Russell W.A.A.F.,
R.A.F. Sennan,
Land's End,
Cornwall.

My darling Linda

No news from you for some time but nevertheless I'll do the generous thing and write to you – your apologies are assumed!

The first subject to spring to mind is the weather and what weather at that – rain, wind, rain, wind, cold, and today a combination of all three. Still I suppose it's pretty cheerless at home at this time of the year tho' I admit that I can think of no better place to spend it. Today has been very quiet as I haven't even left the ship – in fact Hugh came over for tea and we had big eats on the strength of it. Last night, too, was equally quiet as we went for dinner to the mess and then played darts, by 2130 Hugh & I were the sole supervisors as all the others had turned in – our bicycles are definitely in pawn for the moment.

We had one party four nights ago. We decided to honour the American club with our patronage and together with two other bods and an American Air Force type we went to town in a big way. It was the first party for ages but we managed to conduct ourselves in the usual gentlemanly fashion and stay out of all [illegible]! Still it was fun.

I'm afraid the photograph hasn't turned up yet but I'm hoping it will be in the next sea mail – incidentally if you had any snaps taken during the summer I'd love some copies.

I'm still anxiously awaiting my relief but it doesn't appear likely until the New Year. Darling this will be the third Christmas spent away from you and I hope the last. One of our blokes has been out precisely six weeks and drips more than the rest of us put together – I suppose because one tends towards resignation after a time. Still we have the whole of our lives ahead of us and we'll have a hell of a lot of fun together to make up for these miserable times. I love you more and more my darling & I'm only living to be back with you again – lots of leave and all of it spent together. Incidentally under the demobilisation scheme I see all married women will be released which will be an excellent thing. Just keep on telling me that you love me and will always love me then I shall be perfectly content.

Write as often as you can Linda my sweetest

All my love
Ever your own
Don xxx

L Russell,
R.A.F. Sennen,
Lands End,
Cornwall.

4th December 1944

Lieut F. D. Bickerton,
R.N.V.R.
Mess 276,
Coastal Force Base,
Leghorn,
Italy.

My darling Don,

My usual luck to be posted before Xmas! Changes are always unsettling and at the moment I ain't feeling very happy. I'm billeted in a largish hotel which incidentally is beautifully situated overlooking the sea. There are over a 100 steps leading up to the building - which is no joke in this weather, but they say is splendid for the figure!

There are quaint old cottages scattered all over the place, and a lifeboat house on the front where dear old fishermen gather, and where I hope to wangle a crafty lobster later.

If only you were at Falmouth life would be perfect.

Just had your air letter dated 26th Nov which has made me feel tons better. We will make up for these miserable times and promise never to leave me again.

It is great to hear that you have had only one party recently, from which I gather that you are almost T.T. I hope the Americans out there are better than the types I've seen in this country. I couldn't send the photo by air I'm afraid so it will be some time reaching you. I warn you it is pretty ghastly, he has touched up the mouth making it look hard, but hope it will do until I can send another.

Darling, I love you so much, please don't worry about me. I shan't change. I've never been so sure of anything in my life, and come home soon.

All my love,
Ever yours
Linda xxx

Mess 276,
Coastal Force Base,
Leghorn.

31st December 1944

Cpl. Linda Russell W.A.A.F.,
R.A.F. Sennen,
Lands End,
Cornwall,
ENGLAND.

My darling Linda

I know I'm probably in your bad books for not writing for over a week but things have been pretty hectic with both hard work and Christmas parties – am I forgiven once more please?

What bad luck being posted just before X'mas – did it interfere with your leave or did you manage to get home? It sounds a heavenly spot but I must admit I can work up no enthusiasm for any hotel which overlooks the sea! I've had my fill of it recently and in a rather too literal way at that.

I felt horribly dejected on Christmas day as I'd previously had visions of spending it with you and to cap it all no Christmas mail arrived – hasn't done even now. As usual I went down on the mess deck and had all my crew down here. They drank every drop of stuff that I'd saved from our meagre rations and then looked around for more – still it was a pretty good party and I rather enjoyed it.

On Boxing evening we were invited to a dinner at the local Officers Club thrown for us by our Big White Chief but judging by the white faces and shaky hands I don't think many people enjoyed it overmuch. I know that both Hugh and I left early! Anyway it was our last party and I only went ashore again last night to see a flic "Ministry of Fear" and quite a good one incidentally.

Mother tells me that they have received your photograph (luckier than I am) and that they like it immensely and say that you look "a very nice girl" – of course I've had to disillusion them on that score!

Well darling the New Year starts tomorrow and it's one in which I hope we will be able to spend most of our time together. It's been a hell of a long time since I last saw you, and my main fear has been that you might change your mind about me – no darling that's not really true as I do entirely believe you; but being so far away from you tends to warp my better judgment rather badly. I love you, my darling, with all my heart and just waiting for that cursed relief of mine to turn up. At midnight tonight I'm going to drink a toast to us and to one quick, long and happy marriage – I know only too well that without you I haven't anything to live for. Hurry up the photo, my sweet, and write as often as you can.

All my love sweetheart
Ever your own
Don xxx

x for the New Year.

Chapter Thirteen

JANUARY – JULY 1945

Don's first letter of 1945 is dated **3rd January** and he reports that they had a fairly quiet New Year's Eve. He and Hugh arrived about an hour late at a party in the Barracks Wardroom. They left at 20:00 and had seen the New Year in, on one of the boats. Then the following evening they had a quiet dinner at the Officers' Club. He has seen the film *Heaven is Round the Corner* and reckons that Will Fyffe is the only actor worth watching. He plans to see *Hail the Conquering Hero* that evening. He ends his letter in the usual way and stresses how impatient he is to return home.

He writes again on **15th February 1945**, acknowledging receipt of Linda's letter of 7th February (missing). He has also received her photograph. Don has enquired about reliefs and thinks it will be at least a month before anything happens. He has been to Ischia for a short spell (presumably to the same rest camp where he had been before). They also had a good dinner party on Hugh's boat. He mentions that Hugh wants to be his best man and says he likes the idea. That evening, he has seen the film *Thousands Cheer* which, he says, kept breaking down every ten minutes.

Linda must have been very relieved to receive this letter, as his previous letter was dated 3rd January. Apart from a six-week gap during the autumn of 1943 when he had been in hospital, the frequency of his letter writing had been exemplary and seemingly much better than hers. However, she is obviously finding their enforced separation as difficult as he is and all the frustration seems to have come to a head when she receives this letter. The outlet for her frustration at the delay is to write a number of comments against passages of his letter. Next to his apologetic opening paragraph, she writes "7 WEEKS" (presumably the gap between receipt of these two letters) and twice underlines the comment. His excuse, that the delay is unavoidable, is given short shrift with the words "HM! HM!!", and she underlines the word 'still' in the sentence where he says: "I still love you just as much, and more, than ever." When he refers to the photograph that she has sent and declares that she looks "more perfect and sweeter than ever", that receives the word "LIAR!" – she always was self-conscious of being photographed. Her comment against his news that he has been down to Ischia for a short spell is not fully legible. He goes on to say that it is good to meet "old friends" (a phrase which she underlines) and "familiar places" (to which she adds "!!!!" and writes "7 weeks" again). Against his closing paragraph, in which he says that she looks more beautiful than ever, she writes "LIAR". At the bottom of the letter she inserts the words "WHAT A LINESHOOT". Once she has read the letter, it is a fair bet that she folds it up in disgust writing the final words "LIAR! LINESHOOTER".

Don writes again, two days later, on **17th February 1945** (his ears must have been burning!). He recounts how on the previous day, they "spent a lazy afternoon having a haircut and wandering around" and then they went to the YMCA for tea, where Hugh met an "army type" who had been at school with him. They had dinner in the mess and then saw the film *Sweet and Low-down*, which he describes as terribly bad. Don says that he had not realised that Linda had a brother in "crash boats" in Gibraltar and that he is lucky to get home after two years. 'Crash boats' was the colloquial name given to the RAF rescue boats. Linda's brother, Gordon is three years her junior. Don reports that his No. 1 is turning out quite well (Stan Munns with whom Don kept in touch for the remainder of his life).

Don writes on **27th February 1945**, thanking Linda for her letter of 23rd January (which has not survived) and remarks that she sounds depressed. He has been away, but they now have the day off and it is beautiful. He got permission to take his boat out and dropped anchor in a little cove off one of the islands. Whilst his crew explore the hills, he is sitting writing letters and Hugh is reading. They had been visited by an American AMG (Allied Military Government) Major who was disappointed they had no drink on board. The weather is changing and they will soon have to move. Obviously life is becoming much more relaxed out there for the flotilla.

On **3rd March 1945** he writes again. He says the last crew member on board when they left the UK has been relieved, so now he has a completely new crew. He is not keen on training them, as the new CO to take over from him may like things done differently. Don says he is feeling fed up as Hugh is in Ischia. He had been looking through the awards list and noticed Dudley Arnaud had received an MID (Mention in Despatches) for gallantry during the Normandy landings.

He writes on **9th March 1945** complaining that, despite Linda's moans that he has not written, he has not heard from her since 23rd January. On the previous evening, they had travelled down the coast to an army mess where they had dinner and a dance with a number of South African nurses, one of whom jitterbugged. The weather has been wet and windy for a few days. He agrees with his mother that the war in Europe should be over in a couple of months. He wishes the Army would move up the Italian coast as he is sick of Leghorn. There is still no sign of his relief.

Linda writes **the following day,** saying she has received three letters from him this week. She had been about to ask why she had not heard from him for seven weeks. She has now calmed down but asks that he should write at least once a fortnight. She says she looks forward to meeting Hugh. The weather has been beautiful for mid-March and her face got burnt after falling asleep on the beach. She also refers to the photograph that she had sent – and which was such a sore point. She regards it as "<u>awful</u>" and asks him to tear it into small pieces. She did not want to be photographed in uniform and had borrowed a blouse from a girl twice her size. She says she only sent the "wretched thing" to keep her promise. She ends begging him not to wait seven weeks again and declaring that she loves him with all her heart and will never change.

The next surviving letter is also from Linda, on **17th April 1945**. She has not heard from Don for four weeks, which would have been his letter of 9th March, and again chastises him. It seems that the urge he stated, in 1942, to correspond frequently, has left him. One wonders if there is some other reason that has not become apparent. Even around the invasions of North Africa,

Sicily, etc. there were only gaps of a couple of weeks between letters. As the Allies and Russians close in on Germany, the Mediterranean is obviously becoming quiet and, as the prospect of his relief arriving gets closer, one would expect him to find more time to write. It appears Linda feels this way, too.

Linda says that Lands End is deadly and that, when she did not hear from him, she felt depressed and imagined the worst, and her crew suffered. Her comments are reminiscent of his sentiments, many months earlier, when she had been remiss in putting pen to paper. She has been on leave at home in Totland Bay, where her mother is looking after her two nephews (Derek and Anthony) for a few days.

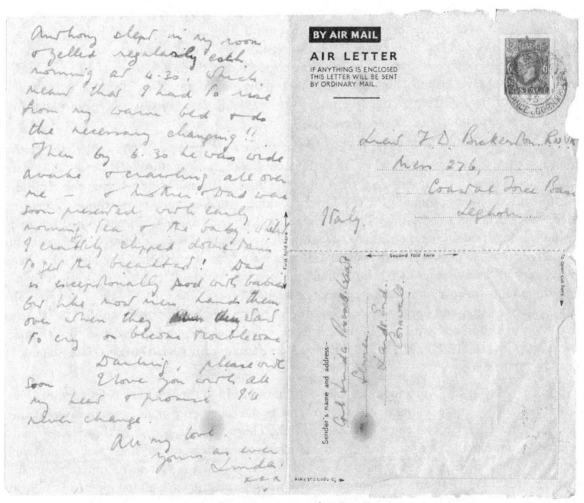

Part of Linda's letter 17th April 1945

Don writes on **21st April 1945**, having just returned from Ischia again. He has received her letter of 10th March and points out that her previous one had been in January, so her complaints appear to be a case of the pot calling the kettle black! He points out that, owing to censorship, he cannot say what he has been doing and there is not much to talk about apart from the weather. He has been assured that his relief is no more than two months away.

On **29th April 1945**, he has just received Linda's letter of 17th March and is feeling guilty for not writing. However, he has explained the reasons in his previous communication and gives her all the possible assurances that he has not changed his mind about their relationship. He has acquired a 14-month-old mongrel and finds he must keep him on a leash because of his behaviour. Things are hectic and he is very busy; he will tell all on his return.

Germany's surrender, on 7th May, prompts Don to write on the following day, **8th May 1945**. He says that, unfortunately, there is still a lot of work to do in the Mediterranean; he will explain upon his return. He may have been referring to the need for minesweeping to make the coast safe. There is also probably a need to ferry supplies not just to the military but also to civilians. At the time of writing, they are cut off from base in a heavenly little place not far from Genoa (see **Map H**, on page 197). However, it is hot and abundant with flies. On the previous evening, they had listened to the King's speech and then, despite only 12 hours' sleep in the last four days, he and Hugh took the dog for a walk and got dragged into a party, which was the best for years. Hugh's relief is more overdue than Don's, and his wife, Betty, has just had another operation.

Linda writes on **18th May 1945**, having received Don's air letter of 8th May. At *RAF Sennen*, she says, they spent a peaceful VE Day and watches continued as normal. The cooks iced an enormous cake with the inscription 'remember the boys in Burma'. She felt that the reminder that hostilities were continuing in the Far East rather put a dampener on things. However, there was a dance in the evening, although she did not have a drink and went to bed in timely fashion. She is hoping to go on leave on 7th June for seven days, with additional allowances for two days of travel each way and two days of VE leave. She reports that her father has been "very, very ill" and that he had "nearly died" the previous evening. The worry is affecting her and she intends to apply for a compassionate posting nearer home (on the Isle of Wight). She has received a letter and photographs from Hugh Gwynn whose wife has been ill. She declares that Don will soon be home and all their dreams will come true, and she advises him to make the most of his bachelor days. Judging by Don's description of his VE Day party, he was not in need of such advice.

On **23rd May 1945**, Don announces that both his and Hugh's reliefs have been appointed but it will be four to six weeks before they can return home together. For the past four weeks they have been travelling around the north coast of Italy. He prefers the people to those in the south – they do not like the Germans and give the British a warm-hearted and noisy welcome. Again, he talks of there being a lot of work to do and of them being at sea most of the time. Presumably this involves mine clearance. Currently, it is too rough and they are at anchor in the Gulf of Spezia (about 70 miles South East of Genoa).

His next letter, dated **19**[th] **June 1945**, is addressed from Ischia, and this is the last in the archives before his return. Don says he is excitedly awaiting a troopship and hopes to be back in UK towards the end of the first week in July. He will then wire and join Linda at some convenient place to marry, if she will agree. He and Hugh are relaxing and bathing in Ischia. (This card advertising the Officers' Club in Ischia, was amongst Don's papers.)

Il "CAVALLUCCIO MARINO,, ha aperto i suoi battenti ai vecchi clienti dell'Albergo Ischia; essi potranno ivi godere le più squisite vivande, al lusso dell'ampio salone ristorante, intrattenersi sull'ampia terrazza al mare per un mondano five-o'clock tea, o gustare al bar le più fini bevande.

PREZZI MODICI

The "CAVALLUCCIO MARINO,, a club for Officers only, is the finest and the smartest place of meeting in the island of Ischia.

If you go visiting this club for the first time, you'll be back there soon.

Remember :

    Dining-Room - Bar - Tea-Room - Bridge-Room.

GRAN RISTORANTE "AL CAVALLUCCIO MARINO,,

C. Vittoria Colonna, 39 - PORTO ISCHIA

Card for the *Officers' Club*, Ischia

Don handed over *ML 338* to Lieutenant L H Nixon who, in his memoirs, would reminisce that he took command of the ship in Ischia. He commented that, now he was skippering *ML 338* and returning to the 3rd ML Flotilla, he had a worthwhile job at last. However, this would not be for long as he too returned to Liverpool in July 1945.

Don and Hugh's passage from Ischia to Liverpool took a week, from 26th June – 3rd July 1945, and he is quick to cable Linda on 4th July at *RAF Sennen*:

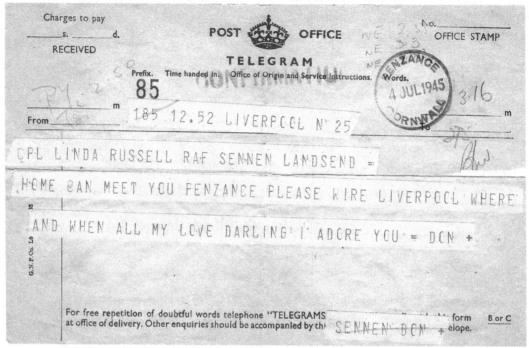

Telegram from Don dated 4th July 1945

Separated for so long, at last the couple can be together. Wasting no time, their Wedding Day is scheduled for ten days later, on 14th July 1945. Three telegrams are sent the day before:

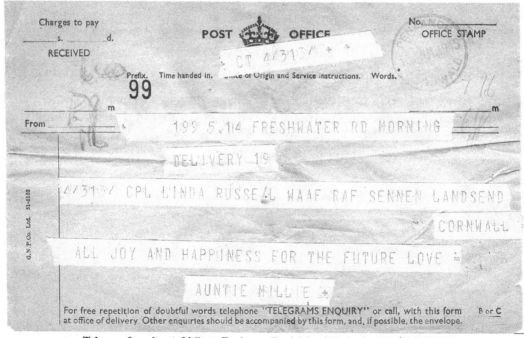

Telegram from Auntie Millie in Freshwater Road, Isle of Wight, dated 13th July 1945

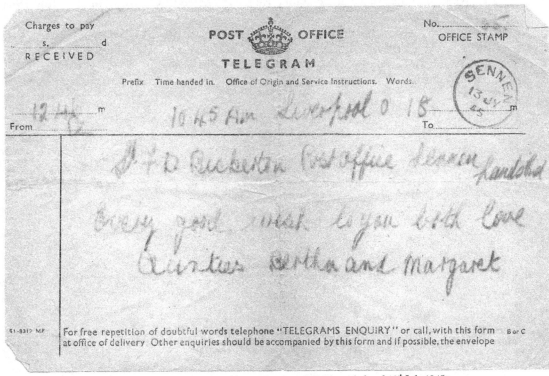

Telegram from Aunts Bertha and Margaret in Liverpool, dated 13th July 1945

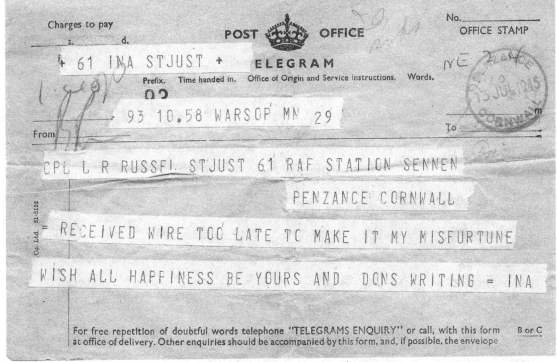

Telegram from Ina in Warsop, dated 13th July 1945

Finally, their wedding takes place at Penzance Register Office in Cornwall on 14th July 1945:

Don's and Linda's Marriage Certificate

Their wedding photographs are taken three days after the ceremony, by which time the flowers have died and the 'happy' couple and guests seem to have lost the mood!

Back row (left to right): Hugh Gwynn (Best Man), Leslie Bickerton (Don's Brother), Frank Bickerton (Don's Father)
Alice Bickerton (Don's Mother), Don, Linda, Betty Gwynn (Best Man's Wife)

Linda must have been saddened that none of her family could attend. As she mentioned in her letter of 18th May, her father had been "very, very ill" and had "nearly died". One assumes that he was still not in good enough health to travel such a distance.

Don and Linda

Cpl. Linda Russell W.A.A.F.,

R.A.F. Sennen,

Lands End,

Cornwall,

England

Letters:
January – July 1945

let you know what progress I'm
making towards getting home. At
the moment I'm here awaiting a
troopship and I hope to arrive in
the U.K. towards the end of the
first week in July with any luck.
As soon as I do get home I'll write
you and join you at some convenient
place and, if you agree, will get
married as soon as possible.

It seems such ages since
I last saw you and I'm feeling
rather excited now that our meeting
is so near. You know how much
I love you my sweetest and you

Anthony slept in my room
Belfast regularly/each
morning at 6.20. Ruth

Mess 276,
Coastal Force Base,
Leghorn.

3rd January 1945

Cpl. Linda Russell W.A.A.F.,
R.A.F. Sennen,
Lands End,
Cornwall,
ENGLAND.

My darling Linda

No more mail turned up yet but after my previous lapse I thought I'd write and try and avoid a lecture from you.

New Year's Eve was fairly quiet – although it looked troublesome at one stage. Hugh and I went to the Barracks Wardroom where they were throwing the biggest party and with more hootch than I've seen since I've been out here. We were about an hour late in arriving and things were well underway by that time – however we made no attempt to catch up as the night was very very young. We left about 2000 with a very hilarious party and went to our own mess for dinner, where people were making all kinds of horrible plans for the remainder of the evening – so we crept quietly away back to the boats. Here we gathered on one boat and talked till the New Year came in, had the usual toasts and a special one for you, and then turned quietly in. Surprised?

The following evening we went for dinner to the Officers Club and found to our surprise that we were the only people there – the hangovers must generally have been pretty heavy. Still it was a pleasant if quiet evening.

Saw a film you want to miss "Heaven is around the Corner" – Will Fyffe is the only bright spot in it and he really is good. The others just hadn't a clue.

Tonight I'm thinking of going to see (is it?) "Hail the Conquering Hero" as all the reviews of it which I've read say that it's first rate.

Well it's a pretty scanty letter I fear but it's about all that does happen in this place – I hope to be away from here for a short time in the near future.

Need I add my darling that I love you and miss you more each day and that I'm still cursing my relief wherever he is. I hope it won't be too long now tho' I feel more impatient each day.

Please write often my angel your letters are the only things worth anything out here.

All my love Linda darling
Ever your own
Don xxx

Lieut F.D. Bickerton R.N.V.R.
Mess 276,
c/o Coastal Force Base,
Leghorn,
Italy.

15th February 1945

Cpl. Linda Russell W.A.A.F.,
R.A.F. Sennen,
Lands End,
Cornwall
ENGLAND

My own darling Linda

Just received your letter of Feb 7th and I'm feeling terribly apologetic for not writing to you for so long, but please believe me that it really was unavoidable and that I still love you just as much, and more, than ever. I've also just received the photograph – which seems to have taken an incredible length of time to arrive – and naturally I'm thrilled to death with it. I must say you appear to have put on weight since I last saw you (God how long ago that was!) which is a good thing as I've been rather worried about your numerous colds. Darling you look more perfect and sweeter than ever and it makes me feel worse than ever to stay away from you. I've been making inquiries once more about reliefs and I fear that it will be at least another month before anything happens – just one of those things I suppose.

We've had very few parties recently tho' I managed to get down to Ischia for a short spell. It was good to be back there and meet old friends and visit the familiar places. We had a few dances – two to be precise – and it was quite fun to be stooging around again, but perhaps our best evening was on Hugh's boat where we held a dinner party. It was actually given in honour of a rather ancient (?) nurse who is terrific fun and who we decided to adopt – she even laughed when Hugh called her Two Ton Tessie, which I thought was fair enough. Incidentally Hugh wants to be my best man when we get married and I like the idea – he's an excellent type and we usually manage to get the maximum fun out of any horrible Italian town.

Been to see a flic tonight called "Thousands Cheer" and found it quite good, but it had the usual annoying habit of breaking down every ten minutes – still it's better than staying on board.

Darling please do take care of yourself as you know I love you more than anything in the world and I'm living for that not too distant day when I can be with you again. I promise you that I'll always love you sweetest so please don't be too harsh with me when there are rather long gaps between letters. Please write to me as often as you can and do please keep writing to Mother.

God knows I'm tired of being out here away from you and when I get home I'll do all I can to ensure that I'll never leave you again.

All my love my darling and I think you look more beautiful than ever.

Your own
Don xxx

P.S. I'll try and write again tomorrow.
And just in case it isn't obvious from the letter I love you far more than I can possibly tell you.

Mess 276,
Coastal Force Base,
Leghorn.

17th February 1945

Cpl. Linda Russell W.A.A.F.,
R.A.F. Sennen,
Lands End,
Cornwall,
ENGLAND.

My darling Linda

No more mail but I've been so naughty recently that I'm trying to ease my conscience a little by writing again – in any case, believe it or not, I like writing to you.

Had quite an amusing evening yesterday. We'd spent a lazy afternoon having a haircut and wandering around so we decided to have tea at the YMCA where Hugh met a bloke who was at school with him – army type. We wheeled him, or rather he wheeled us in his truck, down on board for the odd noggin before going up to the mess for dinner (for once almost edible!). Then we went on to the flics to see the most awful film which can possibly have been made – Benny Goodman and his band in an abortion called "Sweet and Low-down" it really was incredibly bad and we were, not unnaturally, complemented by the Army on naval film taste! After that we returned to the boats and just sat and talked – usual subject, home sweet home.

I didn't realise that you had a brother in crash boats at Gib – if it had been elsewhere in the Med. I might have run across him as I know quite a number of those types; anyway he's pretty lucky getting home after two years.

My No 1 seems to be turning out quite well (under my guiding influence of course) and has become a little more sociable. But I'll still be pleased when my relief turns up!

We've decided to have a quiet game of poker tonight, principally as there's little else to do and I personally don't feel like a hectic night at the Officers' Club – things have a tendency to happen when we get there!

Darlingest, I'm missing you so terribly and I love you with all my heart, life will again become a pleasure when I can hold you very tight in my arms again. It's now nearly two and a half years since I last saw you and it seems its equivalent in centuries, but I hope it won't be too long now and perhaps I'll be back with you for keeps this time.

Write often my angel, you're always in my thoughts and you know that I'll never change.

Please write often my angel your letters are the only things worth anything out here.

All my love Linda sweetest
Ever your own
Don xxx

Mess 276,
Coastal Force Base,
Leghorn.

27th February 1945

Cpl. Linda Russell W.A.A.F.,
R.A.F. Sennen
Land's End,
Cornwall,
England.

My own darling Linda

We've been away and your letter of 23rd January has only just caught me up – however it was extremely welcome even tho' you did sound rather depressed. Darling please believe that I know how you feel and that I too know that even five minutes together would clear up so many difficulties. You must know that I love you and that you are constantly in my thoughts and, for that matter, in my conversation – ask Hugh for confirmation when I get home.

We've got a day off today and as the weather was so beautiful (it's like a July day) I obtained permission to take my boat out and anchor in a little cove of one of the islands. The crew, or rather some of them, have gone ashore to explore the hills and I'm sitting on the quarterdeck trying to write with the letter on my knee. Hugh is loafing around reading and, as you can see, has very cleverly managed to knock over my last bottle of ink.

I've just been visited by the American A.M.G. major who seems most disappointed that one of H.M. ships has nothing for him to drink – I offered him tea but he left before it was even ready! He seems a peculiar type without much of a clue to his name – not that many of them have for that matter.

At the moment it rather looks as though it may start blowing and also as though it may rain which is all rather unfortunate as I'm anchored rather close inshore and it appears that I'll have to shift.

We've been working pretty hard for the last week or so and this break is certainly welcome – I'm sure you'd love this spot as it's a heavenly island and seems very remote from the war, which suits me rather well as the mere mention of the word makes me feel pretty fed up.

As you say it seems incredible that we have known each other for less than three years and that two and one half have been spent apart from each other. But the time apart has only served to remind me how much I love you, how much I miss you and, perhaps above all, how much I need you. Never before in my life have I had that feeling about anyone and now, if I thought you were not waiting for me, I should have nothing to live for at all. Linda my sweetest I'll always love you and I'll never leave you again for this length of time – I know I just couldn't bear it.

Write as often as you can my angel and I promise I'll do the same.

All my love and take care of yourself
Ever your own
Don xxx

Mess 276,
Coastal Force Base,
Leghorn.

3rd March 1945

Cpl. Linda Russell W.A.A.F.,
R.A.F. Sennen,
Land's End,
Cornwall,
ENGLAND.

Linda my sweetest

No more mail but as I'm still feeling rather guilty I thought I'd write and tell you that you are the most perfect girl in the world – and, what's more, I mean it!

The last bloke who was on board when we left U.K. was relieved yesterday so now I have a completely new crew to knock into shape and frankly, I'm not overkeen on the idea as the C.O. who takes over from me may have ideas which don't coincide with mine – still that will be his misfortune.

I'm feeling pretty fed up at the moment as Hugh is down at Ischia and there is no one here whose company I enjoy sufficiently to go ashore with them – actually most of them just bore me to tears when it comes to relaxing in harbour, not half a clue between them.

At the moment I'm contemplating going to a flic but there doesn't appear to be anything on that's worth seeing and a couple of hours on a hard seat in an Italian cinema watching a lousy flic is scarcely my idea of enjoyment.

Incidentally I was looking through the awards and I discovered that Dudley got a M.I.D. for his part in the Normandy business – I must write to him as I owe him one letter as it is.

The weather hasn't been too good since we got back here, been blowing pretty hard and it's bloody cold – the sort of cold one enjoys in England but not out here. Still another couple of months and I suppose it will be pretty hot – not that I hope to be here anyway.

Darling I'm sure that this is a most depressing letter – please forgive me, but I'm feeling so utterly dejected at being away from you for so long. Perhaps it's particularly the recent weeks when I know a relief may turn up at any time and I'll be back with you again. Oh my darling I do love you so very much – as you wrote, all the things I want to say to you appear so futile in a letter so I'll save them up for another month or so until I can tell them to you in person

Write often to me angel

All my love
Ever your own
Don xxx

Mess 276,
Coastal Force Base,
Leghorn.

9th March 1945

Cpl. Linda Russell W.A.A.F.,
R.A.F. Sennen,
Land's End,
Cornwall,
ENGLAND.

My own darling Linda

You know you are a little wretch – you give me terrific bother for not writing to you when the last letter from you was dated 23rd January. What about one a month at least as I also get worried – please?

We had quite a party last night, we went down the coast to an army mess where we had dinner and then a dance with a number of South African nurses who were quite fun. We all got slightly whistled and one of the nurses insisted on jitterbugging – actually it must have looked quite amusing but we were quite serious about it at the time. Roy, the army type who invited us, stayed the night on board as he wanted to come to sea with us today but that, fortunately, was cancelled! Today saw us viewing things in a less rosy light but it was fun – incidentally I behaved myself, in case you were thinking other things!

The weather has been pretty filthy over the past few days blowing hard and rather too much rain and today has been a little better and the wind now appears to be dropping, which is a good thing as I'm due out tomorrow.

I had a letter from Mother t'other day and she is still foreseeing the end of the war (tho' Father seems to have ceased to forecast the actual dates). On this occasion I'm inclined to agree with her and I rather think the next two months will see the end of things, tho' I wish the Army would move up this coast as I'm more than sick of Leghorn and almost any other place would be pleasant for a change.

No sign of reliefs yet but one of the blokes with whom I came out has just been relieved so it shouldn't be too long now and then darling I'll be back home to you quicker than that! Judging by the number of people who have threatened to come to our wedding we shall have at least half of Coastal Forces there – and it will take the full products of at least two breweries to keep them quiet.

Linda darling, if it's really possible, which I don't think it is, I'm more crazy about you than I was even when I last saw you. I think about you, dream about you and, as you've no doubt gathered, talk about you so much that the blokes out here are probably tired of the sound of your name. My angel I love you so much, I'm living only for the day I can hold you in my arms once more.

All my love precious
Ever your own
Don xxx

L. Russell W.A.A.F.
Sennen,
Lands End.

10th March 1945

Lieut F. D. Bickerton,
Mess 276,
Coastal Force Base,
Leghorn,
Italy.

My darling Don,

I've received three air mail letters from you this week, many thanks. Lucky for you they stopped me from posting a letter asking why I hadn't heard for seven weeks – that is putting it politely, of course! Promise to write at least once a fortnight and you are forgiven.

Hugh sounds a good type and I am looking forward to meeting him – in spite of his clumsy habits!! (Trust you have managed to get another bottle of ink, otherwise I can see myself without mail for some time).

Have you written to your Mother recently as she was worried the last time I heard from her. The weather has been beautiful just lately, touch wood! I fell asleep on the beach yesterday for about an hour & my face is so red & sore that I'm terrified it will decide to peel.

By the way, my apologies for that awful photo, isn't it ghastly? Please tear it into small pieces. I didn't want to be photographed in uniform & borrowed the blouse from a girl almost twice my size. I just had to send the wretched thing as I had promised you a photo, and please note I haven't gained weight!!

Darling, write again soon and if possible don't keep me waiting seven weeks, it is too long, and remember I love you with all my heart. I'll never change.

All my love,
Ever your own
Linda xx

Sennen,
Lands End,
Cornwall.

17th April 1945

Lieut F. D. Bickerton,
Mess 276,
Coastal Force Base,
Leghorn,
Italy.

My darling Don,

No letter from you for over a month. The last gap was 7 weeks & now 4 weeks – how can you expect me to write more often when I feel something is wrong?

I fully appreciate that very often you are frightfully busy & away at sea, but surely you can write occasionally, if only a few times.

Lands End is deadly, believe me, & your letters (at least hoping for them) just about make life bearable. When I don't hear I feel depressed & imagine all sorts of ghastly things - & the crew suffer. I often look back three years to those happy times we spent in Tenby & Falmouth etc., which helps. I suppose we have grown apart whilst you have been away, but I feel confident that when we meet there will be no doubt about our future happiness, & we shall continue where we were forced to leave off.

I've been back from leave over a week, & settling down once again to the old routine. I spent a quiet but busy time (mother is without help) with the family. My sister left her two boys with us for three days – Derek aged 11 & Anthony 19 months, so you can imagine there wasn't much peace!

Anthony slept in my room & yelled regularly each morning at 4.30, which meant that I had to rise from my warm bed & do the necessary changing!! Then by 6.30 he was wide awake & crawling all over me - & Mother & Dad were soon presented with early morning tea & the baby, whilst I craftily slipped downstairs to get the breakfast! Dad is exceptionally good with babies but, like most men, hands them over when they start to cry or become troublesome.

Darling, please write soon. I love you with all my heart & promise I'll never change.

All my love.
Yours as ever
Linda xxx

Mess 276,
Coastal Force Base,
Leghorn.

21st April 1945

Cpl. Linda Russell W.A.A.F.,
R.A.F. Sennen
Land's End,
Cornwall,
England.

My darling Linda

I've just returned from Ischia and received your letter of 10th March which must have taken ages to get here – I was pleased because your last letter was written in January. I rather gather I'm in your bad books for not writing more frequently. Please darling believe me when I tell you that you are constantly in my thoughts and that I love you more than I would previously have believed possible. But I'm so fed up with writing anything at all – there just isn't anything to tell you about. I can tell you how much I love you but I hope you know that and in any case that will hardly fill a whole letter. I can't tell you what I've been doing because that is censorable. I could fill a whole book with my comments on the Italian weather but it would hardly bear reading. And so I get pretty slack. But my sweetest believe me when I say that I love you more than anything in the world and that I'm just living to be back in your arms once more. This has been a very long two and a half years but it has at least taught me how very much I need you. I frankly couldn't bear to be parted from you again and I shall do all I can to make sure it doesn't happen.

Hugh tells me that he has written to you. If he was speaking the truth when he told me what he had written you can disregard 99.9% of his letter – the .1% is his name at the bottom.

I don't know how long before I am relieved but I am assured a maximum of two months – I only hope it's earlier.

Darlingest this letter is a hell of a drip and I apologise but I do so much want to be back with you once more. Please write to tell me I'm forgiven and that you love me as much as ever. I promise you my angel that I shall never alter – you're my whole life and always will be.

All my love Linda sweet
Ever your own
Don xxxxxxxxx

P.S. I still think you're beautiful even in the outsize blouse!

Mess 276,
Coastal Force Base,
Leghorn.

29th April 1945

Cpl. Linda Russell W.A.A.F.,
R.A.F. Sennen,
Lands End,
Cornwall,
ENGLAND.

My own darling Linda

I received your letter of 17th March about ten minutes ago and I'm feeling very guilty about everything. Please believe me when I say that nothing is wrong and as you know I tried to explain the reasons in my last letter. Darling I'm quite confident that you are wrong in suggesting that we have grown apart, in fact but for the thought of returning to you soon, very soon I hope, life would be completely unbearable. I, too, wish to continue where we were forced to leave off and the mere sight of you even for one minute would be all the tonic I require to bring me out of the dumps. I don't think you'll find that I've changed at all except that of course, I'm two and a half years older! But I love you more than ever, in fact more than I would have thought possible. Please don't be angry with me – you are always in my thoughts and I left my heart behind me in England with you.

Your leave appears to have been quite hectic especially the care which young Anthony apparently requires – I'd much rather it were an infant of our own.

I forgot to tell you that I've acquired a hound which occasionally answers to the name of Maleesh (not sure of the spelling!) which being interpreted from the Arabic means "It couldn't matter less". He really is terrific, about fourteen months old, a hell of size and of indeterminate ancestry. However he doesn't go much on, but rather for, Italians and Americans with the result that I've had numerous complaints. There was one rather amusing incident while we were last in Ischia. He made a rather vicious snap at one of the Italian workmen who while side stepping quite neatly walked right over the edge of the quay. Of course I had to attempt to keep a straight face and be so very apologetic – so now I keep him on a leash. I'd love to bring him home with me as I'm sure you'd adore him but I fear it won't be possible.

Things are pretty hectic around here at the moment and we have been very busy – I'll tell you all about it when I get home.

Linda my sweetheart I love you and always will love you with all my heart – I promise you I will never change.

Keep smiling my sweetest

All my love
Ever your own
Don xxx

Lieut F. Bickerton R.N.V.R.,
Mess 276,
Coastal Force Base,
Leghorn.

8th May 1945

Cpl. Linda Russell W.A.A.F.,
R.A.F. Sennen,
Land's End,
Cornwall,
England.

My own darling Linda

So it's all over and I can hardly believe it now! But unfortunately there is still a hell of a lot of work ahead of us out here – I'll tell you all about it when I get home. As usual we are cut off from base and at the moment we are in a heavenly little place not far from Genoa. It's hot. There are flies. But the people seemed so pleased to see us and I certainly prefer them to the Southern Italians. I suppose the main reason is that they are so much cleaner.

Last night was quite a night. We listened to the King's speech and then Hugh suggested a walk before we turned in (we were pretty tired as we'd had only twelve hours sleep in the last four days!) I agreed and we set off with the hound. Unfortunately we ran into some of our ships companies who were celebrating VE Day in the traditional naval manner. Please would we come and have a drink with them? Yes we should be delighted to do so, but only one as we were tired and wanted to turn in. That, of course, was our undoing. When we went into the cafe we were immediately surrounded by hordes of matelots and there we stayed until they had enough – still it was a good party and I enjoyed it more than any I've had in years.

Darling it won't be long now and then I'll see you again and be able to hold you so tight in my arms once more. And that's what I've been dreaming of doing for the last two and a half years. I love you with all my heart my sweetheart and this time away from you has been hell – but it won't happen again.

Hugh is pretty fed up as his relief is even more overdue than mine and Betty (his wife) has just had another operation. It's pretty bloody sort of luck especially in view of the promises made to us six months ago.

My own, do take care of yourself until I get home and then I shall take over – or perhaps you think it will be t'other way round!

All my love Linda sweet I'll always be completely yours.

As ever
Don xxxxxxxxx

(Extra as the war's over!)
Maleesh sends his love.

Sennen,
Lands End,
Cornwall.

18th May 1945

Lieut F. D. Bickerton,
Mess 276,
Coastal Force Base,
Leghorn,
Italy.

My darling Don,

Just had your air-letter dated 8/5, many thanks.

Yes, it's all over in Europe, I can hardly believe it myself. You had a fair enough excuse for celebrating this time but twelve hours sleep in four days is heavy going!

We spent a peaceful V.E. day here at Land's End. Watches continued as usual and the majority of people were extraordinarily sane and sober. The cooks iced an enormous cake with 'remember the boys in Burma', which rather put a dampener on things! There was a hop in the evening and I hopped off to bed at 10.30 <u>without</u> a drink – (believe it or not).

I'm hoping to go on leave June 7th which is really worth while this time – 7 days + 48 + 48 travelling + 48 V.E. leave and a crafty get-away, if possible, the night before!!!

Dad has been very very ill. Last week he nearly died and Mother didn't wire as I was so far away. Fortunately, he is getting stronger. I can't stand this worry any longer so I'm applying for a compassionate posting nearer home.

Please thank Hugh for his letter and the photos (it's a very good one of you), I'm so sorry to hear that his wife is ill and hope by this time he has heard good news.

Darling you will soon be home and all our dreams will come true. Write soon.

As always,
All my love
Linda xxxx

P.S. Make the most of your bachelor days!

Mess 276,
Coastal Force Base,
Leghorn.

23rd May 1945

Cpl. Linda Russell W.A.A.F.,
R.A.F. Sennen,
Land's End,
Cornwall,
ENGLAND.

My own darling Linda

The glad tidings have arrived – my relief has been appointed! But just in case this news leads you to believe I will be home tomorrow or the next day, I'd better tell you now that it will be about a month to six weeks before I am with you. You see, darling, he has to be relieved by another bloke and so on until it becomes rather like an endless chain but, as C.C.F. said, he has been appointed and that's the major obstacle out of the way. Hugh's relief has been appointed at the same time so we shall travel home together by the fastest possible route. I suppose it's a selfish attitude to adopt but this seems far more important than the end of the war and to be with you again with no war to worry about will be full heaven Sweetest. I've been dreaming of this day since I last saw you and now it is, at last, within sight.

Are you receiving my mail? We've been poking around the North coast of Italy for the past four weeks and we've just had to get mail away by any means we could and some of the ways weren't at all certain – I know it's ages since I last heard from you and Mother and, of course, Mother does write regularly.

Actually the coast is very lovely out here and I much prefer the people to the Southerners – they are far more generous and not so slimey and obsequious - also they really didn't like the Germans and gave us a most warm hearted and noisy welcome.

The trouble is that there is a hell of a lot of work to be done up here and we've been out most of the time – rather a pity as I think most of us felt like relaxing as far as possible. Today the weather is too bad to go out so we are at anchor in the Gulf of Spezia – plenty of shelters so we are not rolling too badly.

Honestly darling I'm really far too excited for words and just waiting rather impatiently for this bloke to turn up – he may even be at base waiting for me on our return. I'll write and give you approximate dates as soon as I can.

Incidentally please don't stop, or should I say please start, writing as I do want to hear from you. I'm just living for the not too far distant day when you are in my arms again. I love you with all my heart dearest and I'm never going to let you out of my sight again.

All my love my darling
Ever your own
Don xxx

Coastal Force Base,
Ischia.

19th June 1945

Cpl. Linda Russell W.A.A.F.,
R.A.F. Sennen,
Land's End,
Cornwall,
England.

Linda darling

Just a short note to let you know what progress I'm making towards getting home. At the moment I'm here awaiting a troopship and I hope to arrive in the U.K. towards the end of the first week in July with any luck. As soon as I do get home I'll wire you and join you at some convenient place and, if you agree, we'll get married as soon as possible.

It seems such ages since I last saw you and I'm feeling rather excited now that our meeting is so near. You know how much I love you my sweetest and you know too that it will always be that way.

Ischia is heavenly at the moment and Hugh & I do nothing except loaf and bathe – quite a pleasant change but you <u>could</u> improve it by being here.

Take care of yourself for me and I'll let you know more exact dates as soon as I can.

All my love my angel
I adore you
As ever
Don xxx

Chapter Fourteen

AFTER THE WAR

Following their marriage in Penzance, Don and Linda have their honeymoon in Mousehole, Cornwall. Now that they are both together, there is no further correspondence to enable their movements to be tracked.

Amongst their effects are blank pre-war picture postcards of Mousehole in 1935 and Sennen Cove in 1936:

Mousehole from East, 1935   86600

1930s picture postcard of Mousehole
© The Francis Frith Collection

1930s picture postcard of Sennen Cove
© The Francis Frith Collection

Linda's service record (see Chapter Two) shows her release date as 17th September 1945. Don's release document, dated 7th December 1945 (see next page), indicates 28th December 1945, with the three-week period between those dates designated as leave.

Don's address is recorded on his release document as Amos House, Totland Bay, Isle of Wight, indicating that he and Linda are living with her parents. One can only surmise that Don, having returned from the Mediterranean to Liverpool on 4th July 1945, was allowed leave to make wedding arrangements, marry Linda and honeymoon, at least throughout July 1945.

S.1587B (Established November 1944),

ORDER FOR RELEASE FROM NAVAL SERVICE (Class B).

(OFFICERS).

26 C/CF ab.74/12/46

H.M.S

(Date)   7th DEC. 1945.

[See Note 1.]

To   F. D. BICKERTON   (Name)

Ty. LT. RNR.   (Rank)

1. You are being released from Service as a Class B Release, for the purpose of transfer to industry for urgent reconstruction work as a *Individual Specialist*. (Industry Group Letters _____) (Occupational Classification No. _____)-

2. The date of your Release from Service and Transfer to Industry will be *28th DECEMBER* 194 5 .

3. You have been granted leave as follows, starting on the day after the date of this Order :- * _____ days foreign service leave expiring on _____ 194 _ and 21 days transfer leave expiring on the date of your Release.
*Delete this line if no foreign service leave has been granted.

4. You are to report in person at the local Employment Exchange at† *to: The Ministry of National Insurance* within 7 days of the date of this Order. You will not be required to take up your civil employment until after your leave has expired, but you may do so if you wish at any time after the date of this Order.
†Insert Exchange nearest to permanent address.

5. You may wear civilian clothes at any time after the date of this Order and you are to cease to wear uniform after the date of your release, but you should keep your uniform intact in case you are recalled for service.

6. After your release you will be regarded as being in Reserve and you will be liable, until the end of the present emergency, to recall to the Naval Service by revocation of this Order at any time. Besides being liable to recall in an emergency, you will be liable to be recalled should you discontinue the employment for which you have been released or should the necessity for that employment lapse for other reasons. [See Note 2.]

7. Your home address is noted in official records as follows :-

AMOS HOUSE

TOTLANDBAY. I. O. WIGHT.

You are to report all changes to the Secretary of the Admiralty. Failure to do so may involve delay in payment of war gratuity or such other payments to which you may be entitled under naval regulations.

8. You should carry this order with you and produce it when required.

(Rank)

Commanding Officer.

NOTES.
1. This date is the date on which the Officer leaves his ship or establishment.
2. Officers on the permanent lists of the R.N.R. and R.N.V.R. also remain liable for recall to service and for training under the Regulations for these Reserves.

Don's Order for Release from Naval Service

He had talked about the likelihood of being sent to the Far East, but Japan surrendered on 15th August 1945. There is no available evidence to track his movements thereafter, until his formal discharge in December 1945. From his service history, he was attached to *HMS Drake* at

Plymouth. Therefore, he would not have been far from Linda at Sennen Cove – although she was released in September 1945, three months before he received his discharge.

Presumably, after spending Christmas 1945 at his in-laws' on the Isle of Wight, Don would have started work at the Ministry of National Insurance, where he was an Assistant Press Officer. It seems that he was posted to their office at Warbreck Hill, Blackpool, and initially he would have stayed at his parents' address at Fairfield, 93 Thomas Lane, Broadgreen, Liverpool 14. Details of his War Gratuity were sent to him there on 3rd January 1946. The amount of £96 - 5s was payable on 2nd February 1946. In today's terms, that would equate to about £3,800.

Don's War Gratuity statement

In Blackpool, Don found lodgings at 336 Queen's Drive (now Queen's Promenade), which was within walking distance of his office in Warbreck Hill. A letter was sent to him there on 18th February 1946 from the Admiralty enclosing war medals that he had been awarded, namely:

1939-45 Star
Atlantic Star
Africa Star
Italy Star
War Medal 1939-45

ADMIRALTY,

S.W.1.

C.W. 78579/45

18th February, 1946.

Sir,

On the occasion of your release from Naval Service, I am commanded by My Lords Commissioners of the Admiralty to convey to you an expression of their recognition of your services in the Royal Navy during the war.

The good wishes of Their Lordships go with you on your return to civil life.

I am, Sir,

Your obedient Servant,

Lieutenant F.D. Bickerton, R.N.V.R.,
336, Queen's Drive,
Blackpool,
Lancs.

The Secretary of the Admiralty presents his compliments and by Command of the Lords Commissioners of the Admiralty has the honour to transmit the enclosed Awards granted for service during the war of

1939-45.

Campaign Stars, Clasps and Medals

instituted in recognition of service

in the war of 1939-45

NUMBER OF STARS, MEDALS, CLASPS or EMBLEMS ENCLOSED	6

Order of Wearing	Description of Ribbon	Clasp or Emblem (if awarded)
1 1939-45 Star	Dark blue, red and light blue in three equal vertical stripes. This ribbon is worn with the dark blue stripe furthest from the left shoulder.	Battle of Britain
2 Atlantic Star	Blue, white and sea green shaded and watered. This ribbon is worn with the blue edge furthest from the left shoulder.	Air Crew Europe or France and Germany
3 Air Crew Europe Star	Light blue with black edges and in addition a narrow yellow stripe on either side.	Atlantic or France and Germany
4 Africa Star	Pale buff, with a central vertical red stripe and two narrower stripes, one dark blue, and the other light blue. This ribbon is worn with the dark blue stripe furthest from the left shoulder.	8th Army or 1st Army or North Africa 1942-43
5 Pacific Star	Dark green with red edges, a central yellow stripe, and two narrow stripes, one dark blue and the other light blue. This ribbon is worn with the dark blue stripe furthest from the left shoulder.	Burma
6 Burma Star	Dark blue with a central red stripe and in addition two orange stripes.	Pacific
7 Italy Star	Five vertical stripes of equal width, one in red at either edge and one in green at the centre, the two intervening stripes being in white.	
8 France and Germany Star	Five vertical stripes of equal width, one in blue at either edge and one in red at the centre, the two intervening stripes being in white.	Atlantic
9 Defence Medal	Flame coloured with green edges, upon each of which is a narrow black stripe.	Silver laurel leaves (King's Commendation for brave conduct. Civil)
10 War Medal 1939-45	A narrow central red stripe with a narrow white stripe on either side. A broad red stripe at either edge, and two intervening stripes in blue.	Oak leaf

Documents enclosed with Don's war medals

The number of medals referred to in the last of these documents is six. However, only the five listed on page 275 were found.

74 post-war letters have also survived. These were written during their enforced separation between January 1946 and July 1947 but are generally outside of the scope of this book. One such letter to Linda, at Amos House, is dated 21st April 1946 and addressed from his parents' house in Liverpool. Subsequent letters dated 23rd, 24th and 29th April 1946 were sent to Linda at her sister's at 6 Leigham Vale Road, Southbourne, Bournemouth from his lodgings at 336 Queen's Drive, Blackpool.

Linda wrote from Southbourne on 6th May 1946. The address shows that, around Easter time, he relocated to London. Don addressed two undated letters to Linda one from 65 Rutland Place, London and the other from 13A Tanza Road, London, NW3 (perhaps temporary lodgings). From 23rd May 1946 his letters were addressed from lodgings at 10 Priory Gardens, Highgate, London N6, where he remained a guest of landlady, Mrs Thompson for nearly a year.

On 11th June 1946, Linda was admitted to Tuckton Nursing Home, where she gave birth to a son: me. A brochure issued to all inmates of the Nursing Home follows. It lists Mother's and Infant's requisites, fees and visiting hours. The first items on Mother's Requisites are nightgowns or pyjamas, including 'one old one'!

Tuckton Nursing Home

SOUTHBOURNE
BOURNEMOUTH

Phone - Southbourne 54

MOTHER'S REQUISITES

NIGHTGOWNS OR PYJAMAS, INCLUDING
   ONE OLD ONE
BEDJACKET
6 DOZEN SANITARY TOWELS
1 SANITARY BELT
1 OBSTETRIC BINDER OR
1½ YARDS ROLLER TOWELLING
USUAL TOILET THINGS
DRESSING GOWN, SLIPPERS
2 BATH TOWELS
RATION BOOK

   Please Mark Everything

INFANT'S REQUISITES

4 VESTS
4 NIGHTGOWNS
2 SHAWLS
24 TURKISH NAPKINS
24 HARRINGTONS SQUARES
1 3-INCH CREPE BANDAGE
ZINC CASTOR OIL CREAM, SOAP,
   POWDER, SAFETY PINS

FEES - - - 8 GNS. PER WEEK

VISITING HOURS

11 A.M. - 12.30 P.M.
4 P.M. - 5 P.M.
7.30 P.M. - 9.30 P.M.

Tuckton Nursing Home Brochure

On news of the birth, Don responded from London with a telegram:

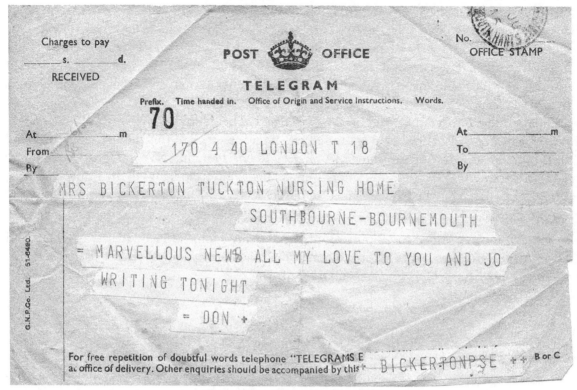

Telegram from Don dated 11th June 1946

It must have taken a little while for them to settle on the name David, as I am referred to as "Jo" in Don's telegram and the first few letters after my birth.

Once discharged from the Nursing Home, Linda returned, with me, to live at Southbourne with her sister and brother-in-law, Peggy and Herbert, and their two children, Derek and Anthony. However, the arrangement was not ideal and, after two months, she decided to move us to her parents' home at Amos House, Totland Bay, Isle of Wight.

In the meantime, Don was desperately trying to find accommodation in the London suburbs that would accept his wife and child. This was not an easy task after the war, as London had suffered extensive damage from German bombing. Correspondence between my parents reveals their frustration at the situation in which they found themselves. Having been cruelly parted for nearly three years, whilst Don was in the Mediterranean, it was not satisfactory that they could only meet on the occasional weekend, when Don would journey by train and ferry to the Isle of Wight. The expense of separation would have prevented them from saving for the future.

In May 1947, Don's address changed from No. 10 to No. 86 Priory Gardens, and the last surviving letter from there is dated 28th July 1947. We must, therefore, have joined my father in his new lodgings at 86 Priory Gardens around August 1947. (He had moved from Mrs Thompson at No. 10 as she was unable to accommodate the three of us.) We remained there until sometime in 1949 when my parents were able to rent Flat 77A, Shepherds Hill, Highgate N6, just a short walk from Priory Gardens. The location of Highgate was convenient, as Don could catch the Northern Line tube from Highgate Station at the end of Priory Gardens to the Ministry of National Insurance office at 6 Carlton House Terrace, London SW1.

On 19th November 1948, Don was enrolled with the Royal Naval Supplementary Reserve:

NAVAL RESERVES, ADMIRALTY,
QUEEN ANNE'S MANSIONS,
LONDON, S.W.1.
19 November, 1948.

Telephone No. -
WHItehall 9444, Ext. 209.

Dear Bickerton,

It gives me great pleasure to enrol you as a Member of the Royal Naval Volunteer Supplementary Reserve and to sign your Memorandum of Appointment.

The services rendered by the Reserves in the late war will long be remembered by the Royal Navy and the fact that officers with such fine records of service behind them are again ready to volunteer in the event of another emergency is, I can assure you, greatly appreciated.

I wish you the best of luck and I know I can rely on you to uphold the past high traditions of the Royal Naval Volunteer Supplementary Reserve, and to do all in your power to see that they are maintained in the future.

Yours sincerely,

ADMIRAL COMMANDING RESERVES.

Tempy. Lieutenant F. D. Bickerton, RNVR.

NAVAL RESERVES, ADMIRALTY,
QUEEN ANNE'S MANSIONS,
ST. JAMES'S PARK,
LONDON, S.W.I.

N.R. 400/1/46

.........19 November.....194 8.

MEMORANDUM.

To_____ Frank Donald BICKERTON

You have been enrolled as a_____ member of _____ i̶n̶/ the Royal Naval Volunteer Supplementary Reserve to date____ 19. 11. 48.

2. In the event of your services being required as an Officer in the Royal Navy in War or emergency, you will receive a telegram or letter from the Admiralty giving instructions for your procedure.

You will at once acknowledge the receipt of such telegram or letter and forthwith comply with the directions given therein.

3. If found physically fit for service, you will be granted a Naval commission in the rank of_____ **Lieutenant** _____, and will then be subject in all respects to the Kings Regulations and Admiralty Instructions.

4. You are to report your address to the Admiral Commanding Reserves on 1st January each year, failing which you will be removed from the Reserve.

You should also report any permanent change of address when such change actually occurs.

5. You may withdraw from the Royal Naval Volunteer Supplementary Reserve at any time, on giving notice to the Admiral Commanding Reserves.

Your name will be removed from the list on your attaining the age of 50, but an extension may be granted in exceptional cases at the discretion of the Admiral Commanding Reserves.

6. In the event of your withdrawal or removal from the Royal Naval Volunteer Supplementary Reserve, this form is to be returned to the Admiral Commanding Reserves.

Admiral Commanding Reserves

Correspondence outlining Don's enrolment with the Royal Naval Supplementary Reserve

Each year, until he was in his eighties and the number of former colleagues dwindled to a handful, Don used to attend the Annual Reunion of the 3rd ML Flotilla at the RNVR Club in London. The programme of 30th April 1949 is the only one he kept, and this includes signatures of his ex-colleagues.

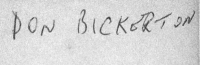

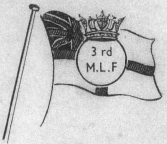

ANNUAL
REUNION

30th APRIL · 1949

at

The R.N.V.R. CLUB
LONDON . . W.1

•

On the occasion of the Third Annual Reunion, the signatories herein were among those present when we were pleased to welcome "Simmy" as our Guest. During the course of the Last Dog and First Watches, glasses were once more well-drained in the manner which typified the friendship of 3rd M.L. Wardrooms during the years 1940/46.

Signed programme for the 3rd ML Flotilla Third Annual Reunion

Those signatures that stand out are:

Stan Munns - his No. 1 in 1945, with whom he kept in touch until his death.

Hugh Gwynn - CO of *ML 462* and other MLs, who was Best Man at Don and Linda's wedding. After Hugh's and Hugh's wife's deaths, Don kept in touch with their son, Rodney.

Gordon Stead - author of *A Leaf Upon the Sea*.

Whether he continued to keep in touch with his former colleagues in 25th ML Flotilla (Dudley Arnaud, Gibby, Max, etc.) is not known.

On 11th September 1953, my brother, Ian was born at Hampstead Nursing Home. In the same month, Don's Ministry combined with the Ministry of Pensions to become the Ministry of Pensions and National Insurance. His new office was located at 10 John Adam Street, and there he became Chief Information Officer. In 1961 he took on the same role at the higher-profile Ministry of Transport, based in St. Christopher House, Southwark Street, SE1 where, in 1965, he was awarded the CBE in the Queen's Birthday Honours. In 1968 he became Controller (Home) at the Central Office of Information, and in 1971 Don was promoted to Director General and Head of Government Information Service, where he remained until his retirement in 1974 at the age 57.

In 1956, Don had managed to obtain a mortgage and, as Highgate was unaffordable, he, Linda, Ian and I moved from our rented flat in Highgate to a three-bedroomed house at 9 Copthall Drive, Mill Hill, London NW7. Linda devoted her time to the upbringing of Ian and me, and to the care of her husband. She was also active for a while in the Townswomen's Guild at Mill Hill.

Don's only experience of driving was a Jeep in the war, so there was no family car until 1967 when Linda learnt to drive at the age of 47. She passed her test the following year, at the second attempt, and would drive some fair distances when they holidayed to the Isle of Wight, Devon, Pembrokeshire, Norfolk and other places, until she was in her seventies. However, in later years, she confined her driving to the Isle of Wight, and she was devastated when she had to stop driving around the age of 80 through poor eyesight.

Following Don's CBE award, the two of them were frequently invited to Garden Parties at Buckingham Palace. One such occasion happened to fall on their 36th Wedding Anniversary, and I found the invitation amongst their papers:

The Lord Chamberlain is
commanded by Her Majesty to invite

Mr. and Mrs. Frank Bickerton

to a Garden Party at Buckingham Palace
on Tuesday, 14th July, 1981 from 4 to 6 p.m.

Morning Dress, Uniform or Lounge Suit

Invitation to a Garden Party at Buckingham Palace

Don used to put in long hours at the office and, in order to relax after work, would stop for a drink (or two) before catching the tube to Mill Hill East Station. Because of the poor bus service, Linda would drive to the station to meet him. Unfortunately, on an increasing number of occasions, he would doze off and fail to change tubes at Finchley Central Station. When he awoke, he then had to shuttle up and down the Northern Line to reach his required destination. It was known for Linda to wait, worrying, for several hours. Once, by way of apology, he bought her a floral bouquet but, after trapping it in the closing tube doors, he finished up presenting her with more stalks than flowers.

When my brother and I reached the age of 18, myself in 1964 and Ian in 1971, we left the family home for university, but Don and Linda continued to reside in Mill Hill until 1975 when, after Don's retirement, they relocated to 6 Diana Close, Totland Bay, Isle of Wight.

On the Isle of Wight, they purchased a 32 feet long cruiser, which they kept at Yarmouth, and during the summers they would cruise in the Solent. Don was also a very keen gardener. In the early period of their retirement, they both spent a considerable amount of time caring for Linda's elderly mother, who lived nearby at 'Oaklands', 42 The Avenue, Totland Bay, until her death on 1st April 1977 at the age of 91.

They continued to be devoted to one another, although Don's drinking did get out of hand from time to time. As she had promised all those years ago, Linda did lecture him. She also had to use more subtle methods. She was able to monitor the amount of Famous Grouse he was drinking by marking the bottle labels. She also perfected the art of adding water to the whisky bottle to within a millilitre, before he would notice.

Don and Linda also had frequent holidays abroad, initially staying with Linda's brother, Gordon, and his second wife in their villa near Alicante, Spain. On one occasion, Corsica was on their schedule. The last time Don had been there was on *ML 338* in 1945. In fact Don and Linda holidayed abroad until 2001, when Don suffered a slight stroke at the age of 84.

Thereafter, Don's health gradually declined. He broke his upper femur in a fall whilst opening the garage door and, a few days after an operation, he fell again whilst two nurses were moving him resulting in 25 stitches to his arm and further damage to his hip area. However, once discharged from a lengthy hospital stay, Linda cared for him at home with limited assistance from daily carers.

Unfortunately, osteoporosis was causing Linda major problems. She was in extreme pain when vertebrae at the base of her spine collapsed. During the Christmas period of 2005, another crushed vertebra meant that I had to take both of them into Seven Gables Care Home, Totland Bay.

Around Easter 2006, Linda was able to return home to Diana Close, on her own, for nine months and look after herself, visiting Don most days but, the following Christmas, another vertebra fracture resulted in her having to return to residential care. Unfortunately, as there was no space at Seven Gables, she had to spend three months in another residential home until a room became free. There, although in separate rooms (Don snored quite loudly), they would sit together in the home's conservatory each day and their devotion to each other never wavered. Nearly 66 years of friendship had proven, beyond all doubt, their love for each other and the sincerity of the poignant words in their wartime letters. On Linda's 87th birthday, I bought a card for my father to give Linda, featuring a puppy. Don wrote in it: "It wasn't puppy love."

On 22nd June 2007, a 90th birthday party was arranged in the home for Don. He thoroughly enjoyed the day and delivered a moving speech to the 30 guests. His chest, however, was beginning to fail him. On several occasions he spent time in hospital. His final admission, for a chest infection, resulted in his death on 14th April 2008 at the age of 90.

Linda became increasingly frail. She was admitted to hospital around her 89th birthday and died a week later, on 30th May 2009. Although Linda had not had a career after the war, she epitomised the saying: 'Behind every successful man there is a woman.' She was most certainly that woman.

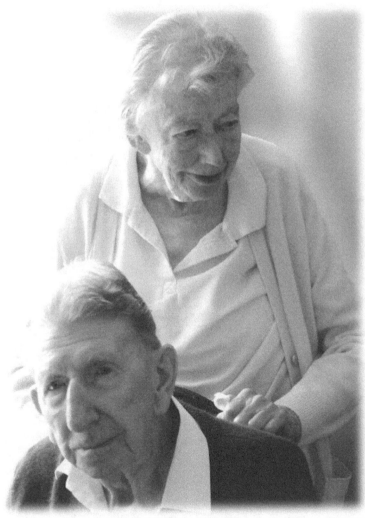

**Don and Linda in Seven Gables Care Home
during his 90th birthday party**

Bibliography / References

Books

Jefferson, David, 'Coastal Forces at War', Patrick Stephens Ltd; First Edition (5 August 1996)

Lambert, John and Ross, Al, 'Allied Coastal Forces of World War II. Volume 1: Fairmile Designs and US Submarine Chasers', Conway Maritime Press Limited (1990)

Pope, Dudley, 'Flag 4, The Battle of Coastal Forces in the Mediterranean', Chatham Publishing (1995)

Searle, Geoffrey, 'At Sea Level', The Book Guild Ltd (2005)

Stead, Gordon W, 'A Leaf Upon the Sea, A Small Ship in the Mediterranean, 1941-1943', The University of Columbia Press (1988)

Valli, José, 'Le Docteur Colonna et Port-St-Louis-du-Rhône', La Compagnie Littéraire (2015)

Other Publications

Admiralty SW reference S.6051, Historical Section, 'HMS Mauritius Summary of Service', Reprint S5553 (April 1962)

Atkinson H C, '3rd ML Flotilla', private paper (7 May 1951)

Jefferson, S, '50th Anniversary Radar at Worth Matravers and Swanage', Typesetting: Amberwood Graphics, Printing: Abbirt Print, Wareham (1990)

Nixon, L H, 'War Memories', private paper (1999), Imperial War Museum, London, reference: Documents.9815

The Secretary of the Admiralty, London SW1, 'The Navy List', Crown Copyright reserved (1940–1945)

Thomson, Eric, 'Some Impressions of the Invasion of Sicily, July 1943', private paper (28 September 1943)

'The Mediterranean Fleet, Greece to Tripoli, The Admiralty Account of Naval Operations April 1941 to January 1943', His Majesty's Stationery Office (1944)

Websites

Briscoe, Martin, 'A Short History of HMS St Christopher', http://www.mbriscoe.me.uk/stchristopher.html [Accessed 26 January 2012]

Catford, Nick, 'RAF Hayscastle Cross – West Coast Chain Home and West Coast Readiness ROTOR Radar Station' http://www.subbrit.org.uk/sb-sites/sites/h/hayscastle_cross/index2.shtml [Accessed 2nd January 2012]

Fabricius, Karl, 'Mount Vesuvius Erupting in 1944', http://scribol.com/anthropology-and-history/history/mount-vesuvius-erupting-in-1944 [Accessed 2016]

Kindell, Don, 'British and Other Navies in World War 2 Day-by-Day', Smith, Gordon, 'Royal Navy Ships, January 1942, Part 3 of 4', http://www.naval-history.net/xDKWW2-4201-40RNShips3WApproaches.htm [Accessed 27 January 2012]

Lt Cdr Mason, Geoffrey B, 'Service Histories of Royal Navy Warships in World War 2', Smith, Gordon 'HMS Mauritius – Colony-type Light Cruiser including Convoy Escort Movements', (revised 5th June 2011), http://www.naval-history.net/xGM-Chrono-06CL-Mauritius.htm [Accessed 10 January 2012]

Lt Cdr Mason, Geoffrey B, 'Service Histories of Royal Navy Warships in World War 2', Smith, Gordon 'HMS Dorsetshire – County-type Heavy Cruiser including Convoy Escort Movements', (revised 8th October 2010), http://www.naval-history.net/xGM-Chrono-06CA-Dorsetshire.htm [Accessed 10 January 2012]

Scott, Len, WW2 People's War, 'Sex in the City: Algiers 1943', http://www.bbc.co.uk/history/ww2peopleswar/stories/72/a2789472.shtml [Accessed 10 January 2012]

Wishart, Ernest George, WW2 People's War Archive, 'ML 238 of 25th ML Flotilla, Royal Navy', http://www.worldnavalships.com/forums/showthread.php?p=68275 [Accessed 12 February 2012]

Peter Rice Destiny One, 'Purchase Tax', http://www.peterice.com/purchasetax.htm [Accessed 2016]

Royal Navy Research Archive, 'A History of HMS King Alfred', http://www.royalnavyresearcharchive.org.uk/King_Alfred_2.htm [Accessed 14 January 2012]

Purbeck Radar, 'Early Radar Development in the United Kingdom', http://www.purbeckradar.org.uk [Accessed 29 May 2012]

Royal Air Force Museum, 'Women's Auxiliary Air Force (WAAF) 1939-1949', http://www.rafmuseum.org.uk/research/online-exhibitions/women-of-the-air-force/womens-auxiliary-air-force-waaf-1939-1949.aspx [Accessed 14 January 2012]

The Guide to Musical Theatre, 'Dubarry Was a Lady', http://guidetomusicaltheatre.com/shows_d/dubarry-lady.html [Accessed 2016]

'The Story of RAF Hayscastle, A West Coast Chain Home Radar Station', http://hayscastle.com/wp-content/uploads/2012/02/RAF_Hayscastle_website.pdf [Accessed 2 January 2012]

From Wikipedia:

'Allied Invasion of Italy', https://en.wikipedia.org/wiki/Allied_invasion_of_Italy [Accessed 2016]

'Allied Invasion of Sicily', https://en.wikipedia.org/wiki/Allied_invasion_of_Sicily [Accessed 2016]

'Battle of Anzio', https://en.wikipedia.org/wiki/Battle_of_Anzio [Accessed 2016]

'Billy Ternent', https://en.wikipedia.org/wiki/Billy_Ternent [Accessed 2 January 2012]

'Damon Runyon', https://en.wikipedia.org/wiki/Damon_Runyon [Accessed 12 January 2012]

'David Wright (artist)', https://en.wikipedia.org/wiki/David_Wright_(artist) [Accessed 2016]

'E-boat', https://en.wikipedia.org/wiki/E-boat [Accessed 11 February 2017]

'Focke-Wulf Fw 190', https://en.wikipedia.org/wiki/Focke-Wulf_Fw_190 [Accessed 2016]

'Gothic Line', https://en.wikipedia.org/wiki/Gothic_Line [Accessed 11 January 2012]

'HMS Calliope', https://en.wikipedia.org/wiki/HMS_Calliope_(1884) [Accessed 13 January 2012]

'HMS Pembroke', https://en.wikipedia.org/wiki/HMS_Pembroke#Shore_establishments [Accessed 13 January 2012]

'HMS Raleigh', https://en.wikipedia.org/wiki/HMS_Raleigh_(shore_establishment) [Accessed 13 January 2012]

'Invasion of Elba', https://en.wikipedia.org/wiki/Invasion_of_Elba [Accessed 2016]

'Ischia', https://en.wikipedia.org/wiki/Ischia [Accessed 2018]

'John Collins (cocktail)', https://en.wikipedia.org/wiki/John_Collins_(cocktail) [Accessed 29 December 2011]

'Marinefährprahm', https://en.wikipedia.org/wiki/Marinef%C3%A4hrprahm [Accessed 11 January 2012]

'Mount Vesuvius', https://en.wikipedia.org/wiki/Mount_Vesuvius [Accessed 2016]

'Operation Dragoon', https://en.wikipedia.org/wiki/Operation_Dragoon [Accessed 2016]

'PT boat', https://en.wikipedia.org/wiki/PT_boat [Accessed 2018]

'Screwjack, RAF Sennen', https://en.wikipedia.org/wiki/Skewjack [Accessed December 2016]

'Rosalind Russell', https://en.wikipedia.org/wiki/Rosalind_Russell [Accessed 1 February 2017]

'V-1 Flying Bomb', https://en.wikipedia.org/wiki/V-1_flying_bomb [Accessed 2016]

'V-2 Rocket', https://en.wikipedia.org/wiki/V-2_rocket [Accessed 16 February 2017]

World Naval Ships Forum, 'Demobilisation at the End of WW2', http://www.worldnavalships.com/forums/showthread.php?t=13958 [Accessed 2016]

World Naval Ships Forums, 'RN Shore Training Establishment: HMS Victory', http://www.worldnavalships.com/forums/showthread.php?p=68275, [Accessed 14 January 2012]

About the Author

    David Bickerton graduated from Leeds University in 1967 and pursued a career in Civil Engineering before his retirement in 2010. He has three children, Pam, David and Julie. David lives with his wife, Dorothy in Hampshire.

H.M.M.L. 338,
c/o G.P.O.,
London,
30th August 1944.

My darling Linda

I might have guessed I was being too optimistic for no sooner had I finished my last letter to you than we (were) whisked away to S. France and although we're working harder than ever (no shore leave!) I'm rather enjoying things.

There have been one or two amusing incidents and of course one or two which didn't amuse us at all. We arrived at one place a day before the army (I didn't know it at the time, believe me) and out came the local life boat, full of bods in gorgeous uniforms, to greet us. I had the chief of the local Maquis on board and he was feeling pretty pleased with life. They brought us grapes and wine (I got the stomach ache) and wrote a long screed on the necessity of closer relations between our two countries. Ashore they had hanged the odd collaborateur and also shaved the heads of all the women who had had anything to do with the

2

Germans. Anyway we enjoyed meeting them and there's no doubt that they hate the Germans and with good reason. Jerry, of course, before he leaves destroys everything he can — and looks for his next line of defence. I also ran across Dennis Venning, who was with me in the 25th and we had the odd noggin to celebrate.

I haven't heard any news for some time — the nearer you are the less you know — but the war generally seems to be going well and I still have hopes that it will be over by the end of October — I'm due to go home then anyway. But I must admit the Germans fight hard and we've had one or two unpleasant encounters with their shore batteries recently — their shooting is good but they don't seem to have the luck — Thank God!

God, darling I am so looking forward to coming home to you soon — tho' I don't quite understand why you should say you are almost frightened to meet me again — especially when I remember some of the lectures you gave me in Falmouth. Still I don't think two years has changed either of us so considerably, I certainly love you as much as ever

M — A — I — L — E —

Army form W 3077

To open cut here →

← To open cut here

Sec. no. fold here

First fold here ←

Mr. Linda Russell W.A.A.F.
R.A.F. Branscombe,
Schools Regi.,
West Sidworth,
South Devon.

From
Lieut. [?] Anton King.

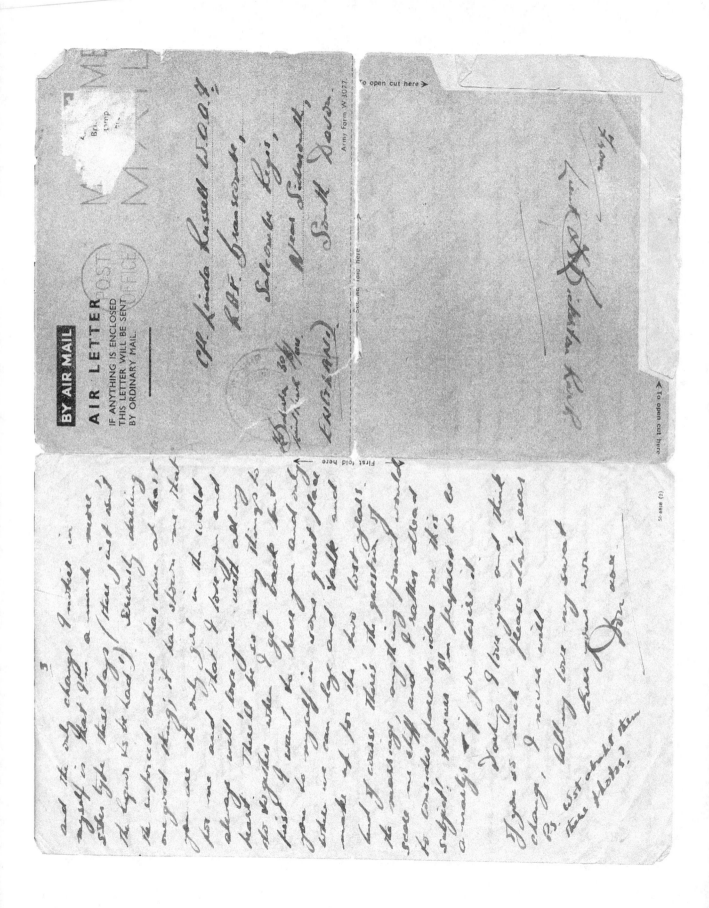

3

and the only change I notice in
myself is that I'm a much more
settled type these days (that just the
it figures to be had!) Everyour darling
the enforced silence has done at last
one good thing; it has shown me that
you are so restful in the world
for me and that I love you and only
always will love you with all my
heart. Thrill to do many things to-
do together when I get back but
first I want to have you and only
you to myself in some quiet place
where we can lye and talk and
make it for the two lost years —

but of course this the greatest of
the marriage, everything I would
scare with stuff and I rather dread
to consider twenty ideas on this
stupid! however the prospect to be
always — if you desire it.

Darling I love you and that
you as much — please don't ever
change. All my love — my sweet
                              Ever your own
                                  [signature]

P.S. Post ordered the
three photos.

(2) 51-9418

CPSIA information can be obtained
at www.ICGtesting.com
Printed in the USA
LVHW05s1656040918
589120LV00001B/1/P